A QUIET REVIVAL

A QUIET REVIVAL

*Geoffrey Bingham
in Life and Ministry*

MARTIN BLEBY

MARBLE MEDIA

2014

First published by New Creation Publications Inc., Australia, in 2012

Second edition published by Marble Media, South Australia

National Library of Australia
ISBN 978-0-9925376-0-9   paperback
978-0-9925376-1-6   ebook

Cataloguing-in-Publication
Bleby, Martin E. (Martin Edward).
A quiet revival: Geoffrey Bingham in life and ministry

Bibliography
1. Bingham, Geoffrey C.
2. Church of England—Australia—Clergy—Biography.
3. Clergy—Australia—Biography.
4. Christian biography—Australia
5. Christian life—Australia.

283.092

Cover and introductory pages to each chapter
designed by Nicole Dunkley

Cover photographs: Full of years—1940, 1966, 2009

Marble Media: 3 Shannon Crescent,
Coromandel Valley, South Australia 5051

Printed by CreateSpace
Available from CreateSpace.com and Amazon.com

CONTENTS

CONTENTS

CONTENTS

ACKNOWLEDGEMENTS

Preliminary Research: Noel Due, Trevor Faggotter,
Elizabeth Klynsmith, John Dunn

Assistance in wordprocessing: Lol Bettany, Gillian Borgas

Proofreading: Bob Pickering, Robin Pickering,
Beryl Skewes, John Skewes

Reviewing: Ian Pennicook, Laurel Bingham,
Noel Due, Trevor Fagotter,
John Dunn

Cover and Graphics: Nicole Dunkley

Typography: Glennys Warren

Photographs: John Dunn, John Kammermann,
Geoffrey Diment, and others

Final Touches: Celia Carter

INTRODUCTION

ORIGINS OF THIS BOOK

GEOFFREY BINGHAM had called a group of us to his home. Now eighty-eight years old, and not content with the two hundred or more books he had already written,[1] there needed to be another one. Biographies of some of his contemporaries had been published,[2] and his should be among them. He had made some attempts at starting one, but it was getting beyond the reach of his powers and computer skills. He needed our help.

Not for his own notoriety—though how can we ever distinguish between our baser motives and the more worthy ones? Milton had written:

> *Fame* is the spur that the clear spirit doth raise
> (That last infirmity of Noble mind)
> To scorn delights, and live laborious dayes.[3]

But Geoffrey was a sinner justified by God's grace in Christ—a man whose heart belonged to God—and he had decided long before, as expressed in the title of one of his recent books,[4] that *love* is the spur. God had used Geoffrey's life and ministry to bring blessing to many. There was a story here that needed telling. The book was to be for the glory of God and His gospel of grace.

GEOFFREY CYRIL BINGHAM 1919–2009

It was to be the story of 'a quiet revival'—God's deep work of love and grace in the life of a man and his wife, that had flowed out richly through preaching, teaching, writing and personal ministry into the lives of so many others, impacting churches and communities in Australia and overseas over several decades.

Should a 'revival' be 'quiet'? Geoffrey was not averse to noisier revivals. Revival, characterised by 'an awesome sense of the

3

presence of God, an overwhelming awareness of the seriousness of sin, an increasing longing for the knowledge of God, an unusual evidence of transformed lives, and a significant passion for the salvation of the lost',[5] had accompanied Geoffrey's ministry in a number of places, with unusual manifestations of the Holy Spirit's power.[6] He had written extensively on the subject.[7] But for the most part it had been a case of 'preach the word, be urgent in season and out of season, convince, rebuke, and exhort, be unfailing in patience and in teaching'[8]—what he called the raising of 'the spiritual water-table' by 'preaching the Scriptures, and especially the great themes' with a view to an eventual 'great outflowing of grace and the Spirit in the truth of Christ', brought about by 'the power of the gospel proclaimed in the power of the Spirit'.[9]

But how to tell the story of a person whose life spanned nine decades, as boy and man, soldier, prisoner-of-war, farmer, husband and father, writer, minister, missionary, Bible College principal, theologian, preacher and teacher? Where do we start, and how do we order it? Geoffrey had asked us to pray about this, and during a holiday break it had come to me that it should be a biographical history of Geoffrey's life and ministry, arranged according to a theological rationale. It would show how each of Geoffrey Bingham's key theological insights arose and developed at particular stages of his life. The time for a full-blown biography might, or might not, come later, and the archival materials were there for when that time came. This book would be a kind of theological biography, compiled from carefully selected extracts of Geoffrey's writings, and contributions from others, joined by a link text. It would be an overview of the person and his ministry, and would give a taste of his writings, in the hope that some might come to read him more widely. It was to be a testimony to what God had done, and it would glory in God's great grace, mercy and peace. It was to serve as an example and an indication of how God revives His people.

I presented an outline of this to the meeting, and it was accepted. I was appointed the editor, in consultation with Ian Pennicook, joined by an editorial committee of Noel Due and Trevor Faggotter, who would help to research various chapters,[10]

4

with Elizabeth Klynsmith as editorial assistant, all under the approval of Geoffrey Bingham, and the book was to be published by the end of the year.

That was in May 2007. Research and preliminary work was done on a number of chapters, but demands of ministry meant that the work did not progress far that year, or in the following year and a half. It may have been that the time was not yet right. Geoffrey's health deteriorated, and he moved to an aged care home. In the last few months of his life, he was given to write once more, this time by hand, in notebooks. The great themes of his life and ministry were rehearsed again, under the title *Finding the Father: Living in the Telos*,[11] yet in an anecdotal and discursive way, with the perspective of one still very much on earth, yet standing on the edge of eternity.

'A LIFE SO DYNAMIC'

Geoffrey died on 3rd June 2009. Over six hundred people gathered in Adelaide for his funeral, from a number of states and from every decade of his ministry. Geoffrey had proclaimed the gospel in twenty-six countries, and had made a lasting impact on our nation of Australia. In 2005 he had been made a Member of the Order of Australia, 'For service to the community through Christian ministry, encouraging cross-cultural theological education and as an author'. A hand-written letter from the Governor-General was read out, paying tribute to 'a remarkable Australian, who gave so generously and so courageously in serving our country, a man who stood for the finest values and principles'.[12] Members of Geoffrey's family spoke of 'a life so dynamic, so vibrant that it defies description . . . A life lived at such pace that sometimes we were left behind, a life that had so much love that we had to forgive his failings because we knew we were loved by someone who understood people, who though a stranger to small talk, could speak to people at the heart of their beings and change lives with what he understood'.[13] The Heads of Christian Churches in South Australia spoke of 'the incredible legacy Geoffrey Bingham has left to the State of South Australia and the wider Australian and International community in the form of his inspirational preaching, and insightful writings around the centrality of the Cross of Christ . . . He was deeply loved and highly respected by everyone who got to know him and his fervency of faith, integrity of heart and intolerance of a cross-less Christianity shone out of him through to the end . . . Geoff's legacy will not be forgotten and his influence will continue to be felt through many generations.'[14]

HEAR THE WORD OF THE LORD

The year in which Geoffrey Bingham died came to an end, and the work he had begun continued strongly, by the grace of God. We decided, and Geoffrey's wife Laurel agreed, that if the book *A Quiet Revival* was ever to see the light of day, now was the time. Much work remained to be done, and time needed to be found to do it. But we were confident that, just as Geoffrey's whole life was a gift from God, so the work and the time for this book on his life and ministry would also be given. And that, if it came thus gift-wise from God, it too would do its work in people's lives.

At Geoffrey's funeral Ian Pennicook preached on Ezekiel 33:33, 'they shall know that a prophet has been among them'. 'Our response', he said, 'as the church, and as individuals, must not be to the prophet *but to the word the prophet brought*. If we are to learn from Geoffrey Bingham, it will be as we believe the word of God and embrace that word—as it embraces us. To honour the man is good, but we must not forget that: "All flesh is like grass and all its glory like the flower of grass. The grass withers, and the flower falls, but the word of the Lord endures forever" (1 Peter 1:24–25). We will *not* honour the man if we do not rise up in repentance and faith and respond to the word given by God through him.'[15]

To encourage us in that response is the aim of this book.

Martin Bleby
Coromandel East
South Australia
2012

[1] See a listing of most of them, in downloadable form from: <www.new creation.org.au/books/indexes/all_bingham.htm> (accessed 9 March 2010).

[2] Stuart Barton Babbage, *Memoirs of a Loose Canon* (Acorn Press, Brunswick East, 2004); John R. Reid, *Marcus L. Loane: A Biography* (Acorn Press, 2005); Marcia Cameron, *An Enigmatic Life: David Broughton Knox Father of Contemporary Sydney Anglicanism* (Acorn Press, 2006).

[3] John Milton (1608–1674), 'Lycidas', lines 70–72, in *The Poetical Works of John Milton* (Helen Darbishire ed., Oxford University Press London, 1958), 449.

[4] Geoffrey Bingham, *Love Is the Spur* (publishing details and a list of Geoffrey's books can be found in the Bibliography at the end of this book).

[5] Brian H. Edwards, *Can We Pray for Revival?—Towards a Theology of Revivial* (Evangelical Press, Darlington, 2001), 10.

[6] See Chapter 10: 'God Sends Revival'. See also Stuart Piggin, *Spirit of a Nation: The Story of Australia's Christian Heritage* (Strand Publishing, Sydney, 2004), 196–197.

[7] See *Dry Bones Dancing!*, *Reviving the Humble*, and *The Revival God Gives*. See also the stories 'Lovefest—I, II and III' in *Twice-Conquering Love*, and in the novel *Beyond Mortal Love*.

[8] 2 Timothy 4:2.

[9] Geoffrey Bingham, undated letter, c. September 1997, quoted in Stuart Piggin, *Firestorm of the Lord: The History of and Prospects for Revival in the Church and the World* (Paternoster Press, Carlisle, 2000), 150.

[10] Trevor Faggotter did preliminary research for chapters 1, 6 and 10; Noel Due for chapters 3, 5, 9 and 13.

[11] This writing remains unpublished, in note form.

[12] Reproduced in Martin Bleby, 'Geoffrey Cyril Bingham 1919–2009: His Public Life and Ministry', Funeral Oration 10th June 2009: <www.newcreation. org.au/pdf/GCB%20Funeral/GCBLifeMinistry.pdf> p. 1.

[13] <www.newcreation.org.au/pdf/GCB%20Funeral/FamilyEulogy.pdf> p. 1.

[14] Reproduced in Martin Bleby, 'Geoffrey Cyril Bingham 1919–2009: His Public Life and Ministry', pp. 3, 4.

[15] <www.newcreation.org.au/pdf/GCB%20Funeral/FuneralSermonGCB.pdf> p. 4.

CHAPTER 1

Remember YOUR CREATOR

With family, 1923

CREATION IS PRIMARY

CREATION HELD a prime place in Geoffrey Bingham's theology: 'the primary doctrine or truth of Scripture', he said, 'is that God is Creator'.[1] This is an unusual statement for an evangelical Christian, many of whom effectively begin with human sin and the 'fall', and trace God's rescue operation through to the cross of Christ. For them, God is primarily Redeemer. But for Geoffrey, 'Creation by God is the doctrine basic to the true understanding of all theology. If we miss out here, we are deficient in understanding everywhere.'[2]

How did creation come to occupy such an important place in Geoffrey's thinking, and what were its implications for his life and ministry?

GOD AND THE BUSH

It began with Geoffrey as a boy in the bush. Born on the 6th of January 1919 at Goulburn, New South Wales, he moved with his family to Wahroonga at the age of five.[3] Wahroonga was then a northern suburb of Sydney surrounded by native bush:

> As a boy I was intrigued by creation. I loved to wander in the Australian bush, search out its insects, birds and animals, and see the beauty—or otherwise—of its flora . . . I had a deep love of the bush, for where we lived waratahs, Christmas bells, flannel flowers and banksia men all flourished. Sometimes there were bellbirds in the shady groves, and at raintime there were the unforgettable songs of the plaintive currawongs.[4]

As Geoffrey relates in one of his short stories: 'On Sundays he would want to explore it, feel the flora and the fauna, and examine the mysteries of birds and their nestings and even trap finches for his aviary'. But on Sundays there was also 'church in the morning and the evening, and Sunday School in the afternoon'.[5] This raised a difficulty for him:

> I had an inbuilt conflict with church and bush. Here were two different worlds . . . I would hear the church bell out in the bush— strong and insistent at the time for Sunday School—and I thought this was an intrusion upon 'nature'.[6]

Yet both worlds drew him in: 'He could not explain to himself the different streams of joy that were his. There was a world of creation which brought him joy, but also a world of worship and love which both awed and gripped him. He had a sense that both joys were authentic but also felt that somehow they conflicted.'[7] He put this down to an unconscious deficiency in teaching and perception at that time:

> Years later, when thinking about it, he concluded that his spiritual friends and teachers had never understood the truth of creation. Somehow within them was a dualism, incipient but unsuspected. The redemptive action of God was focal for them and creation was an almost unknown entity. It lay over the periphery of their thinking—away out on the unseen perimeter . . . the boy was surrounded with the truth of redemption but not of creation, and since both creation and redemption are of the one piece, he was naturally enough confused. He had an instinct for *both* creation and redemption, but was denied support in the former whilst being over-supported in the latter.[8]

'It was when I was much older', he said, 'that I realised there is no inbuilt conflict between theology and creation'.[9]

CREATION AND NEW CREATION

Why is it important to see that 'God gives primacy to creation' as 'what He is about in history'?

If God does not prove to be 'a faithful Creator' (I Pet. 4:19), then He cannot be said to be faithful in any other work He does. Redemption figures largely in our thinking, because we know ourselves to be lost because of our sin. The truth is that redemption is not an afterthought of God, in time, but something which was planned before time. It was not planned merely to rehabilitate fallen man, but it was planned because redemption is cosmological—of the whole creation ... Whilst He is certainly Redeemer in history, He redeems in order to keep His creation true to what He created it to be. At the end of time we will see a new creation, but it will be the same creation renewed, and not an altogether different creation which God has made because the old is broken and obsolete.[10]

This is a vast vision. Everything else hangs on this:

When we ask why it should be said that creation is primary, the answer must be, 'If creation fails, then God fails', in which case He does not prove to be 'a faithful Creator'. In a myriad of ways God would be less than His word claims Him to be ... Those who see redemption as a 'repair job' of God, as though an afterthought—an expediency to meet a contingency—have missed the point. Either redemption is incorporated into God's plan prior to creation—having creation in view—or creation has failed ... creation will reach its ultimate glorified state—the ultimate intention of God for creation. It will reach it by means of redemption, and that gives redemption its right place in history—to bring the creation to its designed end, having defeated all creation-destroying forces ... there is a fascinating verse in Ephesians (3:9) where Paul links the cosmic plan of God with the very creation, as though this were innate in it, 'to make all men see what is the plan of the mystery hidden for ages in God *who created all things*'. 'Who created all things' is not a chance pious observation. It is the revelation that what has come to pass in Christ is of the eternal plan of God for creation.[11]

'For this reason', Geoffrey says, 'creation should not be seen apart from reconciliation, nor reconciliation apart from creation'.[12]

What, then, is God's intention for the creation? It is to share His glory:

13

It is that God wills to glorify Himself, to show Himself with the glory that is His, that is Him. The way of doing this is to glorify His sons by conforming them to the image of His Son, and, at the same time, glorifying all other things of His Creation. Thus all creatures—both celestial and terrestrial—will share in this glory, for to gaze on glory is to become glorious.[13]

This includes dealing with all that seeks to have a 'glory' of its own apart from God:

The other side of His glory and its glorifying nature is the entire loss of glory by all that is evil and opposed to God. All attempts of these creatures to glorify themselves will end in terrible disaster. God will not give His glory to another, but He will share it with His elect Creation.[14]

Thus would come about that which for Geoffrey was 'a trembling in my body, tears in my eyes and a great sense of fear and awe . . . the community by which God will express the truth of His Being, which is His glory throughout Eternity'.[15]

LIVING IN CREATION

What have been the implications of this for Geoffrey Bingham's life and ministry? A keen appreciation of God's creation—particularly the birds, the animals, and the human creatures—remained with him all his life. It came through especially in his short stories—birds in particular feature in twenty-three of them![16]—along with his poems and hymns. Creation, for Geoffrey, was revelatory of God:

If you have paused on any day, a warm, quiet day when the ground is vibrant, and the trees rich with life, and the birds are deliberate in their telling, then you will hear some of the glory. If you traverse continents where it is dry and desert-like and harsh, and you see the salt bush, the little flowers that hide in the dust but are a world to look into with an enlarging looking-glass—if you travel across these and look at the rounder boulders of the near desert, or the harsh hills of the uplands besides them, then you will have seen some of this glory.

If you pass over lush pastures, and wooded groves, and forested mountains, and if you see falling waters over crags, and rushing torrents through the mountains and the gorges, and if you see the long, swift rivers in the jungles, and the broad, blue lakes where the volcanoes once burst, or where the hills settle down to their eternal plains; if you see these then you will see something of the glory of which I speak, but then it will be only a speck of that.

Much of the glory, at the right moment, is hidden within a man.[17] That is correct: it is hidden within a man and a woman. Look into the eyes of a woman at the point where she has conceived life and carries it calmly and proudly within her body; then you will have seen more of the glory. See it in the eye of a man when he has regained his lost nobility and you will see much of what I am speaking about, but see it in the eye of the power to which man belongs, and yet which man himself is not, then you will see it all.[18]

Creation is not all sunsets and rainbows. Knowing the sureness of God's redeeming purpose for His creation also enabled Geoffrey to look squarely at its less attractive elements, and live freely and without fear in their midst:

How beautiful was the dawn, how glorious the day and how high in loveliness the evening sunset. This is our creation! Elsewhere it was not so good. The desert was dry, the crops had failed and famine was in the air. The cries of children in their dying, the panting of the remaining animals and gaping beaks and raised wings of the birds in the dead trees: more of creation. Lush jungles, ancient forest-giants of trees, and the rumble of tractors, earthmovers like ancient dinosaurs. Rebels and insurrectionists moving stealthily behind the thick foliage, rifles erect and ready for defence or attack. Shattered cities in barren lands, gaping with the wounds of war—ghost towns and ghost people—and all of it still the creation in which we live. Prosperous cities, skyscrapers built like temples to the gods of money and of power. High-tech civilisation; new, smooth and suave cultures, burgeoning on the vast mineral and rural wealth of nations old and new.

This is our creation—multifaceted, vital and static, active and passive, freshly living and slowly dying, renewing and tiring, simple and sophisticated, teeming with its expanding and accelerating millions, vivid with new ideas, dreams, ideals and plans, and weary with the failures of ancient cultures, illusioned and disillusioned, hopeful and hopeless—this is the creation in which we are placed.[19]

This is the creation into which we are sent to 'proclaim the good news'.[20]

THE AWESOME ENCOUNTER

'Remember your creator in the days of your youth.'[21] For Geoffrey, it had begun in the bush around Wahroonga. He tells the story of a group of boys who one day saw an enormous freshwater crayfish:

> I reached the creek and stared across at the huge creature. It was thick in the thorax, it was long in the body. It was probably a couple of feet in length, but then I would have said 'three'. Its legs moved slowly, reminding me of a tarantula or even a slow trapdoor spider. I looked at its pincers and thought them powerful. Its eyes were on stalks and they seemed to fix on me. Its antennae waved with what I thought to be grim menace. For a terrible moment I imagined it was an eater of human flesh. I feared to move lest it would scuttle away.[22]

The boy caught it, and they decided to kill and eat it:

> The thing convulsed as I hit it. Then there came a rush of something to my head and I kept hitting him. Its head was mashed, but its legs kept moving. We let the silence drift over all things. I was breathing heavily.[23]

This later played on his mind:

> My feelings were of shock. How did this great creature get to this quiet bush place? How could I have captured it and then bashed its head in? I never knew I could do things like that. Problems loomed up large before me about my future . . . My mind was seeing the

great creature back by the creek, and its ungainly passage along the bank, and then its descent. Even now its eyes seemed to be staring at me. Suddenly I realised we had done a terrible thing. I had killed a creature which had taken many, many years to grow and mature. Maybe it was the largest freshwater crayfish which had ever existed . . . I felt like a murderer. I had killed it, bashing in its head.[24]

He returned the next day to the same spot:

I sat waiting for another grey crayfish to appear on the bank, but none came. I was disappointed . . . I knew could do nothing to bring back our giant crayfish, but I wandered around miserably, hoping to see one. I clambered along the creek bed, jumping from stone to stone.

Then I saw it. It was larger than the one we had seen yesterday. If anything it was more noble. It stood high on its thin legs and tail, and its claws were waving in the air. So were its antennae. That strange feeling I would always have in the bush and in the jungles, plains and veldts of other countries suddenly gripped me. Yesterday I had not seen beauty but today it was nothing else. I swallowed with joy.

Then, out of the undergrowth appeared another companion creature. It was smaller, somewhat delicate in build and I guessed —rightly or wrongly—that it was a female. They showed no affection, but both began their descent of the bank, making towards the creek, antennae waving.

There were tears in my eyes as I saw them enter the clear water. Once in it, their bodies suddenly galvanised as they shot forward in jerks, and were soon lost in the rocks and the debris. I sat for a long time . . . and my thoughts were deep ones for a youngster, even a poetic youngster but strangely enough they have stayed with me for these sixty years.[25]

Sin has intruded into God's good creation, with its attendant guilt and harm. But God has structured creation in such a way that it declares the glory of God and conveys something of the hope and promise of God's grace.[26]

[1] 'The Doctrine of Creation' in *For Pastors and the People*, 5.

[2] *The Things We Firmly Believe*, 44.

[3] 'Geoffrey C. Bingham: A Short Biography, 1919–1995', in *Mr Hicken's Pears*, 261.

[4] *Creation and the Liberating Glory*, viii.

[5] 'The Powerful Presence' in *God and the Ghostown*, 153.

[6] *Creation and the Liberating Glory*, viii.

[7] 'The Powerful Presence' in *God and the Ghostown*, 153.

[8] 'The Powerful Presence' in *God and the Ghostown*, 154.

[9] *Creation and the Liberating Glory*, viii.

[10] 'The Doctrine of Creation' in *For Pastors and the People*, 3, 5.

[11] *Creation and the Liberating Glory*, 73, 74.

[12] *Creation and Reconciliation*, 53.

[13] *The Holy Spirit, Creation and Glory*, 160.

[14] *The Holy Spirit, Creation and Glory*, 160.

[15] *The Beautiful City of God*, 111.

[16] Research by Trevor Faggotter.

[17] Geoffrey Bingham consistently used the word 'man' as inclusive of men and women, as well as to designate the male, consistent with Genesis 5:1–3:

> When God created humankind [Heb. *adam*], he made them [Heb. *him*] in the likeness of God. Male and female he created them, and he blessed them and named them 'Humankind' [Heb. *adam*] when they were created. When Adam had lived one hundred thirty years, he became the father of a son . . .

One of his notes from *The Meaning and Making of Man: A Series of Seven Studies on Christian Counselling*, page 1, is reproduced here:

> The use of 'Man' here is not intended to be sexist. It is the generic use of the word, as against the specific use for the male human. That is, it stands for (i) the male–female entity (cf. Gen. 1:26–27; 5:1–2), and (ii) the entire human race (cf. Acts 17:26; Rom. 5:12).

[18] *Bright Bird and Shining Sails*, 25.

[19] *Creation and the Liberating Glory*, 1–2.

[20] Mark 16:15.

[21] Ecclesiastes 12:1.

[22] 'The Awesome Encounter' in *The Lion on the Road*, 114.

[23] 'The Awesome Encounter' in *The Lion on the Road*, 116.

[24] 'The Awesome Encounter' in *The Lion on the Road*, 117, 119.

[25] 'The Awesome Encounter' in *The Lion on the Road*, 120–121.

[26] See Psalm 19:1; Romans 1:20; 8:19–23.

CHAPTER 2

THE *Word* OF *God*

> The word of God is living and active, sharper than any two-edged sword.
>
> Hebrews 4:12

EAGER TO PREACH

'GOD HAS CALLED me to be a preacher.'

The five-year-old Geoffrey Bingham was standing up in kindergarten class, announcing his vocation to the teacher and all the other children.[1] He was not even converted yet, but the call from God was there.

Geoffrey's mother Eileen, 'beautiful and vivacious' daughter of the bookmaker Jerome Dowling, fostered this vocation, as she 'watched with discerning eyes, and fed me secretly, in her bedroom sessions, with the exalted calling of the "spiritual"'.[2] At Hurlstone High School, Geoffrey was introduced to books and encouraged in writing by an English teacher, John Smith. He took to buying second-hand books, beginning with theological authors John Bunyan, John Newton and Murray M'Cheyne.[3] Yet Geoffrey knew an 'agony that haunted me for years, never entirely abating':

> I loved the land, and wanted to be a farmer. I was obsessed with writing and wanted to be a poet and author. I felt a burning to tell the world about the Presence that never left me, and suffered intolerable guilt as I was torn by these three loves.[4]

The preaching vocation prevailed, while the other two loves never wholly left him. By the age of sixteen, in 1935,[5] after the family had moved to a farm at Box Hill, Geoffrey's heart was set:

> Some nights, after locking the milking cows into the night paddock, I would stand looking at the sun setting in the west. Rarely have I been in a place in this world where sunsets flamed so much, and died whispering such intense beauty, so to speak. They often triggered poems, and if not poems, then tears. I would think of a world which did not know the glory I knew, nor the love that had

come to me on the night of my conversion and which had never departed. I knew there was something brilliant ahead for me, and for others who would open their eyes to see it, so I used to pray that I would one day be sent into many countries and so be enabled to tell many people. It was not an obsession: it was just a conviction that it would happen, and later it did happen.[6]

Born on the day the church celebrates as 'The Epiphany, or the Manifestation of Christ to the Gentiles',[7] here is what he prayed:

Oh, God! Let me go to all the nations of the earth and tell them, each one, your intention for them, so that none will proceed forward without knowing that plan and purpose that you have for them, that they may have it for themselves. No matter what their intentions, draw them into it. No matter what the pain, the horror, the severe demands, please bring them to its summation, its fullness, and spare me not in all that this entails. This, oh Father, is the prayer of love.

This is my prayer, and keep me spiritually alive and alert to it for ever, your Son.[8]

Geoffrey's father, Horace Bingham, a dentist now pursuing his dream of farming, was not so supportive of Geoffrey's vocation. Geoffrey was studying late at night to pass his matriculation, so he could go to theological college, but he was doing it in secret, to keep it from his father. His father then discovered his intention:

He said to me, 'You have to make up your mind whether you are going to stay here and work the farm with me, or whether you are going to be a minister' . . .

'I certainly do want to be a minister', I said. 'I have always wanted that . . . '

He said, 'You can't study and work at the same time. You either give up your studying or you go on with it and leave the farm . . . You make up your mind, now', he said. 'You either stay on the farm or you go to college' . . .

'Then I must go to college', I said.

A number of times I have looked back over that event and regretted the clash between two strong personalities, but what maturity does a boy of nineteen have to declare his deep love for his father, his longing to be a true son, and yet not to lose his integrity for his life's calling?

'Well, I guess I must go', I said.

My father was shouting. 'You go now or not at all', he said.

I found myself also shouting.[9]

He left that night. Later, Geoffrey was able to say: 'I am sure that, behind it all, my father knew of my vocation in life, and that he despaired sometimes of my staying on the farm. He was a shrewd person and discerned much more than we believed he could.'[10] Geoffrey, at age fifteen, had already seen his mother become a Christian. Years later, his father also was converted.[11]

GOD AND THE PREACHER

What is required of those who are called upon to proclaim the word of God? They 'must first know God, hear His word, and then proclaim it under His Kingship, under the Lordship of Christ, and empowered by the Holy Spirit'.[12] They must also know themselves, in God's dealing with them:

> When we know the dark reaches of dread and guilt, the grey, wraith-like *angst* of the fearful human heart, then we can understand what God must do to purge away every stain, and to dissolve the enormous clouds of wrath that lie over the human heart to trouble it up to death and through all eternity . . . This preacher, then, has not only a thinking knowledge of these things, but a living experience of them. He has been drawn down into the depths of intolerable shame. His own heart has been deeply convicted by the evil of the human heart, and he has long ago acknowledged the perfectness of God in His wrath upon evil.[13]

Despite the inevitable opposition, this is to be in no way downplayed, 'lest the cross of Christ be emptied of its power'.[14] 'He must face the cringing, hating world with the unadulterated truth that God is wrathful when they violate His creation, and confront His holiness with their pollution':

If he so much as minimize God's wrath on sin one iota, or maximize the good of man one degree then he shall lose sight of overwhelming grace which works out on the Cross the full meed of wrath, and the full exercise of love and mercy. God-in-Himself deals with the anguish of man's evil and his alienation from the Father–Creator, and reconciles the world unto Himself. The wonderful dimensions of this are what bear down on the human heart and liberate it, and make it love God and agree to do all that He requires, not only in moral obedience, but in the obedience wrought by grace and love to tell others of the God of love. This living, pulsing, warm and palpable thing in the heart is the true *kerugma* which the preacher knows . . . This is the true constraint, and the passing over it, many times, of pain, loss, and persecution will not prevent the kerugmatic utterance, 'God is love!'[15]

This is different from a proclamation 'which sketches out seven points of doctrine, or a mere *schema* of theology'.[16] While 'a formalised theology . . . will be no burden at all to carry . . . he must have a theology of the heart':

His theology of the heart must not simply be one of the emotions, although emotions there must be. It will also be a knowledge of the head. He must know for example the whole nature of the Gospel, and how it fits the creation of God, and how redemption can redeem that creation, and how glorification of the same creation is right and proper, and fits the character of God, and the final, fullest need of man.[17]

No room is there here, then, for preaching that looks and sounds like the real thing, that seems to be 'so real, so sincere, so earnest', but which in fact is nothing more than empty imitation—parrot-like—a 'strange articulated mixture of ideas, concepts, aphorisms, and pot-luck theology':[18]

In practice, what is the preaching of the word of God? Harmless homilies? Topical tidbits? Communication of information which is biblical, moral, social, and spiritual? Exhortation to good living, social justice and social action—including the present ethical issues? Or is it the teaching of the eternities—the proclamation of

Christ, his redemptive and reigning Lordship, the great issues of righteousness, truth, holiness, goodness and love? Does it embrace the state of man and the need for repentance and faith? Does it speak of the new birth, of the new creation, of participation in God's redemptive plan for the world? Does it portray the plan of God for history, the *schema* of God for winning the nations and defeating the massive evil which confronts us in our own generation? Does it envisage the triumphant *telos*—the victory of God at the consummation of the age? Is the great power of the Cross, Resurrection and Ascension so presented that men and women tremble before God and become regenerated in His sight?[19]

As preachers, then, we will 'seek to evaluate the word we proclaim and the manner of our proclamation':

Is it the word of God or is it merely quoting the Bible, the giving of biblical information? Do we preach without power and without fruitfulness? Are we afraid of our hearers, and so seek to satisfy them? Do we seek the praise of men more than the praise of God? Does money and comfort occupy our minds more than the word itself? Do we have presuppositions (critical and otherwise) which mean we do not really believe the Scriptures? Do we have a form of godliness but deny its power (II Tim. 3:5), and is the Kingdom of God words and not power (I Cor. 4:20)?[20]

THE PREACHER, THE WORD, AND THE SPIRIT

For this, 'the pastor must be well-versed in the word':

...all ministry springs from the proclaimed and taught word of God—the Scriptures.[21]

Geoffrey's was a life lived in the Scriptures. So much so, that Geoffrey was once given a vision of himself *inside* the Scriptures, looking out—seeing everything from their God-given perspective.[22] It is a good place to be.

From the Scriptures came his doctrine of the word of God:

... God and His word are identical ... If we look at the word of God in the Old and New Testaments, then we conclude that it is God's own word, identifiable only with Himself, dynamic in its utterance and surely accomplishing what He speaks.[23]

So: 'It is clear that there has always been "the word"'[24]—from eternity. No less is that same word operating when we preach:

The word of God—as we have said—is effective of itself, but God chooses to utter it through human beings.[25]

This gives rise to a very 'high' view of the act of preaching:

P. T. Forsyth, in his *Positive Preaching and the Modern Mind* has said, 'Revelation is the self-bestowal of the living God ... God in the act of imparting Himself to living souls'. He adds, 'Preaching is the Gospel prolonging and declaring itself'.[26] It must, then, mean that it is God who is speaking. Hence I Peter 4:11, 'whoever speaks, as one who utters the oracles of God'. This is why the prophets cried, 'Thus saith the Lord ...' It is also why the apostles kept on claiming they were speaking the word of the Lord. It was not their own word.

The deep agony, then, of preaching is to live where God lives ... Only when the mouth of the preacher is the mouth of God will the word be effective.[27]

From this '*It is safe to conclude that the word of God cannot be spoken in all its awesome and holy truth apart from the Spirit of God*':[28]

The word of God is not merely a reciting of the text of Scripture, or even exhortation from its pages. John 3:34 gives us the principle of true preaching and teaching. Whilst it refers primarily to Christ, it also fits the case of the pastor, 'For he whom God has sent utters the words of God, for it is not by measure that he gives the Spirit'. Doubtless the Spirit was given without measure to Christ, and it cannot be said that we receive the Spirit in the same way, yet we are given that measure of the Spirit which is necessary and sufficient for understanding and teaching the word, as well as living by it.

The point that needs stressing is that Jesus spoke the words of God by the Spirit of God. There are no words of God that are spoken apart from the Spirit, for the Spirit is required in order to have true communication. Men of the word, then, must be men of the Spirit, and if they are men of the Spirit they will be men of the word. It has often been said that the word without the Spirit is dead, and the Spirit without the word is ineffective. This is a strange way of speaking, since the word and the Spirit are inseparable.[29]

FROM HIS MOUTH
COMES A SHARP SWORD

It follows that this word is spoken, not from a position of one's own strength, but by someone who has been humbled in weakness by the Word himself. Someone who has learned that it is not a word of our own making or under our control, but the word of Another. In one of his short stories, Geoffrey wrote of the invisible sword that every man and woman—here in the character of a person called 'Lemery'—carries throughout their lifetime:[30]

Sword in hand he was living, he was strong and he was authoritative. Often he was ebullient. Life around him was lively, sentient. In his mind and brain were great ideas, and his heart found them satisfying . . .

On occasions he would know the sword was no longer in his hand. Some considerable time might have elapsed before he realised it was absent from his grip. He would know this by a kind of lethargy which would come to possess him, much as an old man or woman might discover that the energies they had known in their youth were now gone. Like all persons with a knowledge of vocation and a sense of destiny, Lemery would know a significant loss of energy and driving force, although the sense of destiny and vocation was not diminished. It was a puzzle to him that he was virtually inert, and with an ache in his head that would seem to be a disease. He would wonder why he could not be effective in action.

The strange thing was that the sword would come back into his hand, almost without his feeling that this had happened. He would *know* it had returned because the lethargy, the unwanted passivity and the lack of drive would have disappeared, and his head would be clear. His sense of vocation and destiny would have been enhanced by the return of the sharp instrument in his hand. He would be eager to experience its powers of defence and attack. He would be alert again to the forces which opposed him and which—as required—he must overcome. Once again he knew he was living and, indeed, that all the gifts and talents of his life could now have both meaning and expression. They were not there just for him, but for others—firstly for the One who had given them to him, and then for the humanity of which he had been created to be part.

Lemery had come to understand that without the sword he was helpless and fruitless; that the sword was not of his own making, and that its use was not of his own desire. He had to be doing the will of Another before the sword could and would be effective. The powerful forces opposing him could never be defeated by other than the sword. Sometimes, tempted to devise his own sword, or to use the swords of others, he found this a futile endeavour. The sword was the word he uttered, and that word did not originate from him but from that Other.

It is easy to be caught out in an unthinking and unwary moment. Another story tells of a man who was on his way to a preaching place, when he was waylaid by 'a black insect, like a wiry ant or a thin spider' that 'showed an intense dislike of him'.[31] It jumped at him, growing in size and, instead of using 'the Lord's sword' to hack the creature to pieces, he hit at it with the shoes on his feet. The enraged creature enlarged greatly, and morphed into a crab-like thing with 'waving, whipping, jointed masses of arms or legs'. When the man stamped on it time and again, 'it divided, and became two such terrible creatures'. He then refrained, lest it should multiply even further. As he went, however:

> His mind was occupied with the venomous creature and its surprise attack. Indeed, so occupied was his mind that when he arrived at the place of the proclamation that he was to make, the word had faded from his mind, and he had to set about thinking what he would say. I knew that in the depths he dreaded such situations, for why should he come without a sure word gripping him in every part of his being? He could by no means manufacture his announcement: he must not compile it from materials he had gathered over

the years. He must have a clear word or he would have no word at all. It would be like leaving the sword in its scabbard and making passes in the air, conjuring up the appearance of a sword, and so satisfying his audience that he had successfully wielded such a weapon.[32]

In an earlier part of the story, where the man is wakened in the night by an insistent accusing darkness, the answer is given in these words:

As he lay in that darkness, a strong resolve grew in him. I heard him say, 'I will think only of him who rides upon the white horse.' In his mind's eye he saw that white horse, and he cried, 'He who sits upon this horse is called Faithful and True, for that is what and who he is!' He cried also, 'This is the one clad in a robe dipped in blood, and the name by which he is called is The Word of God'. The one who had cried knew that blood to be of great power, for it had been shed on Calvary's Cross, and it had also been the blood of the wrath of God.

He said to himself, 'I will be in the hands and the arms and the authority of this Great One. I will think upon him, and I will go forth with him who himself goes forth to conquer.' He then saw with great joy and strong confidence that a great and shining sword went forth from the mouth of him who was seated upon the horse, and to his amazement he saw this sword leave no nation unscathed, for with it his Lord conquered all the nations.

I saw in my vision that the powers of darkness relinquished their tenuous hold of the man in the night, and he slept in the power of his Lord.[33]

How did this come across effectively in Geoffrey's life and ministry? Here is one testimony among many:

I went along to my first Spring School at St. Paul's [Chatswood, NSW] (I think it was September 1998), and was astounded by the power of the preaching of this man. He snapped you out of any lethargy that your Spirit might have erred into, and brought home the reality of our calling . . .

After the completion of the School, I left with a new-found zeal in my Spirit, my eyes focused on Jesus, and a certainty of my right standing before God in Christ. In other words, God, through the preaching of Geoffrey Bingham, had cleared the doubts and accusations and made me effective and useful for every good work in the Gospel of Christ.[34]

[1] As told by Geoffrey's teacher to his mother. From Geoffrey Bingham interview with Rob Linn, May 2005, © National Library of Australia, Oral History Collection, TRC 5477/1, track 32. Used by permission.

[2] *My Beloved Family*, 8, 11, 45.

[3] *The Story of New Creation Teaching Ministry*, unpublished document, 2007.

[4] *My Beloved Family*, 45.

[5] *My Beloved Family*, 69.

[6] *My Beloved Family*, 86.

[7] 'The Collect, Epistles and Gospels to be Used Throughout the Year' in *The Book of Common Prayer*, 1662.

[8] *The Story of New Creation Teaching Ministry*.

[9] *My Beloved Family*, 87–88.

[10] *My Beloved Family*, 86.

[11] Marcus L. Loane, 'Geoffrey Bingham', in *These Happy Warriors: Friends and Contemporaries* (NCPI, Blackwood, 1988), 84.

[12] 'The Doctrine of the Word of God' in *For Pastors and the People*, 65–66.

[13] *True Preaching: The Agony and the Ecstasy*, 32–33.

[14] 1 Corinthians 1:17b.

[15] *True Preaching: The Agony and the Ecstasy*, 33–34.

[16] *True Preaching: The Agony and the Ecstasy*, 33.

[17] *True Preaching: The Agony and the Ecstasy*, 34.

[18] 'The Preacher and the Parrot' in *The Concentration Camp and Other Stories*, 15; see also in *Primarily for Parsons*, 15–16.

[19] 'The Doctrine of the Word of God' in *For Pastors and the People*, 135.

[20] 'The Doctrine of the Word of God' in *For Pastors and the People*, 87.

[21] 'The Doctrine of the Word of God' in *For Pastors and the People*, 92, 89.

[22] 'The True Action of Love', Tapes for Life Series, session 31, NCTM MP3 disc 904.

[23] 'The Doctrine of the Word of God' in *For Pastors and the People*, 53, 65.

24 'The Doctrine of the Word of God' in *For Pastors and the People*, 65.

25 'The Doctrine of the Word of God' in *For Pastors and the People*, 66.

[26] P. T. Forsyth, *Positive Preaching and the Modern Mind* (NCPI, Blackwood, 1993 [reprint of the 1907 edition]), 10, 3.

[27] *True Preaching: The Agony and the Ecstasy*, 41–42.

[28] 'The Doctrine of the Word of God' in *For Pastors and the People*, 75.

[29] 'The Doctrine of the Word of God' in *For Pastors and the People*, 48–49.

[30] 'The Legend of Lemery's Sword' in *The Return of the Lorikeets*, 169–173. This notion is developed further with the character Balwone in the trilogy of novels *Strong as the Sun*, *Beyond Mortal Love*, and *Love Unto Glory*.

[31] 'I Saw, in the Night, Visions' in *I Saw, in the Night, Visions*, 101–106.

[32] 'I Saw, in the Night, Visions' in *I Saw, in the Night, Visions*, 103–104.

[33] 'I Saw, in the Night, Visions' in *I Saw, in the Night, Visions*, 101–102.

[34] Darien Khlentzos, 'Lessons from the life & walk of Geoffrey Bingham', 16th June, 2009 (email communication).

CHAPTER 3

Conversion

> when he who had set me apart before I was born, and had called me through his grace, was pleased to reveal his Son to me, in order that I might preach him

Galatians 1:15–16

ALWAYS THE PRESENCE

'WHEN I WAS a boy, in fact a baby, and we were travelling through the Australian bush on a reasonably wide—to me—road. I knew I knew God and that He knew me and that I knew Him.'[1] This was Geoffrey's 'first impression of life—his oldest memory':

> ... being in a basket, having been placed between the front and rear seats of the famous family Oldsmobile, a model invented somewhere about the time of his birth.

He was in the car with his father and mother, four brothers and one older sister—'just how they all fitted in he could not remember':

> The hood of the car must have been down, folded back, because he could remember being driven along a white road between tall eucalypts which seemed to him to reach the sky as he looked up in wonder and with strange yet beautiful contentment. Somehow the Presence was there, and he delighted in the eucalypts which let through the bright light of a summer day on the Southern Highlands of New South Wales. To his mind—in memory—the smooth gums had been like columns—white some, blue others—that reared into the sky as though they were pillars upholding it. Somehow he remembered the dirt road was white and sandy and cool . . .
>
> For him it was just good to be alive, secure in a basket, smelling things that made him stir within, and made him want to express himself in some kind of action. Perhaps he was gurgling or yawping in his joy because the family kept telling him to be quiet. It was certainly a great memory, and some of its greatness lay in the knowledge of the Presence. He just sensed it was good to be a creature and alive and not alone. That was all he knew, but it was

enough. It was social, and that was what impressed itself upon him—so many persons in one vehicle—parents and children. That was how life was and he felt contented in it for the moment, and he never knew what it was not to have the Presence. The absence of the Presence—had it ever have happened—would probably have been intolerable, but then this kind of idea never entered his head.[2]

The consciousness remained with him:

> What I do know is that there was never a time when I was not [conscious] of a presence which was not that of my parents or of our family, or of other human beings for that matter. I think this presence both delighted and worried me. In hindsight I think it delighted me because it told me there was more to this world than our family and other people. It worried me because it caused fear and made demands upon me, much the same as did my conscience.[3]

For Geoffrey the 'presence' was associated with the conventional church-going of the day, but was not confined to that:

> From time to time I would think this presence should be spelled 'Presence' and perhaps be called 'God'. The term 'God' worried me somewhat because my father obviously had no affinity with such a Deity, and my brothers and sisters seemed to think that any God who existed was confined to our local church, St Paul's, situated on Pearce's Corner at the intersection of the Pacific Highway and the Pennant Hills Road. What He did during the week we did not know, but on Sunday a lively congregation worshipped Him, held Sunday school, had a warm evening service and then departed from Him until the next Sunday. Whilst women's, men's, boys' and girls' groups were held during weeknights, God was not really the centre of their activities. Almost all professional and trades people attended the Sunday services as nothing was to be lost by this, and perhaps much was to be gained. Sunday was the Sabbath and my father thought we ought to respect it.
>
> I was never really uneasy about the presence (or Presence) except that I loved wandering in the bush on the Sabbath.[4]

CONVERTED

For Geoffrey, the experience would not ever remain just conventional, especially given 'the immense awe he felt in the presence of the Presence':[5]

> The presence I had known seemed to be working me towards a crisis of soul and spirit. Admiration for new Sunday school teachers who stood for no nonsense, the advent of a child evangelist named Alex Brown—whose rubber face knew no limits, especially when he was dramatising *Pilgrim's Progress*, and the ache to be free of my childhood load of guilt led to my conversion—all of this in my thirteenth year. The presence now became the 'Presence' and suddenly I knew God was real, and that 'his nature and his name is love'.[6]

The change in Geoffrey was dramatic and permanent:

> This is where I should introduce a description of the night when I was converted. I sometimes suppose I was converted before I was born. I see it as having happened 'before the foundation of the world' and certainly many theologians would agree with me. That was when my name was written in the book of life of the Lamb. What I mean is that I knew God when I was born. There never was a time when I had not known him. At the same time I increasingly was conscious of my sinfulness. The evangelistic teaching we were given increased the sense of guilt. It is dawning on me, even as late as this moment I am writing, that my sin has been in refusing the Fatherhood of God in being a true son. Alex Brown, Ernest Reed, Vincent Craven all developed that sense of guilt. Each played a part in my conversion, but it was the night I wandered into the little wooden church in Hornsby and listened to a young man equipped with a set of coloured chalks and a blackboard, and a wonderful power of telling stories.
>
> There was nothing evangelical that man could not tell me. I knew it all but every breath of it all remains with me until this very moment. It was about the Cross, and how Calvary was 'the place of the skull'. I seemed to know every moment of my sin, every place of its happening, and its being indelible as to stain. He would not let me go, I needed the blotting out of it all. It had to be blotted out for ever, and utterly blotted out at that.

Suffice to say it was wholly blotted out and I was relieved—for ever! So many times I have gone back to that small hall, that I say the power of the Cross has proved endless. I have not needed an evangelist to persuade me of God's forgiveness afresh. Not only has Christ set the forgiveness scene for ever but he has made it irreversible for ever. I have no other source of forgiveness for others. Unless every moment is a moment of forgiveness for me, it is not for every other sinner. So where I know my own sins are forgiven I also know the sins of others are forgiven also. I have seen that Cross in so many places, in peace and in war, and at the point of failure anywhere and everywhere!

I did not wait to come forward to an appeal. Why should I have done that? Convinced of the whole matter I ran home. Was that not the place where I should tell what great things the Lord had done? I ran, I jumped, I leapt, trying to reach the hanging branches of high shrubs. I here bear witness to all the world, to all cynics and sceptics that I, Geoffrey Cyril Bingham once for all, in the thirteenth year of my life was forgiven all my sins, was saved, was converted, was born anew, was justified, was sanctified, was utterly cleansed and wholly purified and whatever else was required and all this forever and forever. None of it has been reversed or withdrawn, nor ever shall be. This is all that God demands of a sinful human being. All of this he desires for a sinner and outworks in the sinner. This is the gospel of Jesus Christ, and it is what he commands that I should preach and it is what I have preached. There is nothing more for me to preach for it is sufficient for every person's salvation needs.[7]

Geoffrey preached first to his family, with new-found boldness:

I rushed into the house where all the family, that is, as many of the family as I can remember, and my father asked how my evening had gone and I said, I shouted, 'All my sins have been forgiven and now I am saved from hell, and you all need to believe on the Lord Jesus Christ and likewise saved. If not, you too, will go to hell.'

That was a bit strong talking to all the family like that, including my father, in the exhortation.

He said, 'Now Geoffrey off you go to your room. Don't talk to me like that.'

I was glad to go through to my bedroom. It was not that I had not been thoroughly 'religious' before; it was just that I was taking the initiative outrightly. All the world would know, now, that I was declaring my vocation. The lines were set. What they had known was now in the open. To this I would be adding my message to the world.[8]

It did not stop there. With the teaching he gave as Leader of the Boys' Club, that he says was 'free from heresy and good for true evangelical teaching', consisting of 'many of the great truths' that he later expounded in the books he wrote, 'just about every boy—if not all members of our own Boys' Club—were converted in my time'.[9]

Geoffrey also found that not everyone took kindly to his preaching:

> The results of this conversion experience both delighted and appalled me. I was delighted with the sheer freedom I had in my heart and mind, and appalled because suddenly people put me into the religious category. That category has always seemed dreary to me, and not a little grim. I won't pause to describe it more fully, but the confusing of faith with religion is deplorable. Whatever my feelings were, and are, I felt a coldness between old friends and myself. Unfortunately I took it personally and resented it, and it became the source of conflict. I have seen since that if anyone actually allies himself with God—the Presence—in this world he will discover that the Deity has plenty of enemies.[10]

Nevertheless, this conversion brought him into a revelation of the living Presence, which was indelibly printed on his being:

> I fixed an interiority of being that sought to express itself in good human relationships. I admit to innumerable failures, to the intrusion of my ego into many relationships, and to an ambitious spirit which confused friends and enemies concerning my intimacy with God. Even so, I knew a holy awe of God, the obligation to show Him to others and to live by the innate law of His being. That represents both my joy of life and my pain in failure.[11]

BEFORE GOD

The fullness and permanence of what came to Geoffrey in his conversion never left him, and was the basis of all his preaching, teaching and counselling:

There is a scenario which goes something like this—a Christian who may even be a revered teacher or an effective evangelist, a steady person and well versed in the Scriptures, finds himself or herself in a state of misery because he dare not admit to another Christian that he feels unworthy of being well regarded in the eyes of others. Why? Because his conscience seems to tell him that he is a pretender. He knows full well that thoughts which come to his mind, pressures which come from the flesh, actions which he does and sins he commits all tell him he is far from being perfect, and indeed the claims he sometimes makes in regard to his life seem hollow. He may sincerely believe what Scripture tells him regarding himself and indeed preach the text of the Bible with strong conviction, but even at the point of preaching he may be asking himself questions such as, 'Who am I to be teaching these things?', 'I am so much a failure that it is not seemly for me even to be opening my mouth. Why is this so? I teach others in all sincerity but despair of ever being truly qualified by reason of a proper Christian life and witness.' It appears a bit like Paul's 'For I do not do the good I want, but the evil I do not want is what I do' (Rom. 7:19).

What is our answer to this scenario? Do we just comfort the person by saying, 'My dear friend, you have a sensitive conscience because you are a believer, but it is in danger of becoming a morbid conscience. Sure, the things you deplore are to be deplored, but we are not yet in glory. Once there, these things which depress you will be absent. You will never see them again. Just do the best you can now, but remember we are human, and as such we do fail in the battle from time to time. We are not perfect, but nevertheless will be perfected in the end-time. I encourage you by the thought of Paul, "And I am sure that he who began a good work in you will bring it to completion at the day of Jesus Christ" (Phil. 1:6). Much of the same thought is in 1 Thessalonians 5:24, "He who calls you is faithful, and he will do it".'[12]

That seems a reasonable approach, and as far as many of us would be prepared to go. Geoffrey knew something better:

At first sight this does seem to be a helpful answer, but examined carefully it can be shown to be unhelpful and even misleading. I believe the answer should be along other lines, and that we ought to present the following:

'You are a sinner saved by grace through faith. You have been told that in Christ's cross, along with his resurrection, all provisions have been made for you living a holy and righteous life in Christ Jesus, and by the power of the Holy Spirit who brings the word of Christ to you both for believing it and practicing it. That is what Paul is speaking about in Philippians 1:6 and 1 Thessalonians 5:24. If you add up a number of things which have come to you because by faith you believed God for His salvation, then: (i) by grace you have been saved by faith and this not of yourself it is the gift of God (Eph. 2:8f.); (ii) you have been forgiven all sins (Eph. 1:7–8; Rom. 4:25); (iii) you have been justified by grace when you believed (Rom. 3:24–26; cf. 4:5, 25; Phil. 3:9); (iv) you have been washed, sanctified and justified (1 Cor. 6:11); (v) you have been freed from the power of sin (Rom. 6:1–14); (vi) you have been cleansed from the pollution of sin (Heb. 1:3; 9:14; 10:22; 1 Cor. 6:11); (vii) you have been born again (1 Peter 1:3, 22–23; cf. 1 John 2:29; 3:9); (viii) you are a new creation (2 Cor. 5:17; Gal. 5:16); (ix) you have been sanctified (2 Thess. 2:13; 1 Cor. 6:11; Acts 20:32; 26:18); (x) you have been made a child and a son of God (John 1:12–13; Gal. 4:4–7); (xi) you are being conformed to the image of God's Son (Rom. 8:21, 29, 30; 1 John 3:1–3; cf. 2 Cor. 3:18); and (xii) you have been given the gift of eternal life (John 3:16; 5:24; 1 Tim. 1:16).'[13]

So do we simply try to convince ourselves of these things in our own minds? Is that what it is—a more or less persuasive mind game? Geoffrey knew these things, and could tell them to others, because no doubt he needed to hear them and tell them to himself time and again. It is not a case, however, of convincing ourselves by saying it often enough. The power of these things is that they are already true, by the finished work of Christ in his death and resurrection. They are 'effective through faith':[14]

This is what you are before God, and you must keep this in mind—'before God'. All of this is believed so that by faith all we have said above—and more—is what and how you are. All the time we walk by faith and not by sight. You must always see—by faith, and never by human sight. Your faith can never make anything to be. The whole range of the things in the above paragraph are so by God's work. You have faith that all we have said is so—before God.[15]

FULL SALVATION

Time and again in his preaching, teaching and writing, Geoffrey reiterated livingly the elements of salvation. Here are but a few indications of what he imparted.

Sin

> Not by looking to sin do we discover its nature, but by looking to God. In the light of purity we see our impurity. In the light of His perfection we discover our own depravity. In the light of His glory we see our own dishonour.[16]

> Man's sin is in not being in the full glory of God.[17]

> ... sin is an attitude and an act against the person of God, and is therefore personal. It expresses man's rebellion and hatred.[18]

> A Hebrew understanding of sin ran along something of the lines that follow: Words used for sin were particular and not generic. They covered the ideas of wickedness, confusion, iniquity, perversion, guilt, wrongness, trouble, vanity, lying, deceit, evil, trespass, breach of trust, error, negligence, injustice, disobedience, transgression. They included the component elements of sin so clearly expressed in the Psalms such as restlessness, burden, dread, fear, turmoil, and the like. The Hebrew word *awon* approximates to our idea of guilt. So David can say, 'Thou hast taken away the <u>*awon*</u> *chatta'ti* (guilt of my sin)' (Psa. 32:5). Guilt seems almost to be an entity in itself, although it is vitalistic. Sin, in any case, is vitalistic. Each sin is vitalistic.[19]

> Man then does not seek to extricate himself from sin ... he has no ability to do so. He is morally impotent. Paul says, 'When we were without strength ...' (Rom. 5:6). Most of all man in being evil and unholy is under the judgement of God. He cannot pay the penalty. He cannot expiate his guilt. God is holy, and man's dilemma is that he is doomed because of this.[20]

Wrath

> Experiences of irrational human anger in childhood will certainly give us bad images of any kind of wrath, be it Divine or human. It

will need a view of God as essentially love, and His use of retributive and juridical judgments to be seen as the actions not of Divine irrationality but of His love. We need to be able to speak of 'the wrath which comes from love'.[21]

... the modern saying, 'God hates the sin but loves the sinner' is simply not true. Sin is done from the will of the sinner and it is the action of the sinner which God hates and He does not separate what is done from the doer.[22]

Paul, in Romans 1:24, 26 and 28, speaks of God giving man up to his evil ... Man experiences God's wrath as God's giving him up to (the effects, compounding, and elements of) his own sin. We can then say, 'Whilst God's wrath is not sin, yet sin is God's wrath.' That is, man feels the wrath of God in his conscience as the effects of sin pile up on him. This is felt in guilt, in fear, in loneliness, alienation, pollution and defilement, separation, frustration, confusion, pain, shame, and wounding. So the list could be lengthened. These constituent elements of sin are sin in action, i.e. the wrath of God working in man.[23]

The punishment of sin which is the guilt of sin would have to be borne by the sinner and this would be no less than hell: only if Christ can in some way bear the guilt of sin would that sin be dealt with fully. Christ, in the atonement of the Cross, would have to bear the *guilt* of the sinner which is the same as saying he would be bearing the punishment which *is* guilt, and which is God's wrath ... No man can bear the sin of another which he has not committed. Not being guilty, how can he become guilty? The answer to that—if an answer is possible—would explain the only way one person could bear the wrath on sin, that is, the guilt of sin, would be to become that very person, that guilty person ... somehow Christ becomes the authentic sin-bearer and the receiver of the wrath of God on all sin.[24]

... it is the love of God in wrath which acts to take away the guilt of the sinner and sets him free.[25]

Repentance

... repentance [*metanoia*] means 'change of mind.' It is important to keep this in mind, because the common understanding of repentance seems to incorporate sorrow, anguish, a turning from sin, a turning to God, conversion, and even restitution. Repentance is not all these things, although it certainly involves them.

Sorrow or contrition for sin leads to repentance, and rejection of sin, turning to God, are fruits of repentance, rather than the repentance itself. However we need not be too technical. It does not matter if people see repentance as involving all these. Yet what we must be careful to do is to get to the core meaning of repentance, or 'change of mind' . . . or attitude. We need to see that this is a very deep change, in fact it is a change which affects man totally. Wherever there is true repentance, *the whole person is changed.*[26]

. . . there is a vast difference between repentance and remorse. In II Corinthians 7:10 Paul says, 'Godly grief produces a repentance that leads to salvation, and brings no regret, but worldly grief produces death.' We can say a grief or sorrow that God initiates leads to repentance. A grief that man's spirit initiates is harsh and deadly.[27]

Repentance is a Gift: Two passages make this very clear—Acts 5:31, and 11:18. God has given repentance to Israel. God has given repentance to the Gentiles. That is to say that the gift of repentance is now universal. It is there for any man who will repent. If we ask 'Why is it a gift?' the answer is 'Because man cannot, of himself repent.' The full answer involves the whole fact that, as Jesus said, 'He who commits sin is the bondslave of sin.' He cannot extricate himself. He cannot repent. We would need to see that in fact the whole work of saving and renewing a man is initiated by God. Repentance is a gift, faith is a gift, forgiveness is a gift.[28]

Repentance is Evoked: By this we mean men repent when they have an incentive. Generally that incentive is a gracious one, one that draws out a positive response . . . Repentance simply and naturally follows the revelation of the love of God. When that revelation comes and there is no response, then let us put it this way: *failure to repent is refusal to repent, and is not natural, but unnatural.*[29]

Repentance is always a command, even if it often seems to be couched as an invitation. John commanded; Jesus commanded; Peter commanded; Paul commanded. Yet in fact it was God who commanded. 'God has commanded all men everywhere to repent, for He has fixed a day in which He will judge the world in righteousness by a man whom He has appointed, and of this He has given assurance by raising Him from the dead' (Acts 17: 30) . . . Have we repented? Let us gladly take the gift of God and repent. And if, by chance we be of those who have drifted, let us renew our repentance as we cry, 'Turn us, oh Lord, and we shall be turned'.[30]

Forgiveness

Forgiveness . . . is the personal act of God in forgiving us the violations done to His Person.[31]

Forgiveness destroys the pollution, the penalty and the power of sin.[32]

The question for the reader is this, 'Do you know the forgiveness of sins? Has a voice said to you, "Buck up! Your sins are forgiven!"?' If you ask the question in reply, 'What does forgiveness do for man?' then the answer is, 'Just about everything.' Mainly it releases him from the tension of his guilt, the pressure of his past, and the burden of his shame. He is a free man. A forgiven man is about the free-est man in the world.[33]

Justification

Justification is the removal of our legal guilt, i.e. is a legal acquittal before the law of God from its accusation. The statement, 'There is no condemnation to them that are in Christ Jesus,' must mean the guilt is erased, however much subjective guilt may linger within us, or shame be felt on occasions of sinning.[34]

. . . justification is simply acquittal from the accusation and condemnation of sin. 'Justified,' we tell the children, 'is being just-as-if-I'd never sinned.' That is what it means. It does not mean I have never sinned—for I have. But before God as the Judge of all men I stand as though I had never sinned.[35]

. . . justification is the refusal of God to impute the sin committed against the repentant sinner. This is not because of the sinner's repentance, but because of His own grace and love. He has provided for the demands of the law to be met in full in the death of Christ. Forgiveness and justification, then, both relate to, and spring from, the Atonement.[36]

Sanctification

Paul tells us that the ultimate God has for us is that we shall be 'holy and blameless, before Him' (Eph. 1:4). He means that as God is holy so shall we be, and that we will rejoice in this affinity.[37]

One writer said, 'he made purification for sins', and so another could speak of the conscience being 'cleansed from dead works', i.e. from sins. Yet another said, 'you were washed'. These are profound statements. They tell us—in line with the prophetic promises—that a human being, through Christ's death and resurrection, can become holy. This holiness is both extrinsic and intrinsic. That is why we say, 'Happy he who holy is!' To become pure is like bathing so that nothing of impurity is left. In fact, this happening is called (in the Bible) 'the washing [bath] of regeneration and the renewing of the Holy Spirit'.

Not only does God provide for a *total* washing, but He also provides for a *continual* washing. The first is covered by the words 'you were washed' and the latter by 'the blood of the Lord Jesus Christ goes on cleansing us from every sin'. It is an experienced fact that washed people (Christians) still commit sins, even though they hate them. There is also another fact of great importance. It is this: God declares us to be His holy people when we are forgiven our sins and cleansed from our defilement.[38] It is this fact which we need to concentrate upon.[39]

It is often said that the believer is *positionally* holy, but that he must become that *conditionally*, meaning that his condition must become parallel with his position. This is not a helpful way of speaking. It is better to see that the believer has been forgiven, justified, sanctified, adopted into sonship, given the gift of the Spirit, placed into membership with the whole Body, the Church, and is part of the people of God. This helps him to see that holiness of life will not be an individualistic endeavour, that the basis for a life of obedience is based upon forgiveness, and that he is aided by the Spirit who indwells, and by the members of the Body of which he also is a member. Any consideration of holiness which sets a standard, and demands a work which originates from the believer is doomed to failure, as the effort is certain also to be legalistic.[40]

PEACE WITH GOD

Geoffrey spoke of these things with the immediacy of one to whom they were real, and needed to be real, every moment:

> I constantly say to myself, 'Wherefore, being justified by faith I now have peace with God through my Lord Jesus Christ'. I constantly say this because all around me people are saying other things and talking other things, and I could be swayed by their ways of thinking. Also I am aware that I go through moods and feelings where I even accuse myself of having failed God, both in the past and the present. My only antidote to all this is to say to myself—and certainly not in mantra fashion!—the words of Romans 5:1. I also say the words of Romans 8:1, 'There is therefore now no condemnation to those who are in Christ Jesus'. Also very heart-warming to me are the words of an old hymn; heart-warming because Satan accuses me of all sorts of things, many of which have more than a grain of truth in them:
>
> > When Satan tempts me to despair,
> > And tells me of the guilt within,
> > Upward I look and see him there
> > Who made an end to all my sin.
>
> Standing fast in the reality that the Scriptures teach of this wonderful reality, we refuse accusation that is now untrue, and if it is true, then we accept it, secure in the knowledge that Christ has dealt with it and that it does not endanger the security of justification.[41]

[1] *The Story of New Creation Teaching Ministry.*

[2] *Always the Presence*, part 1, chapter 1, unpublished autobiography of Geoffrey Bingham's life up to 1945, written in the third person, begun in 1988. For a full biblical exposition of God being present to humanity see *The Everlasting Presence*.

[3] *My Beloved Family*, 71.

[4] *My Beloved Family*, 71–72.

[5] *Always the Presence*, part 1, chapter 7.

[6] *My Beloved Family*, 75.

[7] *The Story of New Creation Teaching Ministry.*

[8] *The Story of New Creation Teaching Ministry.*

[9] *The Story of New Creation Teaching Ministry.*

[10] *My Beloved Family*, 75–76.

[11] *My Beloved Family*, 176.

[12] 'The Matter of Power in the Church—4', NCTM Monthly Ministry Study (MMS), 2nd and 7th May 2005, p. 5. See: <www.newcreationlibrary.net/studies/pdf/MMS_2005.pdf>.

[13] 'The Matter of Power in the Church—4', (MMS, May 2005), p. 5.

[14] Romans 3:25.

[15] 'The Matter of Power in the Church—4', (MMS, May 2005), p. 6.

[16] 'The Whole of Forgiveness', study 2 in *Living Faith Studies* (LFS), vol. 1, p. 35. Also published, with some additions, as *Freely Flows Forgiveness* (now out of print).

[17] 'The Whole of Forgiveness', study 2, *LFS* vol. 1, 35.

[18] 'The Whole of Forgiveness', study 2, *LFS* vol. 1, 51.

[19] 'The Whole of Forgiveness', study 2, *LFS* vol. 1, 38.

[20] 'The Whole of Forgiveness', study 2, *LFS* vol. 1, 37.

[21] *The Wrath of His Love: Studies in the Wrath of God and of Man*, 3.

[22] *The Wrath of His Love*, 20.

[23] *The Things We Firmly Believe*, 95.

[24] *The Wrath of His Love*, 57, 58.

[25] *The Wrath of His Love*, 21.

[26] 'Commanded Repentance and Full Forgiveness', *Christian Teaching Series* (CTS) no. 4, 1, 7.

[27] 'Commanded Repentance and Full Forgiveness', *CTS* no. 4, 7.

[28] 'Commanded Repentance and Full Forgiveness', *CTS* no. 4, 8.

[29] 'Commanded Repentance and Full Forgiveness', *CTS* no. 4, 9–10.

[30] 'Commanded Repentance and Full Forgiveness', *CTS* no. 4, 10, 12.

[31] 'The Whole of Forgiveness', study 2, *LFS* vol. 1, 47.

[32] 'Commanded Repentance and Full Forgiveness', *CTS* no. 4, 21.

[33] 'Commanded Repentance and Full Forgiveness', *CTS* no. 4, 12.

[34] 'The Whole of Forgiveness', study 2, *LFS* vol. 1, 47.

[35] 'Faith Justification Conversion and the New Birth', *CTS* no. 5, 9.

[36] 'The Whole of Forgiveness', study 2, *LFS* vol. 1, 51. See further, 'The Grace of Justification in the Pauline Epistles' in *Great and Glorious Grace*, 165–201.

[37] 'Sanctification: The Doctrine of Christian Holiness', study 6 in *LFS* vol. 1, 98.

[38] Geoffrey is referring here to 1 Corinthians 6:11: 'But you were washed, you were sanctified, you were justified in the name of the Lord Jesus Christ and in the Spirit of our God', where cleansing and sanctification are placed prior to, and in the same package with, justification.

[39] 'The Christian Doctrine of Holiness', *CTS* no. 7, 6–7.

[40] 'Sanctification: The Doctrine of Christian Holiness', study 6 in *LFS* vol. 1, 105.

[41] *Comprehending Justification*, 31.

CHAPTER 4

Cross OVER THE Abyss

In Malaya, 1941

PRISONER OF WAR

So WE RAN towards the Japs, and their guns sang, a yammering, rising, falling sort of song that has never died away ... Then the gun wounded. I felt a fury of shock, the left leg buckled and I plunged to the ground ... a wounded man on a smooth black road, a leg smashed, blood running, and the cries and sounds of war again about the ears, the threatening drone of a plane, the explosion of mortars, the incessant shrill shells.[1]

The date was the 11th February 1942.[2] Geoffrey Bingham, Sergeant with the Signals Unit of the 22nd Brigade Headquarters of the AIF 8th Division, 'had been caught up in one of the last battles on Singapore Island and had been severely wounded in an attack on a Japanese machine-gun nest. For his part in this action he was subsequently awarded the Military Medal and was Mentioned in Despatches.'[3] Sir Edward 'Weary' Dunlop reports the clinical diagnosis and treatment:

> ... a compound fracture of the right thigh-bone with damage to a nerve which inflicted foot drop and partial paralysis below the knee.
>
> Most fortunate to survive at all, he lost weight in a few weeks from twelve to seven stone, and after four months bedridden extension emerged with diminishing but permanent lameness to become librarian in the 10th Australian General Hospital.[4]

So began three years in Changi Prison Camp, followed by eighteen months in the Kranji Hospital Camp up to September 1945,[5] which were to prove so formative for Geoffrey's life and ministry. He was indeed 'fortunate to survive'. Rescued from Reformatory Road, he was taken first to Gillman Barracks, improvised as a hospital to take the overflow of patients from the Alexandra Military Hospital across the road.[6] Doctors, nursing sisters, staff and patients in the Alexandra Hospital were systematically bayoneted to death when Korean soldiers, conscripted by the Japanese and probably heavily drugged, burst in there a couple of days later, while those in the Barracks nearby were spared by the Imperial Japanese Guards.[7] Later transferred to the Fullarton building next to the GPO, he was one of nine considered too wounded to shift when ordered to move to Changi by a senior Japanese officer. They were given lethal doses of morphia because they were expected to die anyway in the move. Geoffrey and one other Australian survived.[8] It was later in Kranji, physically weary and weak—so much so that he felt he might collapse and even die—that Geoffrey heard an audible voice telling him: 'Thou shalt not die, but live, and declare the works of the Lord!'[9] And so he did.

'I was naïve in those days. What would you expect of a lad of twenty-three? It was true I had been a person of faith, but that was soon to undergo its own test.'[10] Joining the army in 1940 had catapulted Geoffrey from the comparatively sheltered life of Wahroonga and Box Hill into 'a world we had never known':

> [We] had never met the riffraff of life, including the helpless and the hopeless of the Great Depression, let alone the criminal elements of our cities who wanted an opportunity for a new life. Nor had we met much of the superb breed of men from farms and stations who had come with ideals that stretched back to the Boer and Great Wars, rallying with their love of Britain and the Empire, to stand against the Axis powers.[11]

Geoffrey was intent on not concealing his evangelical faith:

> I remember quietly placing my Bible on the pillow of my palliasse. I thought I would let them know about the Presence which always went with me. The other new recruits certainly got the message. When I returned that night the air was not only blue with cigarette smoke, but was as thick with blue jokes. I began to understand there might be a battle ahead . . . had I been more mature it would not have happened like that . . . yet, even now, I do not regret the impulsive gesture.[12]

As Physical Instruction Trainer, Corporal Bingham had gained the respect of the men by proving himself in the boxing ring, where he earned the title of 'Battling Padre'.[13] But experiences in prison camp were to shake his faith to its core:

> During those years as a prisoner-of-war, like so many others he suffered at times from dengue and malaria, some beriberi, diphtheric ulcer and dysentery. His health was not helped by an inadequate diet or semi-starvation. Added to all this, he had to surmount the psychological and emotional stress of total uncertainty as to the duration or outcome of the War. No one who has not gone through such an experience can fully understand the toll of pain, suspense, and suffering.

Worst of all, however:

> Geoff had a horrified reaction to the general selfishness which the War had shown up. As a result, aggravated no doubt by his own wounds, he went through a phase of spiritual desolation.[14]

He was disturbed not so much by any brutality of the Japanese as by the 'utter moral devastation' and self-saving treachery[15] of his own countrymen:

> I remember the day I had my greatest shock. It was when a friend told me that some of our own troops had broken into the hospital store and stolen precious drugs and tinned foods and had sold them on the black market in order to keep themselves alive at the expense of those who were helpless and less fortunate than themselves. Of course I was appalled because these drugs were otherwise unobtainable and most necessary for bad surgical and medical cases. The tinned food was for those who needed that kind of food to keep them alive during terrible illnesses.[16]

Geoffrey was also told, 'some of the chaplains are in the rackets'.[17] This was life in the raw:

> I had been brought up in a Calvinistic tradition and knew the theological doctrine of the total depravity of Man. I was alert enough as a young person to know there was cruelty, selfishness

and other evil in the world in which I lived even before the war. History is long on that kind of evil of Man, but the fact is that when I now saw depravity in its raw forms, I was shocked. One can live more or less comfortably in a world of theological abstractions, but then one is horrified beyond measure when confronted with the concrete realities of which that theology has spoken.[18]

For a time the only thing that kept him from scornful bitter cynicism was the dogged realisation that this would be like turning into a self-righteous Pharisee:[19]

The high danger in which one can live is to take the higher moral ground in one's judgement of depraved persons. This is the incipient Pharisaism of all self-righteous persons, and how many of us escape it? Everyone takes the high moral ground: everyone.[20]

'For him it was now the end of faith—or close to it.'[21] We will see in the next chapter how this crisis of faith was resolved. Suffice to say at this point:

God had some better purpose in store and brought him through the darkness. A richer understanding of the Atonement was to give him a new sense of inner freedom, in spite of being in a prison camp.[22]

It was not just a 'richer understanding' but a deeper personal experience of the Atonement, reaching through the extremities to which he had been brought. Given a typewriter as Hospital Librarian, Geoffrey wrote—stories, poems, novels—for four hours a day.[23] None of that writing survived—the day came when he burned it all.[24] One short poem remained in his brain:

> Angel wings, beating my face;
> Forcing me into grace.
>
> Dear eyes, loving my soul,
> Drawing me to the goal.

Strong Word, piercing my brain,
Bringing me holy shame.

Pain's cry, welling within,
Lifting me out of sin.

Red hands, clotted with blood,
Thrusting me up to God.[25]

THE WORK OF THE CROSS

The depths of human depravity exposed in this setting called for a matching depth of experience and understanding with regard to God's dealing with evil and sin on the cross, 'which had always been, and still is, central to my thinking and theology':[26]

> Unless we understand the extent of man's depravity in his rebellion against God, we cannot even begin to assess the power needed to regenerate him ... We say, then, that the work of the Cross must indeed be powerful to grip man in his desperate and lost state. We say it must require a work of vast dimensions to move down into man and transform him.[27]

Having lived through something of the worst that the proud human spirit can do—within himself, as well as among others—Geoffrey in his teaching for the rest of his life baulked at nothing that the Scriptures said concerning the grievous offence that the cross is to our proud human spirit as the sole God-ordained means of our salvation. Here is one brief instance:

> We now come to see what God did in and through His Son, and how, in fact He did it. On the night of His betrayal Jesus took the cup of wine and said, 'This is my blood of the new covenant which is shed for you and for many for the remission of sins.' That was clear enough. He was saying, 'My death will take away and destroy your sins—for ever. You will be free of them.' Then He said, 'You will all be scandalised because of me this night, for it is written, "I will smite the shepherd and the sheep shall be scattered."' He was quoting a centuries' old prophecy from Zechariah 13:7 'Awake oh

sword against my fellow. Smite the shepherd and the sheep shall be scattered.' 'Awake' means 'Draw from the scabbard'. 'Make ready'. 'Smite' means 'Cut in judgement'. 'My fellow' means 'My equal'. 'The Shepherd' means, 'the Good Shepherd, the only Shepherd, Jesus!'

That the Cross is a scandal is in no doubt. Paul later said 'The preaching of the Cross is to the Jew a scandal. To the Greek it is (intellectual) foolishness.' And no wonder. Listen to what New Testament writers say about Him on the Cross. Peter says 'He bore our sins in His body on the tree.' He means that Christ did not just bear the punishment of sins upon that Cross, but **He bore the sins themselves**! Of course the punishment was inherent in the sins, but it must be said again, He bore the sins! Paul, in like vein says, 'God made Him (He who knew no sin) **to be sin** for us'. That is Christ became the actual sin. What does that mean, but that He bore its components, its shame, its pain, its fear, its defilement, its anguish, its burden, its impurity, its suffering, its deep sorrows— all the things which we said constitute the personal wrath of God upon man? [28]

This is nothing but 'all that the prophets have declared'—'Was it not necessary that the Messiah should suffer these things and then enter into his glory?'[29]

'Yes,' cries Isaiah, 'We did esteem Him stricken, smitten of God and afflicted.' He was right; so He was. He continues, 'But He was wounded for our transgression. He was bruised for our iniquities. The chastisement of our peace was upon Him, and with His stripes we are healed.' What suffering! As Jeremiah voiced it, 'Is it nothing to you, all you that pass by, Look and see if there be any sorrow like unto my sorrow, wherewith God has visited me in the day of His wrath.'[30]

Wrath and love come together in this action of God:

See, the deep sorrow that a man knows all his life of sin is now borne by this beloved Son. He bares Himself for the sword, the cut of judgement and then cries in intolerable anguish. 'My God! My God! Why hast thou forsaken me?' Only there do we understand both the wrath and the love. Isaiah says, 'Surely He has borne our griefs, and carried our sorrows.' Yes, that is it; there is nothing which needed to be borne, which He has not borne.

Then He cried, 'It is finished.' Ah, yes, the total work is finished. The wrath is borne; sin is destroyed. Man is freed. Man does not now have to receive the judgement.[31]

Geoffrey was not simply content to set it out. He urged his hearers to come in on the reality of it, and many did:

Do you believe this? Do you believe God has revealed Himself in the anguish and love of that Cross? Do you believe every pain and impurity of your sin has been borne to extinction by this beloved Son, sent by the loving Father? Do you trust God? Do you submit to Him? Do you now understand true repentance and forgiveness? Do you really know now what it means 'There is therefore now no condemnation to them that are in Christ Jesus,' and 'Wherefore being justified by faith we have peace with God through our Lord Jesus Christ'?

Friend, let faith—God's great gift to you—have its way, right now. Submit in repentance and faith. Take the gift of forgiveness, and your clearance from guilt. Look, clear-eyed, into the eye of the God who loves. Believe, trust and submit.

Your faith hath saved you, go in peace![32]

Geoffrey preached 'Jesus Christ, and him crucified'[33] tirelessly with many different approaches to bring it through in every way he could. In August 1962, on furlough from missionary service in Pakistan, in a teaching Mission at St Luke's Church, Thornleigh NSW, he spoke for a week on 'Christian Liberty'. Beginning from Luke 1:73, 'we, being rescued from the hands of our enemies', and possibly taking a cue from Martin Luther, he spoke of the 'Eight Tyrants' that are the enemies of humankind from which we have been freed through Christ's cross: Sin and Death, Satan and the Powers, the World and the Flesh, and Law and Wrath.[34] These 'enemies', and our deliverance from them, are set out with variations in a number of his later writings.[35] It was during the Thornleigh mission that one woman said:

'When Mr Bingham was speaking there, he just suddenly disappeared, and there was Jesus there in the pulpit, and he looked right through me, and I know now I am forgiven.' She was a changed woman from that point onwards.[36]

A dramatic instance of this is described from the revival in Pakistan in 1966.[37] A young man was 'shaking uncontrollably' as Geoffrey spoke. 'Only when the testimony was finished, and the final blessing was uttered did his shaking still to quietness':

> His eyes opened, and he saw the speaker. 'Oh sir,' he cried, 'Oh sir, I saw him!'
>
> The speaker nodded. A strong, strange feeling had gripped him around the heart. 'Yes,' he said, 'I believe you did.'
>
> 'Oh sir,' said the man. 'He was on that Cross and, oh sir, I felt so unclean. As you preached you disappeared, and only he was there—on that Cross. Sir, my heart was black, my whole being submerged in my own dark evil. I felt horrible, wretched, polluted.' He paused, pain in his eyes at the memory. 'But, oh sir,' he gasped, 'as he looked down at me, from that Cross, his eyes were filled with love and pity. Then his blood began to drop on me, drop after drop, dripping onto me.' His face glowed. 'Why sir,' he said, with awe in his voice, 'he washed me. He washed me from tip to toe. He made me white as snow.'[38]

At a mission meeting at the Liverpool Town Hall in NSW (with traffic noise outside) one Sunday afternoon in 1975 Geoffrey spoke on 'The Wrath of Love'[39]—'the most difficult of all subjects in the spectrum of Christian teaching'. Geoffrey was brought to tears as he felt he was battling not only to get this across to his hearers but also against some of the powers in the heavenly places, as he set out the full dimensions of the love of God through the propitiation of the cross. It is remembered as a 'powerful meeting' in which 'many were moved'.[40] The recording of that session became one of the most widely listened to of all Geoffrey's talks.

The New Creation Teaching Ministry Summer School at Victor Harbor in 1985 on 'The Power and Preaching of the Cross' was memorable not only for Geoffrey's studies on 'The Cross and Forgiveness', 'The Cross and Justification', 'The Cross and Christian Victory', 'The Cross and Law' and 'The Cross and the

Spirit'—still in demand on audio and video recordings[41]—but also in the ways that whole School was contested in areas of accommodation, furnishings, catering and health.[42]

Many times, from small home groups to three-hour devotions on Good Friday afternoons, Geoffrey has taken people through the seven words of Jesus on the cross, where the heart of God is laid bare:

> ...these words deal with forgiveness, with the coming of sinners into the Paradise of God, with family relationships, with alienation of the sinner from God, with spiritual barrenness and thirst, with the completion of God's plan for man's redemption, and with the offering up of the spirit to the Father Himself.[43]

People hearing these have had their hearts freed and their lives changed.

CRUCIFIED WITH CHRIST

Geoffrey did not draw back from saying that Christ's death on the cross was substitutionary:

> ...Christ's death was primarily legal, that is, it was primarily to bear the penalty of sin.[44]

> There are, of course, many Scriptures which speak of a work of Christ *for* humanity, and that this operation was executed both in his death and his resurrection, e.g. 'He was put to death *for* our trespasses and raised *for* our justification' (Rom. 4:25).[45]

But this is not simply external to us. Not only can we say that Christ 'loved me and gave himself for me', but in that also, 'I have been crucified with Christ'.[46] There can be no effective substitution without thoroughgoing identification. Geoffrey took seriously Paul's statement: 'we are convinced that one has died for all; therefore all have died'.[47] This effectively means that in him we have already *'died the penal death* required for justification'.[48] We are united with Christ—not as a mystical exercise

61

of the mind, not by ascetic practices of attempted 'self-crucifix-ion' in one way or another, and not by regarding ourselves as now above the law[49]—but simply and wholly by faith:

> *The Godward aspect* is that Christ identified with us, in that 'he was numbered with the transgressors' . . . *The manward aspect* must be the acceptance that what happened on the Cross is true. This acceptance comes from being informed, but even more so from being convicted, brought to repentance and faith, and submitted to God in obedience to the Gospel . . . *What matters is that there was a point of faith when we knew* (not necessarily *felt*) *we had died.* This is the manward aspect of co-crucifixion and co-resurrection. Notice that it is a matter of faith and not human works.[50]

Beyond that, Geoffrey urges us not to try to work it out, but accept it as fact:

> The facts then are: Christ died, so we died; Christ was buried, so we were buried; Christ rose, so we rose; Christ is seated in heavenly places, so we also are thus seated.[51]

And to live accordingly.

THE DEEP SORROW AND
THE GREAT SUFFERING

Geoffrey took some pains to trace the impact of the suffering of the cross on Christ's own person—insofar as that is possible:

> All evil powers are present to taunt and to accuse, and he must take the sting of them, as also the sting of death. He must take the weight of sin, its fiery penalty, its innate components of wrath. He must feel the smothering evil of human filth and moral pollution. He must know the dreadful anger of God upon all sin. He must, as man, be taken from the Holy Presence and go out into the place of the damned. He must suffer it all, or not at all.
>   And he does. In doing this he painfully, but fully, explicates the love of the Father. There must be no talk of God being personally

wrathful with His Son, but there must be talk of the Son bearing the wrath of God upon evil, or no theodicy will ever prove valid.

In other words, *he is forsaken*! What almost crushed him to death in the Garden of Gethsemane, is here given its full outworking. The sword which was to be bared against the Fellow of God (Zech. 13:7; cf. Matt. 26:31–39; Heb. 5:7–8; 2:9–10) is not only bared *but it strikes*! The horror of the sinful body of humanity, the evil of the Serpent, the pollution of the human spirit—all of these are borne to extinction, and so the cry is . . . of all pain of humanity, for all time.[52]

Nor is this suffering confined to the Son alone. It reaches into the very heart of the Godhead. In the vision-type allegory *Bright Bird and Shining Sails*, Geoffrey depicts a ship whose centre sail represents the Father, the rear sail represents the Son, and the forward sail, which doubles as a bright bird, represents the Holy Spirit. Here is how he describes 'the depthless suffering':

It was then I looked at the ship. Stark steady it was, and no movement. What I had not seen was the white centre sail move backwards until it covered the rear sail. I cannot deny that it bent down and covered and sheltered and protected and hid the smaller sail within its great self. But then I must say that at the moment of highest anguish—that moment of suffering—a terrible thing happened. It was as though the sail sprang apart in horror, and down through the body of the vessel the great rift suddenly appeared. In my horror I thought the vessel was divided and one part falling away from another. I screamed within and looked away.

There was a sound like a mighty rending, and when I looked back, fearful, I saw high flames shooting up, and a stupendous roar, and a ripping and cracking and the sound of terrible tearing, and all the sky grew black, and the flames leapt high, and the ship swirled and swirled and swirled, turning on its keel like a mad thing, until I was giddy with the swirling, turning movement of it, and my heart was so sick with pain that I was nigh to a mortal retching.

I turned away, breathing with a hot, dry breathing and sobbing so that there was a tearing sound in my own chest. I had to turn and look again, and when I did I could not believe what I saw.

The white vessel was riding on the waters with a serenity I had never seen surpassed. Its white shining flowed out beyond itself, flowing out to all the creation. When I looked for where the crack and the rift had been there was no sign that it had ever been, and I felt like a man in a dream, when the dream has passed and the terror has gone, and unexpected joy presents itself.

When I looked back to where the sorrow had been there was nothing but a white shining. I tell you I was not too late for those last whispered words, and they were a repetition of the truth, the real truth of the sails, and they sang into my heart, and they printed themselves on my mind, and I knew what was the true glory of the white shining out there on the water, and the sheer serenity of the simple sails . . .

One thing I did know. Love was pouring out from where he had been, out of the place of the deep sorrow, and the great suffering. It was also pouring into me, until I was filled. It kept pouring, spilling out of me, and across the land, even into the ocean. It kept overflowing, and I thought that the supply of it would be enough for the whole world, and even beyond it and in that I was correct. It was enough for then, and for the coming-time, and for the time-yet-to-be. In fact that love must surely be for ever.[53]

MAN OF DUST! MAN OF GLORY!

'I will be eternally grateful to God that I spent three and a half years in a prison camp, because it gave me x-ray eyes into the human situation. Men wouldn't look at each other as they passed, because they knew their moral failure and their degradation.' Geoffrey concluded, with regard to the work of the cross: 'I don't see how without that kind of theological surgery we're ever going to have the evil excised from us'.[54]

We might expect that, exposed to that kind of experience, one would end up cynical or despairing with regard to the human race. In reality, the opposite was the case:

Geoffrey Bingham makes no secret of what has been his 'hidden agenda' all along. As a keen observer of humanity, and as a participant in human life and action in many different settings—from prison camp to church fellowship—he has made it his business to see that human beings are accorded their true God-given honour and dignity. Along with this comes his fierce opposition to anything that would belittle or demean human persons.[55]

In his extensive counselling, based on the work of the cross in people's lives,[56] and in his writing on human nature, condition and destiny,[57] as well as in his astute, penetrating and sometimes whimsical novels and short stories, Geoffrey sought to see and call men and women up to their high dignity as grown-up sons and daughters of God, to maturity—'to the measure of the stature of the fullness of Christ'.[58]

For this, the cross is indispensable. One of Geoffrey's poems, now a fine song,[59] gives what is perhaps one of the most profound analyses of the human spirit in the twentieth and twenty-first centuries:

> Out of my nothing I was all,
> Out of my everything was whole.
> Full power was mine to be, to do,
> And I could only upward fall.
> I thought myself no god to be
> Since there was nought, but only me.
>
> I scorned the shiftless schemes of men,
> Their mediocre dreams and plans,
> The best surpassed; my mind was keen
> To go beyond their settled lands.
> I knew myself no god to be
> But I could reach the heights of Thee.
>
> Full height I reared my tower of fame,
> My city walled held me in peace,
> I thought to be as Thee, O God,
> And let my strivings never cease;
> And though my art'ries never bled,
> I owned the city of the dead.
>
> That city dead was mine: I owned,
> I resonated in its power,
> I loved the thoughts my spirit bred,
> Exulting in creative hours.
> No end to treasures I could find
> Nor limits to my brilliant mind.

One day I found the weakened God
Whose art'ries dripped my deadly blood.
I saw Him groaning on a Tree
And I was Him and He was me.
All brilliance mine from Him had fled
Within the city of the dead.

I saw myself as wan and pale,
A skeleton, a dreary corpse.
I hung within His blessèd bones,
He thought my prideful, crassful thoughts.
I bled to nought within His Tree,
And by His death He captured me.

Lord! I was nought when I was full,
Full empty I when rich with fame,
Yet You embraced my wasted self
And all my dreary shambled shame.
I loved You Lord who me had loved,
Dear Father, Son and Holy Dove.

Lord, hold me weak that I be strong,
My shattered tower keep pulverised.
Let not one giddy, heady hour
Return, O Lord. Keep tranquillised
This weeping spirit filled with love
As through its heights and depths You move.

You are my Lord, and I love Thee
Who bled me out upon Your Tree.

[1] 'The Rim', in *Laughing Gunner and Selected War Stories*, 85, 86; also in *The Concentration Camp and Other Stories*, 176, 177.

[2] *Love is the Spur*, 12–13.

[3] 'Geoffrey Cyril Bingham' in Marcus L. Loane, *These Happy Warriors*, 87.

[4] *Laughing Gunner*, 'Foreword', ix.

[5] Loane, *These Happy Warriors*, 87.

[6] See 'The Man in the War Wards' in *Laughing Gunner*, 238; also *Always the Presence*, part 2, chapter 13.

[7] See *Laughing Gunner*, 246; *Always the Presence*, part 2, chapter 13.

[8] See *Laughing Gunner*, 247–250; *Always the Presence*, part 2, chapter 14.

[9] 'A Fragment about Living' in *Angel Wings*, 2; see also *Love Is the Spur*, 63; referred to in Michael Raiter, *Stirrings of the Soul: Evangelicals and the New Spirituality* (Matthias Media, Kingsford, 2003), 235–239. Compare Psalm 118:17.

[10] 'The Power Within' in *Laughing Gunner*, 121.

[11] *My Beloved Family*, 116.

[12] *My Beloved Family*, 116–117.

[13] See 'The Day I Fought Kelly' in *Laughing Gunner*, 211–225.

[14] Loane, *These Happy Warriors*, 87.

[15] *The Story of the Rice Cakes: The Search for Moral Sanity in a Prisoner of War Camp* (Second Edition, 2006), 19–20.

[16] *The Story of the Rice Cakes*, 19.

[17] *Love Is the Spur*, 28; see also *Tall Grow the Tallow-woods*, 73–74.

[18] *The Story of the Rice Cakes*, 20.

[19] See 'Three Rice Cakes' in *Angel Wings*, 81; also in *The Story of the Rice Cakes*, 6.

[20] *The Story of the Rice Cakes*, 20.

[21] *Angel Wings*, 81.

[22] Loane, *These Happy Warriors*, 87.

[23] 'A Life in the Day of a Prisoner' in *Laughing Gunner*, 161–162.

[24] See 'The Holy Holocaust' in *The Artist in the Garden*, 136–144.

[25] Frontispiece in *Angel Wings*: 'G. Bingham, Changi P. O. W. Camp, 1943'; see also *Always the Presence*, part 2, chapter 18. The third and fourth couplets were added 'decades later' when the poem was recalled in 1981—see *My Beloved Family*, 131–132; *Love Is the Spur*, 48. Set to music by Don Priest, *New Creation Hymn Book*, 65; sung at Geoffrey's funeral.

[26] *My Beloved Family*, 111.

[27] *Christ's Cross over Man's Abyss*, 148–149. 'This book is the one the author had always wanted to write—beyond any other' (back cover).

[28] 'Faith Justification Conversion and the New Birth', *Christian Teaching Series (CTS)* no. 5, 11.

[29] Luke 24:25–26; see also Luke 24:44–48; 1 Peter 1:10–12; explicated in *Christ's Cross over Man's Abyss*, 18–22.

[30] 'Faith Justification Conversion and the New Birth', *CTS* no. 5, 12.

[31] 'Faith Justification Conversion and the New Birth', *CTS* no. 5, 12.

[32] 'Faith Justification Conversion and the New Birth', *CTS* no. 5, 12.

[33] 1 Corinthians 2:2.

[34] Recorded on 7 inch reel-to-reel tapes by Fred Rush, reproduced in MP3 format by NCTM, disc 915.

[35] *Christ's Cross and Us* (NCTM June Conference 1979), 14–16; *The Things We Firmly Believe*, 114–117; *Christ's Cross over Man's Abyss*, 25–57.

[36] Interview with John Dunn, recorded 9th September 2008. The woman was John Dunn's mother, not normally accustomed to attending meetings outside her own church.

[37] See Chapter 10, under 'Lovefest Three'.

[38] 'Immanuel', in *The Concentration Camp*, 170–171.

[39] Reproduced by NCTM as ITS 21, included on 'The Cross of Christ' MP3 disc 928.

[40] Personal recollection, Robin Mitchell, 13th May 2010.

[41] Published by NCTM: series CS 37 on MP3 disc 928, 'The Cross of Christ' and on DVD 608; see: <www.videosurf.com/geoffrey-bingham-65231> (accessed 18th May 2010).

[42] Personal recollection, Helen Farmer, 18th May 2010.

[43] *The WORD and the Words of the Cross*, 3. Also available on NCTM MP3 disc 938, entitled, 'Seven Words of the Cross', ITS 20, NCPI.

[44] *Christ's Cross over Man's Abyss*, 164.

[45] *Christ's Cross over Man's Abyss*, 153.

[46] Galatians 2:20, 19.

[47] 2 Corinthians 5:14; see *Christ's Cross over Man's Abyss*, 152.

[48] *Christ's Cross over Man's Abyss*, 165.

[49] 'What Co-Crucifixion Is Not', *Christ's Cross over Man's Abyss*, 159–163.

[50] *Christ's Cross over Man's Abyss*, 157–158. Hear also Tapes for Life Series, session 63, 'Crucified with Christ', included on NCTM MP3 disc 905.

[51] *Christ's Cross over Man's Abyss*, 157.

[52] *Christ's Cross over Man's Abyss*, 69–70.

[53] *Bright Bird and Shining Sails*, 47–48.

[54] 'The Cross and Justification', NCTM Summer School 1985, CS 37:1b, available on NCTM MP3 disc 928 and on DVD 608.

[55] Martin Bleby, 'Foreword', *The Beautiful City of God*, xv.

[56] See *Practical Christian Counselling; A Biblical Way of Counselling; Direct Biblical Counselling; Wonderful Counsellor: Studies in Effective Biblical Counselling; The Meaning and Making of Man: A Series of Seven Studies on Christian Counselling;* and *The Wisdom of God and the Healing of Man*.

[57] See *I, the Man!* and *Man of Dust! Man of Glory!*

[58] Ephesians 4:13.

[59] *New Creation Hymn Book*, 301, music by Christine Dieckmann, recorded on NCPI CD 'Songs of Worship 3'.

CHAPTER 5

THE *Law* OF *Eternal Delight*

> the law of the
> Lord is perfect,
> reviving the soul
>
> Psalm 19:7

THREE RICE CAKES

'THE FOOD WAS very short and didn't have much nutrition in it . . . I was so thin I could put my thumb and my longest finger around my thigh and they'd meet. So, when you're in that situation, there is nothing academic.'[1]

Geoffrey described himself going to a meal in the prison camp:

> He threw his weak legs over the edge of the bed, staring down at their grey pellagrous skin. The flesh hung, weak and lifeless. The wrinkled texture of them was like the scabrous hide of an elephant . . . He placed his feet on the floor, took his walking stick and gripped the haft of the Thomas splint. He raised himself painfully. Somewhere a gong was sounding. The midday meal was waiting. He fumbled for his tin cup, his chipped enamel plate, and made his way along the verandah, shuffling along with all the shufflers.[2]

Not all, however, were in the same condition as he was:

> Some had a better tread than his. There were the few who had no beriberi. Their bodies had a good look, in some cases a sleek look. That look was envied by some, and hated deeply by others. Some envied and hated in the one motion. The sleek ones, of course, were those deeply in the rackets. Some of them were intrepid black-marketeers. They made their way through the barbed wire at night, or bribed the guards, or waited until there was a break in the patrol. Intrepid was the word, and they earned their health and the life they so eagerly preserved. What troubled him and others was their callous disregard for the starving ones, the dying ones, the helpless ones. He wondered vaguely what he himself might have done had he not been wounded.[3]

This revelation of human depravity is what precipitated Geoffrey's moral crisis of faith in about August 1943.[4] 'Every man for himself!' was the cry that broke out at times of desperation, and continued to be whispered in the mind.[5] Geoffrey, true to his evangelical faith, was determined not to be a part of it:

> He looked at the rice cakes on the plate. Every mealtime for months he had gone through the same struggle. Christ had said, 'Greater love has no man than this, that he lay down his life for his friend.' Each meal he had sought to do this. He had taken the smallest rice cake so that others would have more. His stomach cried out for the largest. His conscience approved when he took the smallest. Taking a small rice cake was more than merely symbolic of love. It was love in action, for the whole body yearned for the larger cake.[6]

In these extremities, the matter of love in human living was shown to be literally a life and death issue:

> Taking the smallest cake—and living in every situation by this principle—meant, in essence, that one was laying down one's life for his friends. To take the largest cake and always act on this principle meant, in some sense, contributing to the death of one's friends.[7]

But now 'my moral assets—power to make a choice contrary to common sense and the saving of my life—had by this point completely run out'.[8] It had been a fearful struggle, with a 'dark, sickening horror'[9] looming ahead. Are the laws we live by merely 'enlightened self-interest', or are they something more than that?

> He saw clearly that if law was humanly conceived and evolved then it was simply the expression of societies which had decided it was the best system of society, and essential for its wellbeing...If, however, God existed and He had given this law to Israel, and that law was basically universal in its essence, then to break it spoke of elements of guilt, conscience, judgment and punishment. If law could be shown to be of wholly human origin then breaking it really offended no essential morality.[10]

What then if there is no God, and so no ultimate law?

His mind was saying. 'There is no law because there is no God. Where there is no law and no God, *nothing matters*.' It was the last phrase which horrified him: 'Nothing matters'... Anarchy lay ahead. He knew that. Beastliness was permissible, admissible without prejudice. What he had always seen as wrong would now be neither right nor wrong but just how things would be.[11]

Geoffrey stood powerless on the edge of this abyss:

For himself the end had come. His own moral assets had nigh on given out. He knew all the morés. Take the largest cake and you were avowedly selfish. You gained life—in principle—by pushing others towards death. To take the smallest because you feared others, or sought approval, was also a form of self-preservation. You coveted their acceptance.

This then was the end. He would take the largest. He would be honest in his self-preservation. He would declare it clearly... He was intensely himself as against all mankind. He was a lone, cruel god on his own.[12]

What made him hesitate?

A faint doubt was still there—the doubt cast by the Nazarene. Was he what he claimed to be—Son of God? Did God exist?... Had this man indeed lived in an Eastern country—Palestine—and had he had humans as disciples, and had he interpreted the seeming silence of God by his physical actions? He doubted it, but the faint thought lingered.[13]

The 'faint thought' grew:

The thought had been gradually invading his mind. 'If God exists, and His law is true, then man is eternal; the conscience is his assurance of life beyond. Everything in life then would matter. God would be good: evil, evil. Judgement would be true, justice vindicated, righteousness proved.'
His mind muttered: 'If God exists—if, if, if...'[14]

It was just enough to make him want to ask for help:

> He decided his course of action: if God exists He must help me. He must prove He is God and I am a man by giving me a new moral power—but a new power of love—to take the smallest cake. This must not be for self-elevation, or out of the desire for man's approval or because I fear man's disapproval, but because by doing so I will truly love, for love lays down its life for its friend.
>
> Knowing his utter weakness, his moral exhaustion, his bankruptcy of love, he said, 'Oh God! If you exist—if you are God and law is truly law, love is truly love—then give me the power to take the smallest out of pure truth. I know truth is love.'[15]

What happened?

> He sensed the miracle. His mind was suddenly clear. His heart was quietly peaceful. His body ceased to cry for its rights. He watched, with some amazement, the hand which was his own, stretching out to take the smallest cake.
>
> No one else sensed the miracle . . . The others, intent on the selection of the best, saw him take the smallest, but then they knew he always did that.
>
> For him it was the greatest matter of all his life.
>
> God, law and love, in one beautiful trinity, were suddenly true and the way things really are.
>
> As for him, he could not describe the nature and the power of this new pure peace spreading through him.[16]

OH, HOW I LOVE YOUR LAW![17]

It is to be expected that one who has received such a significant and positive affirmation of God's law will not afterwards speak ill of it or say it no longer applies. Geoffrey envisages an imaginary group of people coming to a realisation of the glories of God's law:[18]

> 'Look at Psalm One,' I said. They turned with me to that Psalm. I began reading, 'Blessed is the man who walks not in the counsel of the wicked, nor stands in the way of sinners, nor sits in the seat of

scoffers; but *his delight is in the law of the Lord*, and on His law he meditates day and night.'

I glanced around the group. All were looking thoughtful. 'That man certainly loved the Lord,' I suggested. There were nods. 'Now look at what his love effects,' I said. 'Look at verse three. "He is like a tree planted by streams of water, that yields its fruit in its season, and its leaf does not wither. In all that he does he prospers".'

For a few moments we sat, thinking. Then Andrew said, 'This man certainly benefited from the law. For him it was fruitful.'

Geoffrey then makes the point that the law 'is not a set of static regulations' but has always been 'dynamic':

> We chatted this over as a group and then moved on to Psalm 19. We read verses seven and eight; 'The law of the Lord is perfect, *reviving the soul*; the testimony of the Lord is sure, *making wise the simple*; the precepts of the Lord are right, *rejoicing the heart*; the commandment of the Lord is pure, *enlightening the eyes*'.
>
> 'See', I suggested, 'the number of things the law effects.' We read on and came to verse eleven. 'Moreover by them is thy servant warned; *in keeping them there is great reward*.'

The speaker then observes: 'the moral law is simply the functional law of God's great creation. The law is truth, and knowing the truth—in this sense—makes you free when you obey':

> Then I added, 'Now let us turn to Psalm 119.' Pages were turned, and we came to the great Psalm . . . I said, 'Look at the very first verse; 'Blessed are those whose way is blameless, who walk in the law of the Lord!' Then we looked at verse 18, 'Open my eyes that I may behold wondrous things out of Thy law!' The Psalmist had added, 'My soul is consumed with longing for Thy ordinances at all times.' In another place he had said, 'I will run the way of Thy commandments when Thou enlargest my heart!' . . . We saw then the love the writer had for the commandments: 'I delight in thy law', 'How sweet are thy words to my taste, sweeter than honey to my mouth!' 'My soul keeps thy testimonies: I love them exceedingly', 'Consider how I love thy precepts!'

There is also 'sorrow when the commandments are not obeyed':

'My eyes shed streams of tears, because men do not keep Thy law.'
His great longing for them says, 'With open mouth I pant, because I
long for thy commandments.'

Nor was this love for the law drawn only from the Old
Testament:

Paul makes it clear that the moral law or the ten commandments
is summed up in 'love your neighbour as yourself'. This is clearly
stated in Galatians 5:13-14, and Romans 13:8-10. Of course Paul has
many precepts, but they are, after all, only the ramifications of the
basic law of love. James is clear in 1:25 and 2:8-12 that the ten
commandments constitute 'the perfect law', 'the law of liberty',
'the royal law'. John in his first epistle constantly stresses love of
God and love of neighbour or brother. He calls this 'an old commandment' (2:7ff), but then a new commandment. The new is the
old; the old has become new.

Peter in his first epistle cannot but stress the holiness and obedience which is incumbent upon the new believers. They are the old
people of God, but now the new people of God (I Peter 2:9-10).
They call on God as Father so they must be holy and obedient
(1:13-17).

The writer of Hebrews sees his readers as those who have access
to the living God, through the living way—Christ—and at the
same time they have the law of God in their hearts, their inner
parts, their minds.[19]

Where did this love for God's law come from? It came from
Christ—the one from whom the 'faint thought' was instilled in
the crisis of the rice cakes:

'Who of us expresses ecstasy over the matter of law, especially of
God's law?' One of those who did was Jesus. He came not to
abolish the law but to confirm and establish it. Indeed he was the
very end, or goal, of the law. It was not only about him, but it was
also from him and for him, and the final meaning of history lies in
his fulfilling its goal. The phrase 'the law and the prophets' was
often on his lips because he saw these two elements as one entity.
He delighted to do this will or law of his Father and wished to pass
on that delight to others, to us all![20]

THE LAWLESS AND DISOBEDIENT

Such love of the law is very different from how law is generally regarded by sinful humanity:

> The human race has a problem when it comes to the word 'law'. Terms such as 'law', 'command' and 'authority' have the connotation of demand, restriction, a hierarchy of authority, and seem to go against the freedom of the human spirit, especially the freedom of the will. For this reason humanity has an inbuilt reaction to the words, and in particular the word 'law'. It must be said that the reaction is linked with the guilt humans know before God. They experience an existential guilt for being less glorious than He made them, and they know personal guilts for the infringements of His law.[21]

While the law is a delight and a freedom for those who live in obedience to it, for those on the wrong side of the law it is 'a tyranny, a hard task-master':[22]

> Whilst law exposes sin as sinful, and acts as a pedagogue to bring us to Christ, yet the law is there for another purpose, and this we might call grim. It is there for rebellious people, people who transgress God's commands. Hence in I Timothy 1:8–11 Paul outlines that the law is not so much laid down for the just, 'but for the lawless and disobedient, the unholy and sinners . . . etc.' This is the dreadful side of law. Sinners are always confronted by law, whether they choose to face the confrontation or despise and avoid it.[23]

Geoffrey cites Romans 3:19–20 and says:

> In this he is saying that everyone is under the guilt of the law—'every mouth may be stopped, and the whole world may be held accountable to God'. 'The whole world' is held accountable to God by the law. None is free of this. Then comes the terrible statement, 'through the law comes knowledge of sin'. At first sight this simply seems to mean what Paul wrote to Timothy; namely, that the law picks out those things that human beings have done which are contrary to the law's commands. This may well be so, but he is saying much more. 'Knowledge of sin' is a fearful thing. It means men and women have been through the gamut of their sins, the acts

of their law-breaking, with the heavy guilts which attach to all their active sins. It catches up the pain; the dislocation of the human spirit and psyche; the anguish of heart caused by sin; the deadly heaviness which comes with guilt; the being given up to the guilt of sin; the compounding of rebellion; the pollution experienced in the heart and conscience by one's evil; the dread of the curse and judgment which is on sin by reason of the law—and further innumerable and indescribable elements which at last expose sin for the dreadful thing that it is. This is 'the knowledge of sin'. Nothing less would hold a person in terror before God. All of this is by reason of the law . . . For the sinner, the law can only bring wrath.[24]

THE LAW AND THE CROSS

Drawing on Romans 5:12–21, Geoffrey depicts the plight of humanity under 'two monstrous tyrants, sin and death':

Both fasten, parasitically, on man. Both grind him down to slavery and servile servitude. Sin is represented as a high, sullen river, flowing black and heavily. Death is a ruthless giant, ruling the inner thoughts of man, who fears, ultimately, to meet that same death. Hence man, through Adam, is beset by darkness, doom, and gloom.[25]

Law, according to 1 Corinthians 15:56, shuts us up to that:

'The sting of death is sin,' I said, 'That is its wrath and judgement. The power of sin is the law, that is its guilt. Take away the guilt of sin and you take away the power of sin.'

I wondered how the group would respond—or react—to this. Most looked puzzled so I tried again. 'Suppose,' I said, 'you are under the guilt of sin. Is it not a fact that the practical elements you will sense and feel, such as a sense of wrong doing, wrong being, alienation, and even fear and apprehension will make the climate more suited for sinning?'

They agreed with that, although still not fully comprehending. 'If you sin, then are you not in some sense under the power of sin, and does not one failure help to trigger off the next?' They saw that immediately, and agreed.

I quoted a theologian who once said, 'Satan only tempts where there is innocence. Where there is guilt he has already obtained power.' They also understood that. Then I quoted a verse of a hymn . . .

> 'When Satan tempts me to despair,
> And tells me of the guilt within,
> Upward I look and see him there
> Who made an end to all my sin.'[26]

Joe liked that. He showed he did. He slapped his thigh. 'By heck,' he said, 'I like that. So when guilt is gone, power is broken.'

I nodded. 'When there is no guilt,' I said slowly, 'we love God because there isn't! We love Him because we know His love. That is a great preventative against sinning.'[27]

This comes about because all that the law demanded of us was borne by Christ for us, when on the cross he 'identified with sinners, taking their sins upon himself':

> Christ, by bearing all the sins of mankind for all time showed that God has never really passed over these sins but that their judgment was effected in Christ (Romans 8:3, 'judged sin in his flesh') on the Cross. The law therefore was satisfied, and so the man of faith can understand that he is 'justified by His grace as a gift, through the redemption which is in Christ Jesus, *whom God put forward as a propitiation.*' This propitiation pleases God and satisfies the law.
>
> Man, then, is released into freedom from guilt and accusation. He is in a whole new world. He can now live.[28]

Galatians 2:14–21 shows that we are not apart from that death and judgement that Christ bore, but are included in it with him:

> . . . through the Cross man died to the law. The Law slays the sinner, being ruthless about his sins. However, it is really Christ who dies, but dies having taken up man's lawlessness and consequent death into himself. Hence, having died in Christ, one is also raised again, in Christ.
>
> This, too, is the great grace of God. Grace brings us to penal (or, legal) death. Grace also brings us to life.[29]

A right relationship with the law of God is dependent on seeing what happened on the cross as fully the love of God:

If you do not see love fully at the Cross then you will not see God fully, for He is the actual love we see—love-in-action. If we then love because He first loved us we will want to obey, voluntarily. We will become His slaves with joy. We will want His guidelines for living—the very moral law itself, but then law translated into our contemporary situation and its language.[30]

To miss this love is to become one of two things: 'a careless antinomian, or a heavy legalist'. Geoffrey identifies these two as 'lawless grace' and 'graceless law'.[31]

LAWLESS GRACE

There are those who, freed from the condemnation of the law, then want to be above and free from law itself in any form:

> The antinomians hate law because it seemed to have dragged them down into guilt and bondage. It never did. It was opposing the law that did that. Never mind. That is how the antinomian saw it, so he backed away from law. He loved being free, but then what was he free to do? Either instinctively love and keep from evil, or go into dreadful license and do anything.[32]

Geoffrey makes clear that 'To be free from the law does not mean to be free to have no law, or free from law observance':

> It would be bewildering to a human being suddenly to have no way in which to walk, and equally bewildering to have to, somehow, substitute a new law for the old.[33]

In an exposition of Romans 8:1–4, Geoffrey insists that 'the law of the Spirit of life in Christ Jesus' and 'the law of sin and death' are not opposed entities but one and the same 'holy and just and good'[34] law of God:

> Paul is saying that the law of God, because of our sin and the law's penalty of death, has become 'the law of sin and death' to us. Christ, by dying the death we should have died, has freed us from the condemnation of the law, so that now his gospel brings us to the

law—and the law to us—as 'the law of the Spirit of life in Christ Jesus'. The law itself could never do this because it was 'weakened by the flesh', but Christ has done it.[35]

The purpose of this was that 'the just requirement of the law might be fulfilled in us, who walk not according to the flesh but according to the Spirit'.[36] This is taken to refer not just to the penal requirements of the law, but to the keeping of the commandments.[37] Yet this is not something we can do of ourselves:

> We ought not to miss one important point, and it is the wording of 8:4, 'in order that the just requirement of the law *might be fulfilled* in us'. For us to go out to fulfil the just requirement of the law might seem to mean that we have to accomplish this demand of ourselves and from ourselves, but the text is saying 'might be fulfilled in us', meaning that the fulfilment does not come primarily from us, from our own unaided efforts, but that the gospel and the Spirit—'the law of the Spirit of life in Christ Jesus'—so work that the just requirement of the law is fulfilled in us . . . we live with the law as a new entity. We have a new view of it. Indeed we have come to the point where we 'delight in the law of God after the inner man'.[38] What was tasted as vinegar is now mouthed as honey . . . We no longer dread the law. It has now become 'sweeter than honey and than much fine honeycomb'.[39] The drippings of it become our delight to taste. The sourness of death has passed.
> We are now in a new delight.[40]

We are 'freed from the law in order to obey it'.[41]

GRACELESS LAW

Perhaps worse than 'a true Antinomian' is 'a true Legalist':[42]

> He knows he should obey the law, and that is good. However he obeys the law to keep in good with God. He does not really know that through the grace of God he is in good with God. He fears not to obey the law because of what may happen to him. Hence

obedience to the law is a heavy thing. He does not enjoy law. In addition, he is never free from guilt because he's never sure whether he has obeyed properly. To see him in action is to see a dreary sort of fellow. He's no credit to himself, the Gospel, or God.[43]

Sometimes there is basically little difference between the antinomian and the loveless legalist—both view the law as an imposition, and both are without real freedom or joy.[44] What we do need to see is the difference between legalism and true obedience:

One is using the law as a helpful and necessary directive. The other is using one's powers—mainly imagined—to keep on the right side of the law, and so on the right side of God. Actually that is not how it is supposed to be.[45]

Grace, rather than law, is now our master:

When we examine the grace which frees from law we see it frees us from the penalty of the law. It also frees us from the foolish notion and practice that to keep the law is to justify ourselves. In doing so grace sets us on an entirely new way of life—law without condemnation, law without self-justifying actions.[46]

Thus we can truly say to God, 'grant me the grace of your law'![47]

THE LAW OF GOD'S OWN BEING, AND OF OURS

While Geoffrey had always maintained that 'the law is the very transcript of God Himself . . . the moral expression of Who He is, and the outshining of His very nature',[48] and that God's 'moral law is the simple way of observing life and creation as they are',[49] his later writings searched this out more vigorously in all its Trinitarian and human dimensions. Central to this understanding is what is meant by 'the image of God'. Geoffrey loved to quote from J. A. Motyer:

Man is the living, personal image of God; the law is the written, preceptual image of God.[50]

Rather than regarding law as something external to God and human persons, this seats law back into God's own being:

> I believe the key to understanding God's law is to see it first as the law of God Himself. By this I mean that God is not a legislator who simply decided what should be the behaviour of Man, and accordingly made a block of laws, but is that Being who, by nature, lives by law Himself. So His law is the law of Himself.[51]

God being triune means that the law of God's own being is the law of love:

> ... the law of God is the law of the three Persons subsisting in total unity. This would not be so if the Father Himself were not love. He is love, and the Son is eternally generated from Him and therefore is the Son of His love. The Holy Spirit proceeds from these two Persons and is the Spirit of love. Thus they are one in unity whilst still being three Persons or hypostases. They are in utter communion which is their love. The ways in which they subsist together is their law. It is not imposed on them from a source other than themselves, but arises from themselves as the divine Community.[52]

Geoffrey expresses this devotionally in a poem:[53]

> This is the law of You, dear Lord,
> The law of Your own true Self,
> The law of life that gives all life to all,
> The law of the endless wealth
> Of the Spirit, the Father, and the Son,
> The Three who are One as love;
> For all creation flows from Them
> As on earth so in heaven above.
>
> Yours is the law we cannot know
> Where the Father Himself is Love.
> The Son is truly the Son of that love,
> And the Spirit in love must move,

> For He is the Spirit of Father-God,
> The Spirit of God the Son;
> And the Three as love must ever be
> For They are the Three in One.

Since 'all creation flows from Them', then this love of God is the law by which all creation is constituted, and in which all are to participate:

> Theirs is the law of love, the law
> By which the Three subsist;
> But Man is the image of that God
> And in covenant must exist.
> The covenant law is one with God
> As God is one with all men—
> Created in love to live with all
> Forever, as now and then.

Geoffrey summarises the reality of God's law in the context of the whole story:

... in one sense there are four images of God: (i) Man as 'the living, personal image of God'; (ii) the law as 'the written, preceptual image of God'; (iii) Christ, the true image of God; and (iv) the church as 'the ecclesial image of God'. It is in the context of these four images that redeemed Man lives. As he was created he was the pure image of God, and the primary law of God was written on his heart, telling him how to live in God. The image was marred, and in some senses lost, by the Fall and the personal sin of Man. Man needs to be renewed in the image, and this happens when he is renewed in Christ. The law of God first judges, condemns and gives sin the power to exacerbate itself in Man, but finally leads him to Christ. Man, having come to God in Christ, is renewed by the Spirit, in the image of God which is Christ. One strong element of the way of that renewal is the law of Christ, which is the law of God so that, as renewal proceeds, so does willing obedience to the law. There is, so to speak, a recovery of knowing the law and living in it. God has now implanted the 'new law' within the heart of the believer through redemption. The context of all this is, of course, Christ, but since the church is the body of Christ, the context is at the same time the church. The church is the company of the faithful who live in communion with God and with one another. The life that obtains within this community of Christ is the same life as that which obtains in the Community of the Triune Godhead, the difference being that way of life which we have called 'the law of God'—intrinsic to the Godhead—is a life that is lived by Man only in dependency upon God. It is a derived life and, as such, needs the constant exercise of faith in the context of the continuing grace of God.[54]

All of this—from three small rice cakes! What follows from this is the whole matter of the love community, as we shall see in the next chapter.

Geoffrey concludes with the ultimate triumph of law in the age to come, where 'the very Presence of the Lawgiver will be the guarantee of obedience to Him':

Of course by that time the perfection of our sonship through being in the Son will have brought us to be the full image of God, and filial love will be the restored ontological order for us. There will be no 'hard copy' law hung on the portals or walls of eternity. With God in the midst, as also He is on the throne, every eye shall see, every ear hear, and every mind recognise things which were beyond comprehension prior to entering eternity . . . It is then we will see with brilliance the beauty of the innate law of God, for this will be the law of the Holy City, the law of the Bride and the Bridegroom who is the Lamb—for it will all be the law of love, love that is holy and captures forever the will of Man. Most powerful will be the awe in which the Father—*fons divinitatis*[55]—will be held. If memory will be part of the 'immeasurable riches of his grace in kindness toward us in Christ Jesus', then we will wonder that a human being could ever oppose so great and holy a law, and we will thus see the measure of redeeming grace and the great and holy love which ordained it.[56]

[1] Geoffrey Bingham interview with Jan Springett, *A Thousand Days to Freedom*, Encounter, Australian Broadcasting Commission, n.d. For the historical background and setting see Chapter 4.

[2] 'Three Rice Cakes', in *The Story of the Rice Cakes*, Second Edition 2006, 4.

[3] *The Story of the Rice Cakes*, 4–5.

[4] 'these eighteen months he had battled for faith', *The Story of the Rice Cakes*, 7.

[5] *The Story of the Rice Cakes*, 2, 3.

[6] *The Story of the Rice Cakes*, 9.

[7] *The Story of the Rice Cakes*, 31–32.

[8] *The Story of the Rice Cakes*, 31.

[9] *The Story of the Rice Cakes*, 7.

[10] *Always the Presence*, part 2, chapter 18.

[11] *The Story of the Rice Cakes*, 7, 11.

[12] *The Story of the Rice Cakes*, 9–10.

[13] *The Story of the Rice Cakes*, 10.

[14] *The Story of the Rice Cakes*, 11.

[15] *The Story of the Rice Cakes*, 11.

[16] *The Story of the Rice Cakes*, 11–12.

[17] Psalm 119:97.

[18] *Oh, No, Lord! Not Law, Lord?!!*, 47–49.

[19] *Oh, No, Lord!*, 93–94.

[20] *Sweeter than Honey, More Precious than Gold: The Law of Love and the Love of Law*, xii; referring to Matthew 5:17-20; 22:34-40; Romans 10:4; Hebrews 10:5–10.

[21] *The Law of Eternal Delight*, 3.

[22] *Oh, No, Lord!*, 22.

[23] *Oh, No, Lord!*, 88.

[24] *Sweeter than Honey*, 34–35.

[25] *Oh, No, Lord!*, 7.

[26] 'Before the Throne of God Above', by Charitie Lees Bancroft; *New Creation Hymn Book*, 92.

[27] *Oh, No, Lord!*, 65–66.

[28] *Oh, No, Lord!*, 10.

[29] *Oh, No, Lord!*, 11.

[30] *Oh, No, Lord!*, 61.

[31] *Oh, No, Lord!,* 61.

[32] *Oh, No, Lord!,* 50.

[33] *Sweeter than Honey,* 45.

[34] Romans 7:12.

[35] *Sweeter than Honey,* 46–47.

[36] Romans 8:4.

[37] Compare: 'If you love me, you will keep my commandments' (John 14:15); quoted in *Oh, No, Lord!,* 45.

[38] See Romans 7:22.

[39] See Psalm 19:10.

[40] *Sweeter than Honey,* 47–48.

[41] *Sweeter than Honey,* 46.

[42] *Oh, No, Lord!,* 35.

[43] *Oh, No, Lord!,* 50.

[44] *Oh, No, Lord!,* 51. For a detailed analysis see, 81–82.

[45] *Oh, No, Lord!,* 77.

[46] *Oh, No, Lord!,* 86.

[47] Psalm 119:29, The Anglican Church of Australia, *A Prayer Book for Australia* (Shorter Edition), (Broughton Books, 1995), p. 351. A subtitle on the cover of *Oh, No, Lord!* reads: 'Reviewing Graceless Law, Lawless Grace, and the Grace of Law'. See also a book drawn upon and highly commended by Geoffrey: Ernest F. Kevan, *The Grace of Law: A Study in Puritan Theology* (Carey Kingsgate Press, London, 1964).

[48] *Oh, No, Lord!,* 53.

[49] *Oh, No, Lord!,* 93.

[50] J. A. Motyer, 'The Biblical Concept of Law', in *Evangelical Dictionary of Theology* (ed. W. E. Elwell, Baker Book House, Grand Rapids, 1990), 624; quoted in *The Law of Eternal Delight,* 167, 193.

[51] *Sweeter than Honey,* 3.

[52] *Sweeter than Honey,* 10–11; drawing on 1 John 4:8, 16; Matthew 3:17; Colossians 1:13; Romans 5:5; 15:30; 13:8–10; Matthew 22:37–39.

[53] *New Creation Hymn Book,* 376.

[54] *The Law of Eternal Delight,* 208–209.

[55] The fountain or source of divine life—that is, within the triune Godhead.

[56] *The Law of Eternal Delight,* 308, 310.

CHAPTER 6

THE *Love* COMMUNITY

> we love, because
> he first loved us
>
> 1 John 4:19

THE LAW OF LOVE

THE FINAL EIGHTEEN months of Geoffrey Bingham's prison camp internment were spent in Kranji Hospital Camp on the north-west of Singapore Island.[1] 'I belonged to the 8th Divisional Signals but I had been transferred to work with the hospital and so I was to go as librarian to Kranji.'[2] The experience of the rice cakes was fresh in his consciousness:

> ... I extrapolated this simple principle of 'the other person first' into my way of living. I have seen this to be the principle by which Christ as the Son of God became Man. He never did so reluctantly but willingly. That is the nature of law. Certainly, I discovered the nature of law that day. But I also discovered that the law, rightly understood, is love. This became the key to me of all life. One does not love from oneself but out of God's love working in and through us. The apostle John said, 'We love because he first loved us'. We could say: 'We love all persons because he first loved us' ... The truth is that we are involved in one another by nature of the case. Whether this involvement is for good or for evil is determined by many factors, but one thing is for certain: we cannot escape each other. That was the great truth I learned in prison days. The matter of the rice-cakes had brought it into full bloom.[3]

Not that this was anything specially high or heroic. It is simply living according to the way things really are:

> When you see that God is really love—I mean when you see that He has been loving all the time, and is now loving, in everything, then you want to love ... God being love, we would be going dead against things-as-they-really-are if we didn't love ... the universe is love-structured ... God is not simply above this world, a Great Reserve of Love, but that in fact, time, space, and all that is happening within them is His thing of Love.[4]

This makes loving quite straightforward:

> We need not make too deep and mysterious a thing of this love. It is very simple. God's love flows to man and man works out of that love.[5]

This love is contested, not only in the starkness of prison camp life, but also in the niceties of ordered civilisation:

> The principle of 'every man for himself' was never far from the surface. Sometimes this was developed into the principle of mutual security action: a corporate standing together. But if this broke down then it was back to the individualistic, self-protecting, self-seeking principle . . . During World War II quite 'nice' people worked the rackets on ration coupons for foods and clothing and saw nothing unethical in it. In what we might call 'the Peace' nothing has changed. The same things go on in commerce, business, institutions, Government departments, schools and churches.[6]

We wonder whether 'there is no final solution to the incessant warring of nations or—if you will—the warring of communities . . . the culture of one nation can never be a home for another culture or cultures . . . as each people grows it comes to have world domination as its aim. Each people is for its own community.'[7]

This, however, is not the whole story. We need to know 'what is Man, and what is a person?':

> . . . true knowledge of Man is a mystery which comes as a revelation. Man has never been an angel. And Man has never been a beast. He is not simply one or the other of these, nor is he a combination of both. Man is simply Man.[8]

The 'scandal of human evil' must be shown 'against the brilliant background of what Man is intended to be':

> Men are intended to be holy and righteous and aflame with the love of God as they live in the community of the human race. If all we had observed in prison camp was Man's depravity then we had missed the better thing—Man in God.[9]

Geoffrey later explained this in a radio interview:[10]

> Generally, we think of man doing evil things. But we also think of him as capable of doing good. But if he's really depraved, he can't do good at all . . . any good that he does isn't really true good or absolute good—at the best, you can say, it is relative good, because he is trying to do it from himself. And so, we will say, he is depraved because he has cut himself off from God, but he can't go against what he has been created, essentially. Now, a friend of mine once said that the image of God in man is irreducible, but reversible. In other words, all those magnificent powers he has been given, he can use selfishly. And while he does that, we call him depraved. But he has the sense of good.

This played itself out in the prison camp. Geoffrey tells of when he was ministered to in a time of utter deprivation and weakness:

> Now in prison camp, you would see for the most part the exercise of that depravity. But then suddenly, unbelievably, you would see a most incredible event happen . . . one day, to my amazement, some of my old mates brought in a feast for me. I can't call it anything else but a feast. It had all kinds of food and fruit and, if I described them to you, you would still not be able to understand what they meant to me. Now, for those men to do that meant they had to make a big sacrifice—they didn't have to make the sacrifice, they did it—and it was a miracle and it was an expression of the image of God. So you see, man will live in his state of depravity and then, suddenly, he will just show this great miracle. And that's the proof that the image of God is there in man.

THE KRANJI CLIQUE

'Our little group (just for fun I have called it 'the Clique', but in fact it was far from being that) had somehow grown spontaneously . . . I think it was the selfishness we found in ourselves which made us come together. We were battling that innate selfishness all human beings know.'[11] As librarian to the medical officers, Geoffrey had begun to make friends with some like-minded men:

One of my friends was Ken Topliss, a physiotherapist, who tried his best to revitalise a dead nerve for me, or at least to give my wasted muscles a bit of tone . . . Ken was a fine man, who had never even dreamed of questioning God about anything. He was an honest worshipper. I would chat the time away when he was trying to get his electronic machine to stimulate nerves and muscles in my leg. He had a close friend, Ted Oliver, who was an Englishman and a fellow therapist. I had recently met Gerry Sampson who was a ward orderly and I suggested casually one day that we four men might get together for a Bible study. They thought that would be a good idea and eventually we found a place to meet. It was the X-ray room. Its windows were covered with blackout paper so that at night no light could be seen coming from it. The Japanese guards, tramping the catwalk, were on the alert to spot any light. Even before leaving Changi American bombers had appeared, and on occasions they bombed strategic targets on the Island. This tiny meeting of ours began a sort of miracle which operated through the months that followed.[12]

One of Geoffrey's closest friends was Alfred Baker, who 'could be seen carrying about with him everywhere a large black Bible'.[13] He and a group of friends had been meeting in Changi, and had been praying for Geoffrey in his 'difficult time of questioning and questing'.[14] Geoffrey had told his rice cakes experience to Alfred.[15] 'Alf was most enthusiastic about us having a small Bible study group.'[16] Others soon joined.

They were a far from homogenous group:

Amongst us were men who had had strange experiences which some might call 'parasensory'. Others were persons who had become disillusioned with the church and Christianity. Some had read their way through many religions and were still dissatisfied. All were thoughtful; some, I think, were brilliant. I suppose we were men who were sick of the separation that individualism brings between persons and persons. We felt there must be something better. Some had become quite cynical of their fellow creatures, and the wonder was that so many of us cared to band together. Unconsciously we trusted one another.[17]

Ground rules were laid early:

We took the first night to discuss how to go about our time together . . . Few men had Bibles and to begin with we never opened them. We set ourselves an almost impossible task. We would try not to remember things we had been taught. If we were to take the Bible on its merit then it also had to take us on our merit. If the Bible seemed obscure, complicated, and unrelated to our prison situation, then in some way it would have to become clear, uncomplicated, and very much related to where we were and our prison life.

This tall order did not make it easy to start with:

We stumbled and fumbled and scarcely knew where we were in our discussions. Gradually, however, we developed the ability to think inside the Bible instead of looking down on it. It was a book that we were beginning to respect and even to love. It was telling us what we were and, as created persons, what love God had for us.[18]

They began at Matthew chapter 5 and went slowly through the Sermon on the Mount. 'How strange and wonderful that long passage was. It seemed every line was given to speak to and help men in a prison, men who might be executed before they would see their loved ones.' At first, questions like 'take no thought for tomorrow' and 'do not be anxious about your life, what you shall eat or what you shall drink, nor about your body, what you shall put on' because 'your heavenly Father knows you shall have need of them all' seemed impossible under the constraints of their situation:

How could God, even, carry out his assurance of enough food, drink and clothing? We talked about that. Almost imperceptibly little things happened in regard to food, drink, clothing and illnesses. Our needs were being met. It was only after these things happened that we recognised that they were linked with our readings and discussion of the Scriptures.[19]

This love from God began to spread:

We decided not to be a club, or a cult, or a sect. We said nothing about our studies to others but we began quiet ways of living for those others . . . We would seek out fellows who were sick and cynical, despairing and looking for death, and we would try to bring comfort to them. Somehow the Sermon on the Mount began to be a living, vital thing in our midst. We found our fear of death was dissipating, and somehow—as though by osmosis—we communicated that to others.[20]

Men with personal difficulties were helped just by being with the group:

At the same time a few more fellows were sent to our Camp from Changi. Someone there thought we would help guys who thought they were going homosexual. After a short time, one of them would quietly be invited to share in our evening chats. They seemed to find nothing strange, since all religious jargon was banned. One by one the new men began to believe they were normal. They were touched with our concern for them.[21]

Meagre personal possessions, including Geoffrey's precious typewriter, were sold on the black market to buy food which was cooked and quietly distributed 'to men whose eyes lit up with unbelief and joy. Quietly the giving of life was taking place . . . We saw fear fade from eyes, and light come back into them.' Love grew also in the group, as they watched over and prayed for one another in times of special need. 'It was all very down-to-earth, but also quite mysterious.'[22]

TWO KINDS OF LOVE

The love these men were discovering and putting into practice was something more than mutual self-interest:

We had talked quite a bit about the principle of love. What I had discovered through the incident of the rice-cakes was that there are two kinds of love: one which we all know and appreciate because it seems outwardly so practical and helpful, and personally stimulating; and another love which is all of these things and outlasts the first kind of love. The first is the kind of love that likes its own act of loving and will do the best for others but, then, at some point, will look for its returns, and if it does not get these it becomes quite angry, savage and even harmful. The second kind of love is God's love which gives without demanding returns. That was shown in his creation of the world, his provisions for its needs, and then in the act of sending his Son into the world to liberate the human race from its bondage to sin and its fear of death.[23]

Geoffrey in his later writing[24] developed this matter of the two kinds of love using the Greek words *eros* and *agapē*:

Human beings are often deceived into thinking that love which springs from themselves can be pure ... this is not the case. Even so, God has so moved that His love, which is known by Christians as *agape* (a Greek word for love), can become the experience of human beings. This *agape* transcends fallen human love, which is sometimes known by the Greek word *eros*. *Eros* in all its forms of noble actions—giving to others, being a friend, and so on—must be seen as a good thing. There is the love of man and woman, love that we call marital, familial and social, and all such forms are fine and proper, yet if they do not flow from the pure love of God, they are always defective. *Eros* has behind it the drive of getting something for what it gives, even if it often seems that this is not really the case. *Agape* is pure love, not giving to get, but just giving which is unmotivated by any form of selfishness.

I am sure many of us think *eros* is *agape*, and *agape* is *eros*.[25]

Geoffrey sets out to show 'the fallacy of *eros* and the sheer wonder and glory of *agapē*':

I hope that my writing shows my admiration for much that is *eros*, but primarily my hope is that many will seek to know the best of love which is *agape* ... *eros* is very powerful. It is so strongly human, because its source is wholly human. It may well be that it is Divine love (*agape*) humanised to become *eros*. Whatever the case, it certainly conquers men and women; yet *agape* makes its way to the very 'secret heart' of a person and there defeats *eros*— the human love. God as love is revealed and so brings a person to the knowledge and experience of *agape*—'twice-conquering love'.[26]

LOVE AND GRACE

Not everyone was pleased with what was happening in the 'Kranji Clique':

> The Nonconformist chaplain used to come into the Officers' library and browse amongst the books. He read quite widely. He rarely talked to me but one day he opened up in a chiding voice, 'How does it happen, sergeant, that you have over thirty men to your meetings and I have only a dozen?' I said that I didn't know. He said, 'You know, Bingham, that you are not authorised to teach the men.' I replied that I entered the Army from a theological college. Did that not give me some kind of a right to teach? 'You know it doesn't,' he said. 'You are a signaller and not a padre. You ought not to do the work of a padre.' 'In fact,' I told him, 'although I lead the discussion and share some of my insights, we all take part. It does not depend on me.' He shook his head. 'What you do is not according to King's Rules and Regulations.'
>
> This book—King's Rules and Regulations—was the legal bible of the Army, and he was technically correct in his protest. I felt disappointed and said in a rush of fervour, 'Padre, don't we work on the heavenly King's rules and regulations? Aren't we all in this together—his people and his children?' The chaplain gave me a withering look and left the room.[27]

This exchange characterises much of Geoffrey's later somewhat ambivalent relationship with the institutional church and its hierarchy. Not that he would hear ill of the church—God's people are His 'prized possession',[28] the Bride of His Son. With regard to hierarchy, Geoffrey never sought to dismantle structures that are in place—any push for an egalitarian or democratic form of church he saw as 'undesirable'.[29] In his theology of both Trinity and church Geoffrey upholds hierarchy to be 'ontological' and 'functional after the manner of love'.[30] He speaks warmly and appreciatively of some of the other chaplains in the prison camp, including those with whom he disagreed.[31] But he does insist that 'All members of Christ's body are ministers', and he speaks against 'the imposition of the biblically wrong clergy–laity division'.[32] Here he simply says:

... the idea of a pastor ruling his people comes close to what we called in the army 'pulling rank'. Ranks there may have to be in society but they are there primarily to serve others, not to rule them.[33]

Earlier in his captivity, Geoffrey had found himself profoundly dissatisfied with a standard expression of 'church':

The Church of England clergyman who led the service was unbelievable. He was dressed in clericals, stock, white collar, cassock and surplice—all of which were regimentally correct. He led us through the entire service of Morning Prayer. I was familiar with every bit of it. We sang hymns that I knew, then he preached. The clergyman was of a lugubrious state of face and mind and theologically correct as he expounded from the Bible. I understood all he said and did, but it was as though I was with him in some English village on a Sunday morning. He was not with me in Roberts Barracks Hospital, in the midst of a prison camp, with my bewilderment and my desire for some answers. I wanted wisdom, encouragement, help. Instead, I had a model service without any dynamic. There was no sharing of our predicament and saying wise words into it. I felt like retching but I didn't. I was transported back to my bed and lay there seething.

'That does it!' I said to myself. 'I'm finished with church and religion!'[34]

He goes on to say, 'I wasn't of course', and tells how he hammered away in his mind about everything, with anyone who would join him in the quest. It was part of his determination only to be real, and to press through to what was real—even in the end to that which we will not know in totality until the age to come. Later in life he was heard to say, 'I do not think I have ever been in a worship situation in which I was fully satisfied'.[35]

Geoffrey has a very different vision of community from what we often find in churches and elsewhere:

Communities are mostly self-serving, self-protective and self-extending. Some communities never seek to enlarge themselves and if they do it is by assimilation. People seem to attend only the local activities. We have *our* suburb, *our* supermarket, *our* service station, *our* school, *our* denomination, *our* football club, and even *our* hairdresser. In the army what mattered was *our* unit and even *our* section. A true community, however, is one which grows not by absorbing or assimilating but by seeking to serve others and seeing them as beloved friends.

The community of Christ does not seek to emphasise itself as something different, rather, it is the community into which all can come and find themselves fulfilled in their relationships with both God and Man. It does not dispossess entrants of other community memberships, but it fills out the heart and mind of the person so that love is now the order of his life. Colour, class, customs and culture do not have to disappear. They remain unless, for some reason, such elements do not make for *agape* love. Legislation may often be necessary for the peace of a society but nothing can establish genuine peace other than this *agape* love.[36]

Geoffrey traces the decline from true community in the life of the church:

Community is a corporate matter in which all are saints and all live by the grace of God and the interaction and support of all others. Community is a living company whose members know the joy of mutual love. But once vast buildings bear down upon us, and choirs intone us into solemnity, and robed clergy transform buildings into temples, and joyous worship is tempered by sacerdotal oversight—then, no matter how beautiful it all may be, we have lost sight of grace. The common company has become divided. The fellowship has been stratified and the joy of unmediated fellowship with God is replaced by ecclesiastical gravity. God is channelled to us by chant and set liturgy. All that is left for us to appropriate in our relationship with God is mediated by the intercession of others who are more worthy than we are.

Such ecclesiastical domination seeks to enshrine our glorious freedom in Christ. I mean that literally. We have been 'enshrining' our faith in all of these ecclesiastical trappings, and once a thing is enshrined it becomes an idolatry. For at least the first two hundred years of Christianity there were no church buildings. There was only the church, that is, the people. They met as community. The church was in homes but homes were not the churches. Then when churches were built they began to look like temples. Originally there were elders and gifted apostles, prophets, evangelists, pastors and teachers—not priests. As the institution of the church developed there were leaders who were above the people, and there were people who were placed below the priests. Worship was to be a matter of deep gravity. It was thought that the only way to preserve spontaneous (sic!) fellowship and its freedom was by a system of mediatorial oversight. The faith was no longer a matter of joy and light and freedom but of careful living before God and holy dread of him. Gratefulness for grace was meted out through sober, if not sombre, sacraments.

What we are saying is that many elements make their way into the true community which impede the spontaneity and warm life and fellowship of the community.[37]

Clearly reformation is needed. 'But the situation in the church is such that a full reformation cannot be wrought just by trying, protesting and campaigning.'[38] Since true community comes by the grace of God, then it can be restored only through the reassertion of that grace. Grace is 'that action and attitude of God whereby He constantly goes towards man to do him good, albeit man does not deserve it'. It reveals a 'brilliant view of God, as demanding nothing for justification but the work of His Son on the Cross and in the Resurrection':[39]

> The battle for grace is the battle for community ... If persons and communities do not get triggered off by grace, then there are many problems which will be bound to arise ... All spiritual and moral exercises will spring from the effort to justify oneself ... What we need to see is that every action of the church changes in nature when dependence upon grace is missing.[40]

THE COMMUNITY OF GOD

'What happens by grace must not be depicted as happening through human effort ... Community cannot be structured out of constructs.'[41] True community comes from within the triune God—Father, Son and Holy Spirit:[42]

> ... God is true Community in Himself ... The Church is the human community which has its origin in the Divine Community, which is the Trinity.[43]

Geoffrey boldly sets out to discover from the Scriptures the quality of relationships within the triune Godhead, and comes to these conclusions:

a) *In the Trinity, each Member prefers the other Members* of the Community, that is, puts the other one first . . . This mutual honouring is, indeed, a glorifying and worshipping—One of the Others.

b) *All Members of the Trinity serve one another.*

c) *All Members of the Trinity give to and receive from one another.*[44]

Since humanity is created in the image of God, then 'Human community is the reflection of the God Community'.[45] This comes about not by imitation or contemplation, but by God's action in pursuing His purpose through all history, as He engages with all that pits itself against this divine life and love:

The great love the Father has for the world He created is indeed a passionate affair when 'he withheld not his only Son but abandoned him up for us all'. And the love of the Son to accede to this with delight and fervour and to carry it out to the giving up of himself upon the Cross to sufferings for sins, the bearing of the wrath upon sin, and the abandonment into the darkness of the terrible limbo of the lost, must be seen in order to understand something of the Divine love of both Father and Son. Likewise, the ministry of the Spirit to, and for, the Father and the Son by his identification with the incarnation of the Son, his part in honouring, serving and empowering the Son, and his participation in the death, resurrection and ascension of the Son thus being the power for these events, as also being the Spirit of glory, tells us of the deep love of the Spirit.[46]

God in this saving love comes to us:

The Father is love, the Son is the Son of His love, and the Spirit is the Spirit of love, and the Persons of this one love have come to dwell in us, and make us to live at home in them. This is how love comes to Man. *There is no other way.* That is the way love goes from us to others.[47]

In this way we see 'the shaping of the Church as His own image, as the Church is being developed to be like the Trinity'.[48] The practical outworking of this is very wonderful:

> The modes of the Triune Godhead are replicated dynamically in the believer and the believing community. For example, love replaces hatred, forgiveness is instant where and when one is sinned against. God's forgiveness and cleansing have purified the heart from all past rancours, spite, guilt, anger—and the like—and so the believer sees the sins of himself and his brother as being 'covered'. He does not seek to be suspicious or critical, but loving and 'covering' where the failure of another is concerned. Only the atonement can actually cover that sin, but *agape* sees it as covered. [49]

So special is this form of love community that Geoffrey is not content to use such words as 'social' or 'gregarious' to describe human coming together. Since the final outcome, planned by God from before the beginning, is the *ecclēsia* ('church'—the gathering of a people together to God), he prefers the word 'ecclesial':[50]

> ... created Man is an *ekklesia* and not just a gregarious community as are birds, fish and animals. God is the Creator of Man. To be human, Man must be ecclesial, since it is in his corporate being and vocation that he reflects the Creator.

We can then take 'the whole sweep from Creation to the *telos* as the nature and destiny of Man':

> Man's nature as 'community' is dependent upon his relationship with God vertically and with the human race horizontally.[51]

This is not just a religious gloss. So embedded is this in the structure of humanity as created by God, that Geoffrey is prepared to discern 'such a fellowship of feeling' and 'uninhibited delight' in something so secular and evidently 'ungodly' as a country football match![52]

For 'humanity created by God for eternal greatness', this gives us more than just a trifling or partial gospel. We are to 'become participants of the divine nature'.[53] Not in any way by being 'divinised' or taking on deity ourselves, but by being 'one with God who is love'[54]—one with God in His action of love—such that we can be called, boldly, God's 'peer community':

> The whole counsel of God is what God in His wisdom has chosen to do in creating the universe . . . If what we have seen . . . is the true goal of God for His creation, then we have a magnificent message to bring. It is that by creation and redemption and the revelation of God and His intention for eternity we have a glorious vista of the God of love to give to sinners under wrath, and under the misery of their guilt. It is to show that God's plan from beginning to end is being fulfilled out of His love, and that He is making us into a people of love who, having been forgiven, justified, sanctified, glorified and perfected, will now be one with Him—the love community of the Godhead—as that community so united to Him, and in Him, that it will be His peer community, the community utterly one in love, working with Him in all eternity, filling out with Him the plan He has for the future of all creation.[55]

LOVE LIVED OUT

As the last days of Kranji drew to a close with the liberation of the prison camp, the final meeting of the 'Kranji Clique' was 'a time of great joy, and also of great sadness'.[56] Some feared that the love they had known for each other would be lost:

> We used to talk about what would happen when we returned home. I remember Toby saying to me, 'You'll marry for sure, and you will naturally love your wife more than us.'
> I understood Toby . . . 'Love has no favourites,' I said. 'That is what we have been learning. Love of wife and children may be in different modes, but it is the same love.'
> They all agreed with that. We all seemed genuinely happy about that understanding.[57]

Lord Mountbatten arrived at Kranji, and opened the gates. 'Go out and be free!' he said. Most of the prisoners were still so dispirited that they could not take this up:

There was silence. Scarcely anyone moved towards the gate. I moved, and a number of the men in our group moved, and we walked through the gate. None followed us.[58]

These men were noticeably different. One of the British officers who had been incarcerated in another camp mistook them for liberating soldiers. He couldn't believe they were POW's. One of the English women explained: 'They don't look like the others. They look different in the eyes.' Geoffrey comments: 'I suppose that was when I knew that in some way our love—His love in us—was sealed'.[59] Years later Geoffrey recalled:

> For those past forty or more years I have been working this out in living in society—it is as real to me as the day when it became a revelation to me in that prison camp—and it's a thrilling thing for a human being to be a human being, especially when he or she comes to know that he or she is made in that special image of God . . . When we first came home and when I was first married after the war, my wife and I went into a situation in NSW where we just tried to work that out in the community where we lived—to serve people rather than look to be served. Not to try to gain advantage, but to give loving service. And we sought to do that all our lives and this seems to be the medium into which God has led us. And we have a whole team—almost a community of people—who are dedicated to this and who see this truth and love it and they're sharing it with many others.[60]

In later years, Geoffrey was known to have a photographic memory for faces and names. One of his friends explained it simply: 'He loved people'.[61]

[1] Marcus L. Loane, *These Happy Warriors*, 87; *Love Is the Spur*, 44.

[2] *Love Is the Spur*, 45.

[3] *Love Is the Spur*, 39–41.

[4] *Where I Love I Live*, 59. The title is taken from a poem by Robert Southwell (1561–1595): 'Not where I breathe but where I love, I live'.

[5] 'The Love Builders', *God and the Ghostown*, 173.

[6] *Love Is the Spur*, 34.

[7] *Love Is the Spur*, 126.

[8] *Love Is the Spur*, 40.

[9] *Love Is the Spur*, 40–41.

[10] Geoffrey Bingham interview with Jan Springett, 'A Thousand Days to Freedom', Encounter, Australian Broadcasting Commission, n.d. See also *Love Is the Spur*, 16–17.

[11] 'The Kranji Clique', *The Boy in the Valley: and Selected Short Stories*, 249.

[12] *Love Is the Spur*, 49.

[13] *Love Is the Spur*, 49.

[14] *Love Is the Spur*, 52.

[15] *The Boy in the Valley*, 254.

[16] *Love Is the Spur*, 50. The account in 'The Kranji Clique' (1992) includes Alf in the original four—there it was Alf who 'suggested we should study the Bible together'—along with Gerry and one called Frank. There was also someone called Toby, a returnee from the Burma-Thailand Railway (see *The Boy in the Valley*, 250-251, 254-255). This differs from the account in *Love Is the Spur* (2004), though Toby does appear there later (pp. 54-56). Events can become mixed when recalled over fifty years later. Both accounts agree the group began with four and grew from there. They also indicate that this coming-together arose from beyond just Geoffrey's initiative.

[17] *The Boy in the Valley*, 249.

[18] *Love Is the Spur*, 53.

[19] *Love Is the Spur*, 54.

[20] *The Boy in the Valley*, 254–255.

[21] *The Boy in the Valley*, 255; see also *Love Is the Spur*, 62–63.

[22] *The Boy in the Valley*, 255.

[23] *Love Is the Spur*, 63.

[24] Love is a major theme of Geoffrey's published works. *Liberating Love* (1960) was written when he was a missionary in Pakistan, and was translated into Urdu. 'Two Muslim officials were captivated by the book and declared themselves—as a result of reading it—to be secret disciples' (Preface to the

1988 edition). *The Authority and Submission of Love* (1982) comes to the upending conclusion that in God, authority and love are one and the same. *Constraining Love* (1985) is a reprint of *Living Faith Study 1*, 'The Nature and Meaning of Love' (1978). *Where I Love I Live* (1977) is a discourse in the form of conversations that take place over the course of a house group weekend where love is discovered. *Ah, Strong, Strong Love!* (1993) is a detailed and unashamedly theological treatment. *Twice-Conquering Love* (1993) seeks to convey the same theological truth through the medium of short stories, essays and poetry. The opening short story from this book 'The Golden Egg of Love' is expanded into a trilogy of mediaeval fantasy-type novels: *Strong as the Sun* (1994); *Beyond Mortal Love* (1996); and *Love unto Glory* (2003). Songs which encapsulate this theme include 'Ah, Strong, Strong Love' (1990); 'Ah, Tide of Love' (1990); and 'God Is All-loving, He Is Our Father' (1977) (*New Creation Hymn Book*, 30, 149, 48).

25 *Twice-Conquering Love*, Foreword, ix.

26 *Twice-Conquering Love*, ix–x.

27 *Love Is the Spur*, 57; see also *The Boy in the Valley*, 256, where Geoffrey says: 'I refrained from saying the King's rules and regulations, as in sacred Writ, were probably justification enough'.

28 *The Beautiful City of God*, 17–19, the whole of that book sets out to answer the question as to why God prizes His people so highly.

29 'The Church the Priesthood of All Believers—IV', NCTM Monday Pastors' Study Group, 4th June, 2001, p. 9; see: <www.newcreation.org.au/studies/pdf/PSG2001.pdf>.

30 Elucidation to p. 5 of 'The Apostolic Ministry of the Church of God—II', NCTM Monday Pastors' Study Group, 15th October 2001: 'The whole creation works in hierarchy because hierarchy is functional, and not barely ontological as ontology is sometimes seen to be. At the same time *it is ontological to be functional after the manner of love.*'

31 *Love Is the Spur*, 31, 138.

32 *The Beautiful City of God*, 149.

33 *Love Is the Spur*, 57–58.

34 *Love Is the Spur*, 30.

35 Personal recollection, Martin Bleby.

36 *Love Is the Spur*, 137–138.

37 *Love Is the Spur*, 152–153.

38 *Love Is the Spur*, 153.

39 *Christ's People in Today's World*, 187.

40 *Christ's People in Today's World*, 187–188.

41 *Love Is the Spur*, 152, 156.

[42] Geoffrey expended vast labours of research and writing in this area of Trinitarian theology. His doctoral thesis (unpublished) is *The Glory of God and Human Relationships: A Study in Trinitarian and Human Relationships* (1990). This is summarised and developed in *Trinitarian Theology: Human Unity and Relationships* and *Relationships: Divine–Human* (NCTM Pastors' Schools 1991, 1994); see: <www.newcreationlibrary.net/studies/schools/sch_index.html>.

[43] *The Beloved Community of God*, 2, 99.

[44] *The Beloved Community of God*, 171–172.

[45] *Love Is the Spur*, 155.

[46] *Ah, Strong, Strong Love!*, 111–112.

[47] *Ah, Strong, Strong Love!*, 155.

[48] *The Beloved Community of God*, 2.

[49] *Ah, Strong, Strong Love!*, 264–265.

[50] 'The Fullness of Created Man', NCTM Monthly Ministry Study, March 1st & 6th, 2004, p. 4, n. 5. Here Geoffrey is 'indebted to Edward Farley for his book, *Ecclesial Man: A Social Phenomenology of Faith and Reality* (Fortress Press, Philadelphia, 1975), in which he speaks about Man having been created as an ecclesial being. Ecclesial being is inherent in creation and not just a state to be attained. Along with this book but more emphasising the solidarity of the human race is Russell Philip Shedd's book, *Man in Community* (Epworth Press, London, 1958)'; see: <www.newcreationlibrary.net/studies/pdf/MMS_2004.pdf>.

[51] *God and Man in the Mission of the Kingdom*, 193.

[52] 'The Football Match', *The Days and Dreams of Arcady*, 82–89.

[53] See 2 Peter 1:4.

[54] *Ah, Strong, Strong Love!*, 267.

[55] 'The Purpose and Plan of God's Mission—1', NCTM Monthly Ministry Study, 1st & 3rd March, 2003, p. 12; see: <www.newcreationlibrary.net/studies/pdf/PSG2003.pdf>.

[56] *Love Is the Spur*, 89.

[57] *The Boy in the Valley*, 256.

[58] *Love Is the Spur*, 85.

[59] *The Boy in the Valley*, 257; see also *Love Is the Spur*, 87.

[60] Geoffrey Bingham, interview with Jan Springett, 'A Thousand Days to Freedom'.

[61] David Hewetson, interview with John Dunn, 27 January 2009.

CHAPTER 7

THE *Profound* MYSTERY

Wedding Day, 1946

Farm at Eungai

GEOFFREY AND LAUREL

GEOFFREY ARRIVED back in Sydney in October 1945 on the *Oranje*, the first hospital ship to bring prisoners-of-war back from the Far East, to a tumultuous welcome.[1] He returned to the family home at Box Hill, but needed to be in the Repatriation Hospital for tests and treatment.[2] After what he and others had been through, reconnecting with the world they had been out of for some years was not necessarily going to be easy. 'Prisoners of all kinds form a life of their own and have a fear of open spaces and of meeting others who do not understand them.'[3] This included the girls who had now grown up into young women: 'The young women I met were fine persons but quite out of my league. They did not know what I was talking about.'[4] Geoffrey says, 'I was looking for someone who could understand some of the pain I was feeling as I tried to adapt to the society to which we had returned':[5]

> I was ambivalent about women. I wanted a wife, having reached the mature age of 27 years. However, women flowed everywhere, and most of them seemed empty to me. I wanted a thoughtful person who was also goodish to look at, fun to know, and who had quiet understanding. To that point I had not found one, nor did I think at this very point that I would find one. Little did I know.[6]

This 'very point' was the moment when Constance Edna Laurel Chapman of Turramurra[7] had decided to visit Geoffrey Bingham:

> ... a pert young woman sailed up the aisle of the ward that I was in. At first I did not recognise her. But when she said her name recognition came. Within a week or so of arriving home after the war I had received about ninety letters. One of these had been writ-ten by Laurel Chapman. Laurel was at the coaching college where I

had studied along with other Moore College men. At that time she was but sixteen and I was twenty so I looked on her as a child. Now she was a full-grown woman, twenty-four years old . . . I thought she was a fine, mature woman. I . . . was interested . . . I learned that Laurel was now a fully qualified nursing sister.[8]

While still at school Laurel had met Geoffrey with his sisters in a church group at St Paul's Wahroonga—'only he was a boy and so of no interest'—as well as later at the coaching college where 'I felt he was very poor [he had a hole in his trousers that showed his skin] but full of fun'.[9] Laurel gives her own account:

Some time after the war ceased the ex-prisoners of war (POWs) came home. And with them one I knew from the coaching college days and had prayed for regularly . . . So in my last months of nursing Geoff came into my life. I wrote him a small hastily written welcome home note when I heard he was at the Concord Repatriation Hospital. Just a few lines and he replied and invited me to visit. I went on my four hours off duty after a morning shift and of course it wasn't visiting hours but I bustled in all oozing bumptious confidence which underneath I didn't have. I wasn't even sure I'd recognise him. The ward sister, a much feared virago, as they thought, somehow knew I was scared and told me his bed number.

I found his bed and introduced myself . . . I had my hair in two long plaits and was wearing sandals and a dirndl skirt, sunburnt and uninhibited we just knew there was a drawing together. We chatted breezily.[10]

Geoffrey noticed:

She was dressed for the beach, or, I think, from the beach. A bit tousled in the hair, cherry red from the sun, and slightly dishevelled in what they called a dirndl skirt. She wore sandals. By no means dressed up to kill. Nor was I to be killed, I resolved. So we chatted. Not emptily, but then not with great wisdom either. She skirted away from the subject of the prison camp. She may have wished to know, but she was wary. So was I. Nevertheless there was plenty to talk about.[11]

Both remember what happened at that first parting. Geoffrey says: 'we chatted until it was time for her to leave. In pyjamas and dressing gown I walked with her to the gate':[12]

> We moved along the walkway, talking quietly. She linked her arm loosely with mine, and her hand rested along my elbow.[13]

Geoffrey later said, 'the simple movement brought a sense of warmth that I would now describe as "communion"'.[14] What happened at the time was more than just theological:

> I was quite shocked. Far from being horrified I was pleased, but then I had not expected that touch. The shock was faint, but it was there, a lingering tingling. I thought, 'That is a very gentle, sensitive touch.' The thought was pleasing. Then I thought, 'It is not an invading touch, but a gentle one. In fact it is timid but reassuring.'[15]

Laurel has her own version of how it happened:

> Geoff got up to walk me to the gate and I slipped my arm into his to steady his feet as he had a decided limp with a tendency to trip.

Even so, she admits, 'with that contact we were smitten'.[16] Geoffrey agrees:

> The touch had done it. It had put me into full contact with another human being, and especially a feminine human being. In due course it led me, inevitably, into marriage. Nor, over some thirty-five years, has that touch changed. It is evenly the same, and still most satisfactory.[17]

Geoffrey says Laurel later told him 'she had been sure I would return and had years ago set her mind to marry me'.[18]

MARRIAGE AND FAMILY

In Laurel, Geoffrey had found 'a nurse he needed and a future wife and mother for our children'.[19] Also a soul-mate and 'a helper fit for him'.[20] As a 'mature no-nonsense woman',[21] a Laurel-like character appears in many of Geoffrey's short stories:

> ... she was sensible, but also sensitive. She went to the heart of any matter quite quickly, and for the most part, too, understood his ways of thinking.[22]

Laurel was involved in both the Church Missionary Society League of Youth, which 'gave me my mission zeal',[23] and the CSSM (Children's Special Service Mission—later Scripture Union) Beach Missions.[24] Reared into 'moral, ethical upright adulthood' through 'one hundred percent law and not of grace'[25] by a hard-working mother married to a daredevil father, she was confirmed as 'an Anglican but semi Catholic'. Taken by a friend to an evangelical meeting at the Methodist Central Mission, she had been 'soundly converted'.[26] In Laurel Chapman, Geoffrey had found 'a woman of faith',[27] 'a person of the Presence' whom he sensed 'had more than an inkling' of the ways of practical love that Geoffrey and the others had discovered in the prison camp.[28] Laurel comments:

> Even in our beliefs there was no conflict. We were both disillusioned with the churches although each firmly loving the Lord.[29]

Laurel found that 'This debonair good looker was full of repartee and fun', bought her chocolates and orchids every time they went to the pictures, and 'was more than generous in every way'.[30]

After a three month engagement, they were married in the St James Church at Turramurra, followed by a reception on the front lawn at 20 Kissing Point Road, on 25th May, 1946. Geoffrey writes looking back on such a wedding in one of his stories:

> The wedding day had been a time of torment and delight—torment because he had wondered whether it would really happen, and if so, then would he be an inadequate husband? ... Anyway she had looked beautiful, and so beautiful that he had been terrified. For all her beauty she was simple and shy.[31]

For their going away, Laurel says, a family friend 'had made me some trousseau of the most unsuitable and quite out of this world nighties and undies. Daring for her and Mum and with the best of love... This was a tremendous step.'[32] Geoffrey tells what happened as they began their honeymoon, after they got off the train at the Blue Mountains resort of Blackheath:

> They walked along the empty platform, he struggling with the two heavy suitcases, and she with her overnight bag.
>
> The moment had been unforgettable. The catch on her small case had not been fastened. Suddenly the lid flew open. There, on the railway line, were all her intimate flimsies. 'First-night things,' they called them in those days. She stared, crimson-faced and astonished. He was no less embarrassed. He hid his feelings by climbing down on to the track and picking them up, one by one.[33]

Laurel remembers how Geoffrey 'would buy me a new set of earrings each day and there are many lovely memories of trips and walks we did'.[34] Geoffrey recalls a 'honeymoon of passion and peace, of intimacy and assurance'. This was in contrast to 'these days—if the TV screen was to be believed' when 'there was nothing new in marriage—no excitement, no surprise':

> Couples unwrapped the present of marriage long before they came to it, and the parcel was found to be empty. Not for her, and not for him! For them it had been a richly packed parcel.[35]

Geoffrey was not ready to return to theological study, and needed time 'for the recovery of health and some readjustment of faith', so their first home was on the north coast of New South Wales, 'where he settled down to farm and to write':[36]

> Laurel and I married and we went to a small farm in Eungai on the north coast of New South Wales. I had purchased this with money that had accumulated during our prison days, and the gratuity we received on discharge. By this time my writing had received some recognition, so that with a bit of general farming and a reasonable income from stories we were able to live.[37]

Here Geoffrey and Laurel sought to put into practice what they had learned about living for others:

> At Eungai we were seeking to live as I had learned in the prison camp, as selflessly as possible, taking opportunities to help others in their work and to bring the principle of practical love to the community. I had frozen against the church because it seemed to me that its message and practice were not what I had learned in the days of our suffering . . . The Eungai days stand out in my memory, and in Laurel's memory also, as almost idyllic times. Pain was submerged in joy and the delights of farming and writing.[38] Later I wrote a book on those days called *Days and Dreams of Arcady*.[39]

There were hard times as well. Laurel recalls:

> Our stay in Eungai Creek was a period of any early marriage and we had our moments. Geoff got so busy helping others that he neglected or didn't have time to fix our house fences and the poddy calf raided his veggie garden and worse, into my garden of flowers at the front.[40]

Geoffrey admits 'it was not all fun and laughter, intimacy and joy':

> He remembered the battles they had had—with each other . . . they had struggled until the misery of it drove them back to each other, and it had been like starting all over again. They both had the sense to know that this sort of thing was universal. Knowing that helped them.[41]

They later joined Geoffrey's brother Stan on his dairy farm at Woodhill in the Kangaroo Valley on the south coast, until Geoffrey was ready to re-enter Moore College in March 1950 under the Repatriation Benefits scheme, living in an available house in Beecroft.[42]

Their first child Richard was born when they were at Eungai, and Carol when they were at Woodhill. Anne was born during their time at Beecroft. Elizabeth and Ruth were born while they were at Miller's Point, and Mary-Grace in Pakistan.[43] Ruth died in a vehicle accident in 1974.[44] At Geoffrey's funeral, his children reflected on their parents' marriage:

> He always, always, saw the best in others and especially in his beloved wife, and family.
>
> His marriage to Laurel, his bride in post-war 1946, was a great love story of 63 years although not always smooth sailing with two feisty strong spirits together. He could not have done what he did without her support of his ministry.

They also sought to sum up their own experience of family life with Geoffrey:

> ... for us, what made him the husband, father and grandfather we loved was his passion for life; whatever he did, he did ... For his children he was a strict disciplinarian—we knew we were in for it when he would line us all up! He never really understood teenage girls at all and mum often had to rescue us from his wrath. But he was keenly aware of his failures as a father. He set high standards for himself and others, and his family were no exception—that made it difficult for some of us growing up but we know now he loved each of us deeply.

The eleven grandchildren added their bit:

> Thank you for telling us to be quiet during the Christmas story, Thank you for praying for us everyday, Thank you for your Grandpa newsletter when we were growing up. And mostly Thank you for showing us what it means to love the Lord and love your Grandkids. We love you with all our heart.

In all of this, the gospel was at the forefront:

> Truthfully he was for our early years often an absent father and husband, not only spending many weeks away preaching and teaching but hours in his study writing. He would inevitably have huge regrets for doing this and promise to reform but we would know that very soon he would be unable to resist what he had to do. After every meeting he would come home and be amazed at the way God had worked—each time was 'the best we ever had'.

119

We knew he could no more stop preaching and writing than breathing.[45]

Laurel sums it up:

> No one can ever say my Geoff has any other mind but that of doing the Lord's work and will. He lives and dreams of it...he is one eyed, one mind, in the Gospel. I don't mean to say he hasn't gardened or had birds everywhere we have gone, but it is all unconsciously to the glory of God the Creator.[46]

THE LAMB AND HIS BRIDE [47]

It was in the realities of his own marriage and family life that Geoffrey forged his biblical theology of marriage, from which he taught and counselled hundreds. What gave Geoffrey's and Laurel's 'feisty' marriage its lasting resilience was the merciful love of God in Christ. Geoffrey sets this out in a poem entitled simply 'Laurel':[48]

> Whence came this love?
> It was born of you
> In your love for me.
> Yet beyond even you
> It came from Him
> Who is love Himself.

This love exposes and replaces our 'love' that is otherwise centred on self:

> I am in Him
> And He in me.
> I, with all others,
> Am also His Bride,
> But this He did for me,
> He gave me His Bridegroom's love
> To love you for ever.
> To love you where my mind,
> Lost in its loveless ego,
> Loved me more than others.

This love from God is enacted at the cross:

> I, too, have been to Calvary,
> First to curse and then to kiss.
> His love destroyed the ego,
> Bringing it to life again
> As the new self, lost in Him.
> Else I had never loved you
> With ought but ego love,
> Seeking you for myself
> And not for you.

What God did at the cross must do its work each day:

> Each day His Calvary love kills
> Old ego that would rise.
> Each day His pristine love
> Repristinates my own
> Until I love afresh
> With Calvary love—
> God's *agape* that grows
> Beyond romantic love
> Which hides Man's ego love:
> So does His love
> Love you, through me.

Thus 'marriage in the present is real/And some reflection of the Wedding to be':[49]

> This love's a mystery.
> Daily the Marriage Feast
> Draws nearer in our time,
> But in our time delights to be
> As it one day will be
> In time's full time.
> Now in our love the Feast is here
> And you love me
> As I love you
> With Calvary Bridal love.
> And ever will.

Central to Geoffrey's understanding and teaching of marriage is 'the climax of history which will be the glorious wedding of redeemed humanity to the Son of God—the Divine Bride-groom—and so the incredible uniting of God and Man in the mystery of the Divine Family—God and Man becoming one forever'. The uniting of man and woman in the beginning to be 'one-flesh' (see Genesis 2:18–24; compare Ephesians 5:31–32) indi-cates that all man–woman relationships, and particularly mar-riage, are really prophetic and protological—a foretaste and a forecast of this glorious wedding.[50] Geoffrey quotes with awed approval these sentences from Jonathan Edwards:

> The end of the creation of God was to provide a spouse for his Son Jesus Christ, that might enjoy him and on whom he might pour forth his love . . . heaven and earth were created that the Son of God might be complete in a spouse . . . There was, [as] it were, an eternal society or family in the Godhead, in the Trinity of persons. It seems to be God's design to admit the church into the divine family as his son's wife.[51]

This goal is reflected in the way men and women are constituted by creation. Their distinctiveness and their unity bear witness to the triune nature of God in Himself and to God's ultimate rela-tionship with His people. Geoffrey Bingham draws on Geoffrey Bromiley to make this point:

> In creating man—male and female—in his own image, and joining them together so that they become one flesh, God makes us copies both of himself in his trinitarian unity and distinction as one God and three persons and of himself in relation to the people of his gracious election.[52]

Accordingly, marriage is not just some convenient mutual arrangement that men and women make between themselves, nor is the union of Christ with his people just an interesting comparison with marriage as we know it to be. The ultimate marriage of Christ and his Bride is what marriage in the present is really all about. As Geoffrey says:

All of this alerts us to the fact that 'one-flesh' union and marriage are of far-reaching importance.[53]

UNITY AND ORDER

Whatever the distinctiveness and relationships of women and men with regard to one another, the most important thing for Geoffrey is that they are to be one with each other. Together they constitute 'the one image and likeness of God',[54] and they are themselves defined by the archetypal relationship of Christ with his Bride:

> The Woman is not seen fully as she is except in relation to the Bridegroom, and in union with him. It is his masculinity which etches her feminity, as her feminity delineates his masculinity. One cannot be viewed wholly apart from the other. The two, together, show the glory of God.[55]

This unity is, first of all, not just in marriage, but across the human race. Commenting on Genesis 2, Geoffrey says:

> We must notice that until verse 24 nothing is spoken about marriage, but everything is spoken about the oneness of the man and the woman, and thus of all males and females of the human race.[56]

'Sexuality', he says, 'rightly understood, should be a useful term for covering the whole range of man–woman relationships, catching up the idea of families and society as a man–woman community'.[57] It is in this context that Geoffrey treats the matter of so-called 'singleness'.[58] But it has particular expression in the marriage relationship:

> This union was to be the type of the one who was to come, whose marriage as Bridegroom to the purified Bride would be the goal and meaning of history.[59]

True and full marriage, then, involves participation in the action towards this goal of God's purpose for His creation:

If then we view man and woman merely in regard to a romantic alliance or in procreation and the rearing of children, we will miss the fact that the point of their being and living was the vocation God gave them ... The marriage that is going nowhere, goes nowhere. Human marriages are often pathetically pointless, apathetic, and lethargic, just because the husband and wife (and, later, the children) do not understand that marriage is for vocation, and vocation with a goal.[60]

With a view to this goal, there is a certain ordering of the relationship between man and woman in marriage that corresponds to the relationship between Christ and his Bride. Geoffrey does not shy away from what the Bible has to say about matters of headship and submission,[61] but he treats it with a strength and tenderness not always present in such discussions. In one of his writings he imparts a vision he has had of the true Woman, the Bride of the Lamb:

She was not, of course, True Woman without the True Man. His presence delineated her true being, as her true being was the glory of him. Only when they were together did the wonderful truth of womanhood and manhood come through to me. And come it did! ... I know that a man can understand womanhood, as womanhood can understand manhood, and there need be no barrier between the two ... As I gazed at the beauty of this holy Woman I saw her adoration of her Spouse. She was for ever looking at him with pride, with admiration, and with joy. Whilst she was greatly animated with her pure affection, she was not merely excited, as though passion were an end in itself, but she showed great tranquillity. What came to me strongly was that she was wholly one with him, and trusted him. There was not one doubt in her mind concerning him. So then, when I say she was submitted to him, her acceptance of her femininity in the presence of his masculinity was not that of an inferior to a superior, but of a lover to the beloved. She was gladly dependent upon him, for her task in their partnership was a high and lofty one, and could only be accomplished in the mutuality of their unity.

When I looked at the Holy Man, Son of Man and Son of God, my heart was gripped for ever by his lordly mien, his high regality, which though firm was yet tender and yielding and of infinite compassion and love. As he looked at the Woman I knew that I—with all the elect race of the Father—was contained in that Woman, and that our race was beloved in his sight, and loved for ever. We were all in the feminine to his masculine . . . I saw then, in the presence of the Man and the Woman, what was, and is, and ever shall be—the indissoluble nature of the unity of masculinity and femininity.[62]

Geoffrey admits that 'the person who is justified is in the best position to examine the meaning of man and woman',[63] but that otherwise it is likely to be contested:

When it is said that to be subordinate is not to be inferior, and to be superordinate is not to be superior, this statement is often brushed off impatiently by persons who have already decided that to be subordinate is to be inferior. Nor is any reasoning likely to persuade them otherwise. Yet the whole matter of creation, functionality, purpose and goal-achievement lies in the principle that one who is superordinate is not superior in quality, character, work or substance to one who is subordinate.

Again it comes back to the very nature of the Godhead:

The Son . . . is not inferior to the Father in quality or nature, but he is subordinate in regard to function, although his function is not inferior to that of the Father. When he says, 'The Father is greater than I', this does not conflict with, 'I and the Father are one'.[64]

BROKEN MARRIAGE

Such union in the beginning never envisaged a 'putting asunder'.[65] Yet perhaps because it embodied and set forth the very purpose of God, 'the serpent was out to discredit the man–woman union and communion . . . To attack marriage on the human level is to attack it as it is on the Divine plane.'[66]

Geoffrey is no stranger to the 'deep abyss' that can open up between a husband and a wife:

When the division comes,
When the anger spurts upward
In the disturbed heart; then it is
That the rending comes,
The intolerable pain, the anguish
As other-centred self returns
To self-centred otherness.
This is the deep pain,
The searing of the tender nerve
The cruel cauterization.[67]

As long as the curse of the human fall into sin continues, the husband will now 'rule' the wife.[68] Apart from the grace of God:

> The man left to himself will be arrogant, and use the ruling of the curse to his advantage and to her hurt. He will regard her as separate. His sexuality will seek to use hers—for himself. He will hide his fallen nakedness so that she cannot know him. For her part she will desire him, i.e. seek to have him, even to rule him, and will exploit his sexuality, hiding within her own so that mutuality does not exist, but there is a warring of the genders, each sinfully hiding from the other but seeking to exploit the other.[69]

Geoffrey upholds 'the radical nature of Jesus' view of marriage which was that marriage was inviolate and permanent; there should be no divorce; and remarriage was inadmissible. It could only cause adultery.' Geoffrey says: 'I am aware of the varying exegeses on these Synoptic passages but believe Jesus' words have the intent I here outline'.[70] While 'honestly prepared to have to change some of these ideas', they were confirmed as he sought to grow in understanding of these matters.[71] At the same time he says: 'Those who differ in interpretation must make allowance for differences of understanding in others'.[72] He also eschews the path of legalism: the Bible 'is not a law book' which yields to those who come to it strictly 'to find out what is permitted and not permitted' apart from its witness to 'the true Bride and [the True] Bridegroom'.[73] What he sees is that the 'union given in creation' is 'a union or fusion of two which cannot be divided simply by the pronouncement of divorce'.[74] Geoffrey maintains: 'Loss of communion does not mean obliteration of union'.[75] Allowance for divorce in the Old Testament was made 'because of your hardness of heart':[76]

> ...my own reading of the matter is that there ought to be no divorce and so no remarriage. What I concede is that where there is hard-heartedness, then allowance is made for a spouse to be freed from the marriage; but, properly speaking, the soft-heartedness of love and forgiveness should seek to maintain the marriage.[77]

This does not prevent Geoffrey from facing the realities of divorce and remarriage, or from relating warmly with those who are in these situations:

> In over forty years as an ordained minister I have never married any person who has been divorced. I have, however, counselled countless persons whose marriages have been breaking up; who have divorced or been divorced; who seek advice regarding divorce and remarriage, and in almost every case have felt my counselling was helpful and comforting. It did not mean, of course, that the advice I gave was always heeded, but the friendship and support given seemed to tide some folk over their most painful periods.[78]

A sample of Geoffrey's extensive marriage counselling is given in one of his short stories, where a young man, jaded in his second marriage, visits an older man for counselling. In the end he is told:

> We need a rich revelation of the true image of God. We need to see God, and to come to know Him. We need a new life from Him. Change your life-style and you don't change much. You revert, after a time, particularly as the new life-style becomes boring. Get a new life and you automatically have a new life-style ... you can only have a new life from God. His is the life of love. He is the One who scrubs the past clean. He takes the monkey off your back. He lifts you out of your little passions, and mediocre loves. He gives you true identity. You really become someone, your true self, the person you have smothered by your dull, self-centred living.[79]

Whatever people have been through, it is only in the True Marriage that lives can be restored:

> There is no place for spouse to hide,
> Or orphaned child to find security
> But in the heart of Father-God.
> He Husband is to lonely wife,
> Is comfort to the brideless man
> And Father to the child bereft
> Of natural love. In Him alone
> The hurt is healed. In Him alone
> Such love returns.[80]

MARRIAGE AND THE FAMILY OF GOD

Geoffrey recounts an incident where a young woman whose life was already sexually complicated was listening to him expounding what happened on the cross, and its meaning for those who believe. She came up to him afterwards: 'If what you say about the cross is true', she said, 'then I am a virgin again!'[81] She had by faith become part of the holy city, the glorious bride of Christ. Geoffrey says:

I believe we should teach these things we have been neglecting to open up to our congregations and to those folk who come for counselling. More than ever, too, we need to grasp hold of the gifts of marriage, of sexuality and of parenthood. Those of the Community of Christ need to know their identity as the Bride of Christ; the nature of Christ's Lordship in this age and the age to come; and the nature of the Church as it is 'helpmeet' to the Son of God in his outworking of history. Not only will the triumphal Messianic Bridal Feast bring living hope to us all as persons, and thus stimulate us to present action, but it will also help us to know our vocation now in history.[82]

Some of Geoffrey's short stories engage these themes from his actual experience of marriage and family life, with both profundity and lightness of touch. 'The Eagle and the Woman'[83] captures something of the grandeur and nobility of man and woman together in their vocation in God's creation. It relates an encounter from the Pakistan days. A man is watching an eagle hovering: 'only a pin-spot in the high sky of cloudless blue' above the Himalayan hills:

> In some way he correlated to the high, flying creature. He had a spirit in him which soared above the mundane and the mediocre. Also he had long, keen sight which saw beyond where most men saw. He saw into other men, and then through them to beyond them . . . Man is not limited to the three dimensions of his locale, nor to the five senses which seem to bind him . . . There is something beyond the horizons of our being!

A woman—his wife—has also seen the eagle. But her mind is intent on other concerns:

> The woman moved towards the bassinette. She was a woman through and through. She had always felt this way. Her husband was her man, and there was none other. Her babe-in-arms was the sixth and, she knew, the last. The others had lived, filling out her warm maternity. She moved with confidence, the soft flesh cradled in her arms. Then she laid it in the bassinette. She paused for a moment, filling her own eyes with the wonder of pink flesh, and its slumbering serenity.

She looks up and sees 'her man gazing down at her'. He waves, and points to the eagle. She sees it again:

> It seemed suspended for a few moments, but with almost imperceptible movements of its wings it faintly fluttered aloft. She smiled at it, and then at her husband. He smiled back. Then he fixed his gaze on the eagle whilst she went towards the house . . . His eyes were hungry for the beauty of the bird. He loved its powerful body, its muscled wings, even the strong talons. What he admired most of all was the regal head, the deep-set but gleaming eyes, and aquiline stance of its sweeping head and beak . . . in his own land he had climbed high mountains to seek out the eyries of these great eagles . . . he had never ceased to marvel at the truth of their being, their unique identity, and their authentic regality.

Suddenly the bird plunged with a squealing cry 'as it swooped over the bassinette, its long talons barely clearing it':

> Nobody moved but the woman. The man watched her suddenly wheel and go plunging towards the bassinette. High in the sky the eagle had risen, and now was poised. So was the man... Every muscle within him tightened, and suddenly he was catapulted down the hill, rushing towards the woman and the baby.

As though in slow motion the man 'could see the bird dropping, wings arched high, talons forward, its whole body rushing in perfect direction, centred on the bassinette and the new baby within it'. He could also see 'his woman':

> ... rich and motherly in body, taut and strong, her voice rising in indignant rebuke to the great bird above her. There was nothing of despair in the cry. She was not a fearful, hopeless person. She was in command; let no eagle defy her! Her shrill cry split the air. So did her two fine arms. Upward they went as she slewed backwards, turning to face the eagle even as her heels dug into the grass and soil... The man caught the glint in the eyes of the eagle. His own strong cry rose with his running. Together their cries would defeat the royal eagle, descending like some brown and feathered arch-angel. The man's arms were high too, as he ran, and in a flash he was there, almost as his wife had arrived.

Even as he did so, he could still take in 'the magnificence of his woman':

> Every part of her was strong and vibrant with protective love. An eagle of sorts herself, she anticipated the moves of the flashing bird. She cried out from her depths against its invasion. She poured all her moral rights into one great and terrible cry: 'No!' The man could scarcely contain his passion of pride and admiration. 'No!' he shouted with her, and ran the extra yard.

The eagle swooped—and missed the bassinette. The man and the woman were together, looking up at the 'magnificent bird' they had battled. 'Somehow this was what life was all about':

They stood there, he loving his wife as never before, and holding in his heart an admiration for the great creature up there in the sky. He could have sworn that as the bird flew off it gave a great salute with its wings . . . both he and the woman knew that the bird would not return. It would leave them with the child. They knew that as well as did the eagle. They found now that they loved the child fiercely as they had not loved it before.

Even so, hand in hand they watched the eagle as it lofted higher and higher until it was a pin-spot, and then no more.

One other story, 'Trouble in the Toilet',[84] celebrates with high humour the resilience of ordinary human family life, in the midst of its foibles and fallibilities. 'Grandpa' is treated to a surprise sixty-third birthday party by members of the family, during which one granddaughter, taking time off from social-ising with cousins, locks herself in the toilet, panics, and screams. No amount of coaxing can induce her to undo what she has done. Her father goes next door for a ladder to attempt to get in through the window. Grandpa ends up breaking the door open with a crowbar, to find the diminutive grand-daughter 'crouched upon the floor, almost hidden behind the S-bend':

> Mighty of voice, forceful of character, she was now a pitiful mite of helpless humanity . . . Even so, as all the faces appeared she rallied. Hers was an incredible recovery rate. Her large and beautiful eyes smiled, charming the assembly. 'I didn't get hurt,' she said, salvaging her dignity and personhood. 'Look how I got behind the toilet!' . . . She uncoiled from behind the toilet bowl. Slightly brushing herself she made a dignified exit. She was soon lost in the remainder of the children.

The adults are left to survey the damage to the door, and to resume the party. Just as they are wondering 'whether she'll carry this all her life' the granddaughter returns:

> . . . a golden streak shot past them . . . She came back a moment later. She had been to the toilet. 'I forgot my pants,' she said, giggling. 'I had to go back and get them.' She wiggled into them,

hoisted them, jetted through the door and down to where all the children were playing on the lawn.

Grandpa had just said, 'Kids are pretty resilient', and the parents agree.

1 Marcus L. Loane, *These Happy Warriors*, 88; *Always the Presence*, chapter 28, part 2.

2 *My Beloved Family*, 138.

3 *Love Is the Spur*, 95.

4 *Love Is the Spur*, 108.

5 *My Beloved Family*, 139.

6 'The Touch', in *The Concentration Camp and Other Stories*, 19.

7 *These Happy Warriors*, 88.

8 *Love Is the Spur*, 108.

9 C. E. L. Bingham, *Laurel's Story*, private publication, 2000 (used by permission), 23, 24.

10 *Laurel's Story*, 33–34.

11 *The Concentration Camp*, 19.

12 *My Beloved Family*, 139.

13 *The Concentration Camp*, 19.

14 *My Beloved Family*, 139.

15 *The Concentration Camp*, 19.

16 *Laurel's Story*, 34.

17 *The Concentration Camp*, 20 (written in 1981).

18 *My Beloved Family*, 138–139.

19 *Laurel's Story*, 34.

20 Genesis 2:18.

21 *My Beloved Family*, 138.

22 'The Photograph', *The Boy in the Valley*, 8.

23 *Laurel's Story*, 25.

24 *These Happy Warriors*, 88.

25 *Laurel's Story*, 14.

26 *Laurel's Story*, 22. 'My mother said she'd believe this conversion when she saw my room tidy and more co-operation in the home. That was a challenge.'

27 *The Stranger in the Cemetery*, 242.

28 *My Beloved Family*, 139.

29 *Laurel's Story*, 34.

30 *Laurel's Story*, 34–35.

31 *The Boy in the Valley*, 8–9.

32 *Laurel's Story*, 35.

[33] *The Boy, the Girl and the Man*, 94.

[34] *Laurel's Story*, 36.

[35] *The Boy in the Valley*, 9.

[36] *These Happy Warriors*, 88.

[37] *My Beloved Family*, 141.

[38] 'Geoffrey's writing career began when he was thirteen, his first short story being published in 1941. After the war he had a meteoric rise in literary fortunes; *The Bulletin* published 34 of his stories within a few years, the highest rate of acceptances by that journal. He had some years writing and farming on the North Coast of New South Wales, a number of journals accepting his stories throughout Australasia. *Coast to Coast* published some of his tales and, much later, he was included in *Great Short Stories of Australia and New Zealand*, an anthology published by *Reader's Digest*, and yet later a German language anthology published in East Germany' ('Geoffrey C. Bingham: A Short Biography, 1919–1995' in *Mr Hicken's Pears*, 262).

[39] *My Beloved Family*, 142.

[40] *Laurel's Story*, 40.

[41] *The Boy in the Valley*, 9.

[42] *My Beloved Family*, 141–142; *Laurel's Story*, 41; *These Happy Warriors*, 88.

[43] *Laurel's Story*, 38, 41, 46, 51–52, 55–56, 64.

[44] <www.newcreation.org.au/pdf/GCB%20Funeral/FamilyEulogy.pdf, p. 1>.

[45] Family Eulogy, pp. 1–2.

[46] *Laurel's Story*, 132.

[47] See Revelation 19:1–9; 20:1–22:17.

[48] *All Things of the Spirit*, 143–145.

[49] 'The End Marriage', *All Things of the Spirit*, 134.

[50] *My Beloved Family*, 177–178.

[51] *The Profound Mystery: Marriage Love, Divine and Human*, 53–54; quoting from Jonathan Edwards (1703–1758) *Miscellanies*, as reproduced in *America's Theologian: A Recommendation of Jonathan Edwards* by Robert W. Jenson (Oxford University Press, New York, 1992), 42–43.

[52] *The Profound Mystery*, 14; see also 35; quoting Geoffrey Bromiley, *God and Marriage* (T. & T. Clark, Edinburgh, 1981), 77. Geoffrey says, 'In my thinking this book is one of the finest and clearest we have in English on the subject we are discussing of marriage, divorce and remarriage'.

[53] *The Profound Mystery*, 43.

[54] *The Profound Mystery*, 144; see Genesis 1:26–27; 2:18–24; 5:1–2.

[55] *God's Glory, Man's Sexuality*, 123.

[56] *The Profound Mystery*, 16.

57 *The Profound Mystery*, 28 footnote.

58 See *Man, Woman, and Sexuality*, 57–74; *God's Glory, Man's Sexuality*, 227–235; also 'Singular Love', *Twice-Conquering Love*, 183–193.

59 *The Profound Mystery*, 24.

60 *God's Glory, Man's Sexuality*, 85, 86–87.

61 See 1 Corinthians 11:3–12; Ephesians 5:21–32; Colossians 3:18–19; 1 Peter 3:1–8.

62 *The Heavenly Vision*, 64, 65–66, 67.

63 *God's Glory, Man's Sexuality*, 28.

64 *God's Glory, Man's Sexuality*, 98.

65 *The Profound Mystery*, 15; see Mark 10:6–9.

66 *The Profound Mystery*, 24.

67 'Flesh Calls to Flesh', in *The Vandal*, 180–181.

68 See Genesis 3:16.

69 *God's Glory, Man's Sexuality*, 117.

70 *The Profound Mystery*, 80–81. Passages referred to are Matthew 5:31–32; 19:3–12; Mark 10:1–12; Luke 16:18.

71 *The Profound Mystery*, 147.

72 *God's Glory, Man's Sexuality*, 265. Geoffrey's approach to counselling in this area is set out in 'The Dynamics of Sexuality—for Saints Only' and 'The Dynamics of Sexuality—for Sinners Only', *The Wisdom of God and the Healing of Man*, 153–171. See also 'Conquering Love' and 'Love Never Fails', *Twice-Conquering Love*, 38–48, 194–208.

73 *God's Glory, Man's Sexuality*, 242.

74 *The Profound Mystery*, 101.

75 *The Profound Mystery*, 22.

76 Mark 10:5.

77 *The Profound Mystery*, 106.

78 *The Profound Mystery*, 147.

79 'The Man and the Not-Man', in *The Concentration Camp*, 106.

80 'Flesh Calls to Flesh', in *The Vandal*, 183.

81 Tapes for Life Series session 1 (NCTM MP3 disc 904); cited in Martin Bleby, *Marriage and the Good News of God* (NCPI, Blackwood, 2010), 98.

82 *The Profound Mystery*, 147–148.

83 *Mr Piffy Comes Home*, 216–225.

84 *Mr Piffy Comes Home*, 33–45.

CHAPTER 8

THE *Day* OF THE *Spirit*

Couple in ministry

MILLER'S POINT

GEOFFREY STUDIED at Moore Theological College from 1950–
1952. 'His spiritual maturity and happy personality made him a
first-class member of College.'[1] Through his studies he obtained
first class honours in the Australian College of Theology Th.L
course, and second class honours in the Moore College
Diploma.[2] Marcus Loane takes up the story:

> Geoff was made a Deacon by the Archbishop in St. Andrew's
> Cathedral on March 1st 1953, and was ordained to the Priesthood in
> the following December. He was thirty-four years old, a veteran in
> the school of suffering, a man with a wealth of experience in his
> background. Archbishop Mowll had the eye of an eagle in his search
> for spiritual promise among his ordinands. He had made up his
> mind that Geoff was just the man he was looking for to initiate a
> strong spiritual outreach to young people scattered through the
> city, and to stir up younger clergy with a trumpet call to deepened
> dedication. This led the Archbishop to take the unusual step of
> bypassing the normal requirement of a curacy in order to appoint
> Geoff at once as the Minister-in-charge of the Garrison Church of
> Holy Trinity Miller's Point.[3]

A story of Geoffrey's, told from the point of view of one of his
children, sets the scene:

> Our house is called 'the rectory' and it is three storeys high. We
> sleep on the second floor and we look out of our window down to
> the Hero of Waterloo, which is a hotel on the other side of Lower
> Fort Street where the tram runs up as far as Kent Street and then
> returns, going past us again until it reaches George Street in the
> Circular Quay area . . . at night my two sisters, my brother and I
> often creep out of our beds and come together in my room where
> we look down, through a window, to what is happening below in

139

the streets. You can hear the trams swinging up Lower Fort Street, and they make a grinding sound as they turn sharply into Argyle Place. There are also the sounds of the ships' sirens blasting away with great hootings, and some of them making thin, piping sounds. Behind us you can hear the trains rumbling across the Sydney Harbour Bridge. Behind the church, which is not far from the rectory, is the big powerhouse where they make the electricity for the lighting of the Bridge and other things. Often we just look down into the Hero of Waterloo hotel and we can see the fathers of some of our friends. Sometimes there are horrible fights. Of course, the hotel has to close early, at six o'clock.[4]

Here Geoffrey was in contact with a wide range of humanity:

Because we are so close to all the places where the ships tie up, we have plenty of sailors who walk through our streets. They never harm us, and they never touch my dad because he wears a minister's white collar and black bib. Sometimes he doesn't wear them, and even then the rough people around the place never hurt him. They seem to have respect for what my dad calls 'the clergy'.

On Sundays we have visitors to our church. Some come because they want to get married in the famous old building, and they talk to Dad about that. Others are visitors from the suburbs who are interested in history. Many have heard of the beautiful stained-glass windows. Others just wander in out of curiosity. Dad talks to them all. He is interested in all kinds of people. He also likes to chat with the drunks who drink methylated spirits in which they mix boot polish. He tries to help them.[5]

Laurel, with her growing family, had less idealised memories:

The next move was to a dirty old rectory in the Sydney city area, called The Rocks situated right near the pylons of the Sydney Harbour Bridge. Miller's point was for me a nightmare ... A kitchen you wouldn't believe existed except in third world situations. A stove that was completely blocked by grease and the fridge covered in a black sticky soot ... Our laundry was a line of tubs and the deep enamel one for the washing up all along the side of the kitchen and a gas boiler in the corner ... The tension of trying to have enough nappies as no washing was allowed on Sunday.[6]

There were times that Laurel later shuddered to think of—'Talk about the angels working over-time':

> The top floor we turned into a play room and the hotel opposite often had clients turn cold sober as they saw Dick climb onto the sloping roof to the gutter to rescue a toy . . . The time he climbed up the drain pipe to get into the rectory when I went to hospital and Geoff had forgotten the children . . . Dick had no fear of heights and would climb around the first edging of the pylon of the Sydney Harbour bridge, coming out a small hole onto the ledge.[7]

The pace was exhausting:

> Life at the Rectory was one hectic pace as we had, it seemed, endless visitors. People coming to see Geoff for counselling. I'd often have them in the kitchen waiting. [One of the children] tells how she squatted against the wall outside the office for Dad to see her . . . One Sunday [another of the children] tipped her meal onto the floor as she carried it to the table and when asked, she said she just wanted attention. Even that didn't register with our busy-ness.[8]

It may be from about this time that Geoffrey recounts Laurel saying to him, 'Until you are a better husband to your wife and father to your children, I will never listen to another of your sermons!'[9]

Geoffrey's ministry at Miller's Point was innovative for that time. He cancelled fetes and raffles as fundraisers and insti-gated direct giving through an annual 'Temple Day'.[10] He started monthly guest services—'There was a strong emphasis on soul-winning and evangelism; small bands went out to find idlers on the street and persuade them to come in'.[11] John Dunn, a teenager from Thornleigh, first met Geoffrey at one of these services:

> Young people in the Bible study group which Geoff ran would go out onto the streets of Miller's Point and round Dawes Point and down to Circular Quay, and they would give people invitations to come back with them to the guest service that night, and they would do the pubs and people coming off the ferries and so on, and

so the church would be packed jam full on Sunday nights at this once-a-month guest service. And that's when a lot of conversions took place. Geoff would invite people forward at the end of the meeting, and they would have counsellors out in the vestry to talk with all these people.[12]

People came from far and wide. Fred George, one of the men impacted during Geoffrey's ministry in the College days as a catechist at St Luke's Church Thornleigh, 'used to round up all the kids at Thornleigh and cart them up and down to Miller's Point for this guest service.'[13] John Dunn remembers Geoffrey 'up there in the pulpit in his surplice and cassock, waving his arms around, preaching with great vigour and fire—I thought he looked like Moses . . . I had never heard anything quite like this before'; and afterwards at supper when 'Geoff came over with his big bushy eyebrows and x-ray vision'.[14] Geoffrey also developed a seamen's mission for Pacific Islanders:

> Geoff was able to lead them to the true understanding of faith. They came from a nominal Christian background or none. It was beautiful to hear them sing in church as they gathered in a circle, got their quarter notes and then sang.[15]

'Geoff found himself in demand for Conventions and also held regular meetings for a small group of the younger clergy who were eager to seek a closer walk with God':[16]

> Bingham's remarkable ability to draw huge crowds meant that he was a popular leader of local missions: an estimated 1,500 people came to hear him at one week-night meeting at St Stephen's Newtown. With energy and dynamism, he preached about the power of the Holy Spirit to transform Christian lives.[17]

Geoffrey had much to offer, and many came to talk with him. Former fellow-student from Moore College, David Hewetson, was among those to whom Geoffrey extended 'generous hospitality'—'after we left College and worked in different churches I was still welcome in the Bingham household and often went there on my day off', staying for lunch. 'It was a great centre for students and nurses and whatnot in those days.'[18] Laurel filled the bill:

Then on Sundays Geoff had a pile of students from the Bible College come to teach Sunday school or just to worship. Geoff invited approximately twenty to lunch every Sunday. Which meant I had to cook a roast dinner and huge pudding.[19]

'Of course all for the Lord', says Laurel. But then she comments, 'Nowadays I wonder'.

SOMETHING MISSING

'There was also a strong emphasis on the need to cultivate a life of true personal holiness . . . Geoff's friends knew him as one who was always ahead in his quest for personal holiness.'[20] There had to be more to this, however, than just an application of law. David Hewetson writes:

> Whatever else we had in common I think there was a sense in our spirits that, although College had been great, there was something more, something missing in our spiritual experience.[21]

Geoffrey concurred:

> I was quite headstrong in the ministry I was exercising. Brought up as an evangelical person, having my faith tested in a prison camp during the war, emerging afresh as a man of the Scriptures, I knew that something of the doctrine I held was dry, factual, and in some ways without the dews of fresh, personal love upon it.[22]

David Hewetson relates how 'Geoff began to share with me some of the things he was discovering in a search for what we sometimes called "the deeper life"'. Keswick Conventions had been influential, and what they discovered was 'very much in line with the authentic Keswick message',[23] a movement that sought the 'Higher Life' in which 'the natural proclivity to sin' required 'the countervailing influence of the Holy Spirit'.[24] About this time a book came Geoffrey's way:

> In my need I discovered a book which took me into a richer and deeper understanding of the Cross.[25]

It is likely that this book was *Born Crucified,* by L. E. Maxwell.[26] This book 'shows Christians how to have victory over sin, and power in God's service':

> When God declares the ungodly sinner just, He makes no mere legal and lifeless imputation of righteousness apart from a real and deep life-union of the believer with Christ . . . Christ's death *for* sin is automatically my death *to* sin.[27]

For David Hewetson:

> The concept of our being 'crucified with Christ' *à la* Romans 6 and the necessity to 'reckon' on this was an exciting new possibility to me and I began to launch myself into it wholeheartedly. [This] brought changes to my life accompanied by a new discipline in living and an exhilaration in daily life. Was this what we had searched and waited for? [28]

'It was a relief to realise that whatever else there was for us in the spiritual life it was, in a sense, something we already had though perhaps we had not fully appreciated it.' They were not teaching any kind of 'second blessing' but 'a newer appreciation of what God had so richly given us at our conversion'. There was a danger, however, 'that in so strongly espousing our line of teaching we had sometimes implied that those who had not yet "arrived" at it were in some sense lesser Christians'. Later, as Geoffrey and David corresponded with each other between Pakistan and Tanzania, Geoffrey 'indicated that some of the central emphases of our teaching had been incorrect'.[29] Being 'crucified with Christ' could be taken as something you strive for by a kind of 'mental gymnastics'. After reading Haldane's commentary on Romans, Geoffrey had come to the conclusion that 'it wasn't a kind of mental position that you took up; it was just something that you simply accepted [as a] fact theologically'[30]—that is, by faith.[31] When David Hewetson asked, 'How could we have been so wrong when God blessed us so much?' Geoffrey replied memorably, 'God didn't bless our muddled heads; he blessed our obedient hearts'.[32]

A RICH REVELATION

At about this time Geoffrey was speaker for a convention at Katoomba in the Blue Mountains. Here he came to a crisis:

> I was crushed by the revelation of my own self-assertiveness, my own human planning of a divine ministry.[33]

He later described it as being shown that all his flourishing ministry was nothing more than a castle of sand, built on his own personality:[34]

> In the toils of an all-night conflict with God, I felt that I wanted to die. Morning found me physically spent and exhausted. As I consciously surrendered my will to the loving care of God I tasted a little of the trust that Christ had when he said on the Cross, 'Father! Into your hands I commit my spirit.' Then, at last, I slept—the peaceful sleep of a small and trustful child. When I awoke it was to a sense of quiet joy and incredible serenity. Many, many years before I had come to know the joyful truth and experience of forgiveness. Now I knew, in an even richer way, the peace of being in the hands of God.[35]

The same weekend, Laurel was at a Church Missionary Society conference at Moss Vale. She had to make her own way there with four children:[36]

> I have a clear picture of two huge brown suitcases and Anne so very obstreperous and Carol and Dick and a baby in my sling—I probably had Anne on reins, I have a picture of her in them with the others—and how we must have got the tram outside to Central and the country train to Moss Vale—and I don't remember at all the transport from the station but I can still hear them say 'Put her down there' and I with my howling struggling kids and those two huge suitcases going down cement steps to the gym basement and in a corner of this vast cement semi-underground place were three beds—and I stood there and whether I screamed it aloud or silently I'll never know—but I said 'If there's a God and I don't believe there is He better show Himself and do something'—and in came through the partition door an old man . . . and he took the screaming baby— chatted to the children . . . I remember clearly as the old man came

in I was flooded with His peace and His Holy Spirit and KNEW His presence.[37]

So Laurel was then able to make the beds with the sheets she had brought—the girls head to toe in the one bed—they all went exhaustedly to sleep, while she fed and slept with the baby in her bed. Next morning a matron on leave from Africa diagnosed and treated the baby's projectile vomiting. The conference speaker 'could have been the biggest bore' but what he said 'was so much life because I had come into a freshness of life—and the Lord was so present . . . I was on cloud nine and I knew His presence and when times I feel like to give up—I pray in the Spirit and He hears'.

Laurel's 'one worry the next day was how was I to convey this to the man so much of a "law" and absent father—and then when we met we both saw something had happened'. Laurel comments, 'of course we were preparing/being prepared for overseas'. For Laurel the change lasted:

. . . though Geoff never did alter that much in his busyness nor the Sunday ease much from the huge meals of twelve or so people I had to feed each Sunday lunch—it somehow didn't bother me as before.[38]

For Geoffrey, 'The results of this experience were both beautiful and appalling':

On the one hand, on the nights which followed, I could scarcely sleep for the wonder of the new discovery I was making in the Scriptures. I could manage only a few hours sleep per night. My wife Laurel had made similar discoveries and we were very much one together.[39]

This showed in their ministry:

. . . it was as though a new man mounted the pulpit one Sunday. His old fierceness was gone, but with its going a new authority and power had come. If he was more gentle he was also more insistent. What he said cut with the edge of a prophetic sword, and for some it was frightening . . . The rector's wife was different. She had a new, fresh acceptance of the Point and its inhabitants. Suddenly the distance between her and the people had diminished; indeed it had vanished . . . The services throbbed with a richer warmth and vibrancy than they had known.[40]

On the other hand, this was not to everyone's liking:

However, our congregation dwindled rapidly. We were accused of heresy. One of these was the heresy of sinless perfection.[41]

Marcus Loane fills in the background:

. . . Geoff was not without critics, though their criticism all too often sprang from nothing more than hearsay. Geoff's emphasis on holiness undoubtedly caused a ferment in church circles. This was in the aftermath of a movement which some twelve years or so before had led to a grievous schism among contemporary Evangelicals. The most influential leaders in this movement had taught that God's purpose for His people is that they should live day by day free from the stain of all known sin; some of them had begun to claim, or so it seemed, that there was now no known sin in their lives. This was described by some as Christian Perfection, by others as Sinless Perfection, and it split the ranks of bodies such as the Inter Varsity Fellowship and the Crusader Union. This had never been lost to view during the next decade; people were nervous of any teaching which seemed to point in a similar direction. As a result, Geoff came under fire from those who feared what they did not know.[42]

Geoffrey himself hardly qualified as a sinless perfectionist. As one adherent of that view scornfully observed, 'He doesn't understand what this truth is, much less practise it'![43] Geoffrey was on about something else:

His own teaching owed much to *The Gospel Mystery of Sanctification* by the veteran Puritan Walter Marshall;[44] it was all in keeping with the hidden life and ardent desire which galvanized his ministry . . . he was, as it were, up at the frontier of New Testament demands for a life set apart without reserve for God . . . Therefore he would go as far as the New Testament authorized him to go, but no further. If his language were sometimes open to misunderstanding, he was always willing to revise it in the light of the New Testament. But he was sure that God had far more for him to experience than he had yet attained, just as he was sure that the God Who is holy wanted him as a man of God also to be holy.[45]

The dwindling congregation was replaced by something better:

> There were dark days when friends slipped away and dropped their contacts with us. At the same time amazing things began to happen. The numbers at the Tuesday evening Bible class suddenly began to rise. From a small group of twelve it rapidly grew to over sixty, and then even higher, folk sitting in the church pews for two hours, and not seeming to notice it. Other wonderful things were happening. Night after night people who felt the barrenness of their lives would ring me, and make their way to our home, even in the early hours of the morning. A group of clergy and laity would meet monthly in a quiet place away from the demanding telephone, to study the Scriptures, to share the truth and its life, and to ask God for renewal of the nation. Because Australia had never known a true revival, we were asking God to visit our land and heal it.[46]

THE CROSS AND THE SPIRIT

What happened to Geoffrey and Laurel that weekend was undoubtedly an experience of the Holy Spirit, and Geoffrey has since called it this.[47] But it is interesting that Geoffrey did not speak of it in a way that magnified the Spirit as such, but emphasised rather what the Spirit came to bring: 'a rich revelation of God's love in Christ and His Cross'.[48] This remained central to Geoffrey's extensive teaching and writing on the Spirit of God. Geoffrey maintained that 'Pentecost was with a view to Calvary, i.e. to revealing the great mystery of God in the work of His Son, Jesus Christ'.[49] Not everyone sees it this way:

> ... others may say, 'Calvary (the Atonement) is a fair enough beginning, but being baptized in the Spirit is so dynamic that it must be seen as greater, even, than conversion. It is really the Spirit

who brings victory and triumph. All things are done through him, and there is no need for us to stay at the Cross. We pass through the Resurrection and come to Pentecost. It is in Pentecost that the dynamic resides, and when that power gets free we are enormously transformed and dynamic in our operations. We can now go to the ends of the world, proclaiming the words of God.'[50]

'Whilst one may wish to agree with this statement', says Geoffrey, 'in essence it has some weaknesses'. The Spirit does not take us beyond the Cross. The events of Pentecost 'did not simply follow the Cross in time':

They were events rooted in the Cross, and part of its wide dimensions. They are beyond the Cross only in the sense that the fruits of a tree may seem more than the tree, when in fact they are dependent upon the tree. When we realize this principle, then we can understand it as it shows itself in so many ways and so many things.[51]

It is this that has led historian Stuart Piggin to say:

I have always taken Geoff to be the archetypal evangelical . . . From my understanding of the history of evangelicalism it originated in a movement of the Spirit which was not all about the Spirit but was all about Jesus—what Jesus had done on the cross for us . . . he maintained those features of early revived evangelicalism . . . Geoff didn't lose any of the theology . . . but he did retain this emphasis on the importance of the experience—he put them together . . . evangelicalism without that emphasis is not evangelicalism at all . . . Geoff is the purest evangelical that I have come across.[52]

THE SPIRIT OF ALL THINGS

This rooting of the work of the Spirit in the central action of the Cross enables Geoffrey to explore the 'wide dimensions' of the Spirit's work with an all-encompassing freedom. 'What we must see', he says, 'is that the Spirit has no other aim, than to see the plan of God fulfilled'.[53] At the beginning of his vast *magnum opus* on the Spirit, in a section characteristically entitled 'The

Spirit, Creation and the Plan of God', Geoffrey sets out nine elements of 'the multiple intention of God', based on passages in the New Testament that refer to God's intentions from 'before the foundation of the world', and then goes on to demonstrate the Spirit's participation, with the Son and the Father, in every aspect of the outworking of that great plan:[54]

> He has been sent not only to transform and further edify God's people, but also to carry out the will of the Son, who, in his turn, is carrying out the will of the Father. That is to say, the Spirit is to continue that action which will bring creation to the ultimate intention God has for it . . . The creation created and sustained by the Spirit of life is now to be redeemed by the same Spirit. That is to say, the Spirit is to take the work of the Father and the work of the Son—the work of redemption—and apply it to the human race and to the whole creation in order to bring redemption, glorification and the ultimate unification of all things.
>
> This is what the Spirit—with the Father and the Son—is all about.[55]

In particular, Geoffrey traces the working of the Spirit in every part of Jesus' life and ministry—from conception, through baptism, temptation, and ministry, to the cross, resurrection and ascension—to show that 'all that Jesus did he did by the Spirit'.[56]

Because of the Spirit's involvement in 'the strange work of Jesus', the day of Pentecost 'was a day which was to change the human situation and, indeed, the situation of Creation itself':

> The Third Person of the Triune Godhead descended upon the human race. For the moment this great miracle was contained within one city, and one place in that city. Yet its significance was for all time and ultimately it would embrace the whole world in glory, for God's glory covering the whole earth was its aim and its goal.[57]

'It has been a conviction of mine that this era in which we live is the time when the Holy Spirit trains us for eternity.'[58] It is with a view to this coming reality, beyond present human experience or comprehension, that the Spirit prays within us:

... the Spirit knows our inability to pray intelligibly in this vast convulsion of Creation, in this work of proclamation which will bring about the new birth of Creation, but He knows we agonise to do so, and to do so properly, so He prays *as though He were us*. So intimate is His loving being with our beings, since God's very love was sent into our hearts through Him, and He has remained in this love, that we know all our prayers are prayed. The Father knows the mind of the Spirit which is one with the mind of our hearts and He takes these prayers and uses them as the authentic yearnings and true intercessions of the heart.[59]

Thus the Spirit, as 'the Spirit of the man', the exalted and gloried man Jesus,[60] has transformative effects in the lives of individual persons:

For Him to come to a man; for Him to work first upon a man, and then in a man, is a most glorious thing. Man is so lost, so degraded, so filled with dark cavernous depths of sin, and so much a sink of iniquity that we wonder this Holy One should even venture near him. Yet He is the Spirit of love, and again we are left breathless at the mighty measure of His love. No one can compute the tremendous thrust and drive of that love. It has to find its way down into man's lost and despairing system; into places of hurt and fear and terror, into realms of indescribable filth and hatred. Yet there is no place into which that Spirit does not go. He undoubtedly so works that man is glad to come to repentance and faith. Man hungers for the forgiveness of sins, and longs for the love of God. The old shattered image is transfigured and renewed by this great Lover of men. New powers of holiness begin to surge through the depths, not only purifying, but renewing the joy, love and peace that is the need of every man born, and every sinner redeemed.[61]

BAPTISED IN THE SPIRIT

From this strong position Geoffrey was able to address authoritatively and pastorally issues that arose from the charismatic and Pentecostal renewal of the 1960s and 1970s:

As one who sees great value in the gifts of the Spirit, including tongues, yet as one who does not hold a Pentecostal view of the question, Bingham stands in a unique bridging position—one which has enabled him to speak to those on both sides. His thesis in this book is an attempt to build a bridge—and an excellent attempt at that—but whether those on either bank will trust themselves to walk on it remains to be seen. The security of the bank is often more favoured than the uncertainty of a crossing![62]

The coming of the Spirit in Acts 2, 8 and 10 are seen as 'principial outpourings', 'as the opening of the Kingdom to the Jews, the Samaritans and the Gentiles (nations)', and so 'not wholly normative now that the Kingdom has been opened to all'. Prerequisites to receiving the Spirit, set out in Acts 2:38, are the same as what is normative for those coming to the Gospel:

> Thus faith and repentance are the two main requisites for receiving the Spirit. The Spirit has been operative prior to faith and repentance. He also brings the gift of forgiveness, and himself comes as the gift of the Father when repentance and faith have taken place.[63]

This is not to deny post-conversion experiences of the Spirit, but rather to welcome them, for 'power, once given, must be replenished by continuing infilling or—where there are lapses—successive infillings':

> ...whilst believers may have post-conversion experiences of the Spirit, they can be explained on grounds other than ... that Spirit-baptism is posterior to, and not coincident with conversion. This in no way is a rejection or denigration of what appear to be post-conversion experiences.[64]

This is consistent with part of the 'Doctrinal Stance' later spelled out for the New Creation Teaching Ministry and New Creation Publications:

> Their doctrine is biblical and Reformed, without prejudice to the movements of God's Spirit which come at times of revival and

renewal of the Church. Whilst recognising these and wishing to share in them as they follow the truth, they do not feel bound to accept theological rationalisations of any movement or group.[65]

Certainly Geoffrey is insistent that 'genuine preaching of the gospel is by those upon whom Christ has poured out "the promise of the Father", that is, the Holy Spirit, the Spirit of revelation and of power'.[66] No less insistent was he that those who live by the Spirit must also walk by the Spirit:[67]

We who are sealed, who have the earnest of the Spirit, and who are enabled by Him in love, unity, fellowship, worship and prayer, how shall we have power unless we depend upon Him entirely? He it is who relates us to the Father and the Son, and He it is who causes us to stand up, 'an exceeding great army,' to be in the forefront of the battle of the Lord, and to share in the might and victory of the Kingdom.[68]

Martin Bleby was one who was greatly helped in the 1970s:

I had met Geoffrey Bingham one afternoon at Meningie, when he had come by invitation to teach us about the Holy Spirit. While nothing startling had seemed to happen at the session he gave, I reflected ten years later that virtually all my teaching in that time about the Holy Spirit, and my avoidance of many of the pitfalls of charismatic renewal, had grown from what he imparted on that day.[69]

AH! SPIRIT GENTLE, SPIRIT HALLOWED

Geoffrey and Laurel's experience of the Spirit at Miller's Point led to a permanent change in the lives of many:

Sadie remembered the night he had preached, and the different note in his voice, and the new fresh light in his eyes. His preaching was wholly uncalculated. It had a freedom about it which had nothing of wildness in it. It was strong and deliberate. When the service finished there were pools of tears on the floor.[70]

One person had earlier, on occasions, seen around Geoffrey as he was preaching a visual radiance that she called 'the Glory':

> The Glory never really left...That night when the Glory was around you and you preached like you never had before, and we were all brought to tears, that was when the Glory came to stay amongst us.[71]

Certainly the Spirit stayed with Geoffrey:

> You lead the weak in holy power;
> You intercede within the heart;
> You cause us to cry 'Father! Abba!'
> Ah! You, who never will depart.
> You cause us to share all the glory,
> Of all the grace and all the love.
> And when we've told the matchless story
> You take us to our home above.
> Ah! Spirit of our Holy Father,
> Ah! Spirit of the loving Son,
> Through You we'll sing the praise forever
> Of You, the glorious Triune One.[72]

'I believe it was Geoff and Laurel's experience of the Spirit at Miller's Point—and what subsequently happened there in the church—that was the springboard for their call to Pakistan. It laid the foundation for him in so many ways for what happened from then on.'[73]

[1] Marcus L. Loane, *These Happy Warriors*, 88. Marcus Loane was Vice-Principal of Moore College during these years.

[2] Unpublished document, 'GB's Biography 29_7_04.doc' (expanded version of 'Geoffrey C Bingham: A Short Biography, 1919–1995' in *Mr Hicken's Pears*, 261–264).

[3] *These Happy Warriors*, 88–89. A 'curacy' is a time serving as an assistant minister.

[4] 'John the Fuzzy Wuzzy', in *The Artist in the Garden*, 23, 25.

[5] *The Artist in the Garden*, 23–24.

[6] *Laurel's Story*, 49, 51.

[7] *Laurel's Story*, 49, 51.

[8] *Laurel's Story*, 50, 51.

[9] Martin Bleby, personal recollection.

[10] See 'The Glory on the Inside', *3 Special Stories*, 13–19.

[11] *These Happy Warriors*, 89.

[12] Interview with John Dunn, 9 September 2008.

[13] John Dunn in interview with David Hewetson, 27 January 2009.

[14] John Dunn, 9 September 2008.

[15] *Laurel's Story*, 53.

[16] *These Happy Warriors*, 89.

[17] Stephen Judd, Kenneth Cable, *Sydney Anglicans: A History of the Diocese*, Anglican Information Office, Sydney, 2000, 257–258.

[18] David Hewetson, 'Memoir of G.C.B.', email to Geoffrey Bingham, 18 April 2007; also interview with John Dunn, 27 January 2009.

[19] *Laurel's Story*, 51.

[20] *These Happy Warriors*, 89, 90.

[21] Hewetson, 'Memoir of G.C.B.'

[22] *3 Special Stories*, 90.

[23] Hewetson, 'Memoir of G.C.B.'

[24] <http://en.wikipedia.org/wiki/Higher_Life_movement>, accessed 15th June 2011.

[25] *3 Special Stories*, 90.

[26] L. E. Maxwell, *Born Crucified: The Cross in the Life of the Believer* [first published 1945], First British Edition, Oliphants Ltd., London, 1958. L. E. Maxwell was Principal of Prairie Bible Institute, Three Hills, Alberta. Geoffrey later spoke of the influence this book had on him (conversation with Geoffrey Bingham, personal recollection by Martin Bleby). See also Stuart Piggin, *Spirit of a Nation: The Story of Australia's Christian Heritage* (Strand Publishing, Sydney, 2004), 150.

27 Maxwell, *Born Crucified*, 14, 16, 17.

28 Hewetson, 'Memoir of G.C.B.'

29 Hewetson, 'Memoir of G.C.B.'

30 Hewetson interview with John Dunn.

31 Hear Geoffrey's later mature teaching on this in 'Crucified with Christ', Tapes for Life series, TLS 63 (available on NCTM MP3 disc 905).

32 Hewetson, 'Memoir of G.C.B.' and interview with John Dunn.

33 *3 Special Stories*, 90.

34 Personal recollection by Martin Bleby.

35 *3 Special Stories*, 90.

36 *Laurel's Story*, 52.

37 Letter from Laurel Bingham to Ian Pennicook, 12th January 1992.

38 Letter from Laurel Bingham.

39 *3 Special Stories*, 90.

40 *3 Special Stories*, 19–20.

41 *3 Special Stories*, 90.

42 *These Happy Warriors*, 89.

43 *3 Special Stories*, 90.

44 Geoffrey told how he was put onto this by his teacher and mentor T. C. Hammond at Moore College (personal recollection, Martin Bleby).

45 *These Happy Warriors*, 89–90.

46 *3 Special Stories*, 91.

47 *Principles of New Creation Teaching Ministry: Some Thoughts from the Discussion of Geoffrey Bingham and Ian Pennicook*, January 1998, p. 3.

48 *3 Special Stories*, 89–90.

49 *Beyond the Cross*, 26.

50 *Beyond the Cross*, 40.

51 *Beyond the Cross*, 26–27.

52 Dr Stuart Piggin, Senior Research Fellow in the Department of Modern History at Macquarie University, in an interview with John Dunn, 5th December 2008. Stuart Piggin was impacted by an experience of the glory and holiness of God during a mission called 'Break into Life' led by Geoffrey at St Philip's Church Eastwood in 1966. He says of Geoffrey, 'He had exceptional heart and spirit . . . one sensed that this man was holy, and he was close to God . . . to be with him was to run the risk of actually experiencing God . . . Every contact with Geoff was meaningful.'

53 *The Christian and the Holy Spirit* (Christian Teaching Series 6), 11.

54 *The Day of the Spirit*, 12–14.

[55] *The Day of the Spirit*, 72–73.

[56] *Spirit-Baptism: Spirit-Living*, 14; see 13–16; also *The Person and Work of the Holy Spirit* (Revised edition 2009), 32–39; *The Day of the Spirit*, 48–73.

[57] *The Holy Spirit, Creation and Glory*, 110, 111.

[58] *The Holy Spirit, Creation and Glory*, 123.

[59] *The Holy Spirit, Creation and Glory*, 119; see Romans 8:26–27.

[60] *The Day of the Spirit*, 72.

[61] *The Christian and the Holy Spirit*, 11–12.

[62] Dr Barry Chant, *New Day International* magazine, quoted on the back cover of *Spirit-Baptism: Spirit-Living*.

[63] *Spirit-Baptism: Spirit-Living*, 104, 105.

[64] *Spirit-Baptism: Spirit-Living*, 106.

[65] Geoffrey Bingham, 'An Account of the New Creation Teaching Ministry and New Creation Publications Incorporated, from 1973 to 1996', April 1996, p. 6.

[66] *The Baptism in the Holy Spirit: Christ Pouring Out His Spirit in the Last Days*, 44.

[67] See Galatians 5:25.

[68] *The Christian and the Holy Spirit*, 24.

[69] Martin Bleby, *The Vinedresser: An Anglican Meets Wrath and Grace*, NCPI, Blackwood, 1985, 14.

70 *3 Special Stories*, 20.

71 *3 Special Stories*, 23, 24.

[72] Geoffrey Bingham, 'Time Was When Spirit, Fallen, Human' (1992), *New Creation Hymn Book*, 260.

[73] John Dunn, email to Martin Bleby, 14 April 2012.

CHAPTER 9

ABBA! *Father!*

> when we cry, 'Abba! Father!' it is the Spirit himself bearing witness with our spirit that we are children of God

Romans 8:15–16

PAKISTAN

WE WERE MISSIONARIES for many years in what was then known as West Pakistan. We were feeling very strange when we arrived in Karachi, and were faced with a wholly foreign situation with our five children on hand. We all loved the new sights and sounds, if not fully the smells, but we had that uneasiness which comes from being in a different climate and culture.[1]

Since he had been participating in 'Deeper Life Conventions' at Miller's Point, Emu Plains, Picton and elsewhere, always with a missionary thrust, it was perhaps inevitable that Geoffrey, with others, would end up being a missionary himself.[2] Marcus Loane writes:

> Early in 1957, Geoff made a fresh and unexpected move: he applied to the Church Missionary Society with a view to service in Pakistan. Everything, humanly speaking, seemed to argue against such a move. Archbishop Mowll did not want to lose him from his exhilarating ministry at Miller's Point; he was thirty-eight years old; he had five children, and a sixth would be born during that year. But the Society had no hesitation, and in April he found himself stationed at Hyderabad in Pakistan. This was to be his base for a remarkable missionary career during the next nine years.[3]

Geoffrey wrote about how he was accepted by CMS:

> When he confessed the burden of his calling to missionary friends, he found that they had been praying and that his calling was already confirmed in their hearts. Next was the CMS, where he was told 'I am sorry, by our rules we cannot accept you. You are too old to learn the language. You are painfully wounded. And

Hyderabad is no place for your young daughters.' But the burden remained and the calling would not leave. So next to the presiding elder of the missionary society, Bishop Hugh Gough, where he recounted his meeting with the CMS, saying 'I well understand the difficulties stated by the society but, Hugh, *I have to go!* I am called and I must go.' And as the Holy Spirit quietly gave witness over several moments of silence, out of the heart of a humble, obedient, and hearing servant, came the simple, clear reply 'Well, Geoff, if God has called you, you shall go and with our blessing'.[4]

Laurel gives her account:

> The Church Missionary Society accepted us although they had a ruling that over thirty five was too old to learn a new language and assimilate to the culture. Also they had a limit of three children and so we paid for the youngest children. We didn't dare tell them that we had another on the way. When I think of it all I shudder, but that was our pattern of life in those days.[5]

Language school at Murree in the Himalayan hills came first: Geoffrey 'learnt to speak Urdu without loss of time, and was soon able to teach and preach in that language with uncommon fluency'.[6] Two of the language teachers stayed in Geoffrey and Laurel's back room, and were converted under their ministry.[7] Then to Hyderabad on the Sindh plain, where they needed to brave 'the broiling sun, and the perpetual *loo*—the hot desert wind that blew fiercely day and night':[8]

> It was a fascinating place, with its ancient walls that encircled the original inner city, but long ago it had sprawled out onto the plains, and had its special areas of occupation, the main one of which was the Cantonment. Cantonments were built by the British at the edge of every large city ... At first we lived on a Mission compound in the city, but later graduated to the Cantonment, where we renovated a much neglected church of cathedral dimensions, getting rid of the pigeons and their years-old droppings, the rats that infested the pigeon manure, and the snakes that preyed on the rats. The church was turned into a Bible college, and a new home was built for us.[9]

The Pakistan Bible Training Institute was opened on 26 February 1960, and Geoffrey was its first principal for the next five years.[10] 'I—along with others—did the teaching, whilst my wife held a medical clinic for the students, and generally acted as a mother to them.'[11] Laurel recounts:

> There were fourteen students that year and they increased by one or so every year because of the limited accommodation. Lectures commenced mid July and closed mid May each year with a break at Christmas of a few weeks.[12]

A second year course was added in 1963, bringing the total of students to twenty-four.[13]

It was a learning experience for Geoffrey no less than for his students:

> In Pakistan I soon realised that what seems to be effective in one culture may prove impotent in another. Soul-searching is probably helpful, and I did plenty of that. As the founder and principal of a Bible college where men trained for ordination, I had my theology well-honed to help men become good pastors.[14]

Meanwhile Geoffrey also 'was in wide demand throughout the country as a Bible teacher and evangelist, and was warmly welcomed in other denominations and most missionary societies':

> The hill station at Murree and the Sialkot Convention found him year by year ministering to fellow missionaries, and his impact on the younger clergy in Sydney seemed to reproduce itself in West Pakistan. Invitations began to flow in from elsewhere. Bangladesh, Sri Lanka, India and North Borneo received him with hungry hearts and open arms.[15]

On one such occasion, at Colombo in what was then called Ceylon, 'I estimated that in 14 days I spoke to about 30,000 people including the school groups . . . the last meeting had over 3,000, some hundreds standing to the final appeal . . . we saw remarkable conversions, and a sheaf of letters tells of deep conviction'.[16]

OH, FATHER!

It was on one of these occasions away that Geoffrey received 'what I can only call a revelation of the nature of God as Father'.[17] It is significant that it began with an in-depth conversation on the message of the cross, and how the difficulty in receiving it is not so much a matter of cultural differences as of the hardness of the human heart:

> Early in 1965 I was a speaker at a convention in Calcutta. Whilst I could preach fluently in Urdu, most of the audience spoke Bengali, and a fine Indian pastor from Assam translated messages for both a Madras preacher and me. One night, after the meeting, the translator, whose name was Subodh Sahu, talked with me. We went long into the night. He confided with me that my message had not been easy to translate. The matter of my English, my words and my pronunciation presented no difficulty.
>
> He said, 'It is your message of the Cross which is hard to communicate. I know and believe all you say. Indeed, it is the heart of my own life and the substance of my theology, but human beings of all races oppose this Cross. As Paul the apostle said, it is a scandal to the religious and foolishness to the intellectuals.'[18]

Yet by that message God brings Himself through to us:

> We talked until we were weary. Subodh and I prayed together and he then went to his room to sleep. Restless but yet elated, I knelt on the floor, leaning against the bed. It was then that something of a remarkable nature happened to me. It came unbidden. Something like waves of extraordinary peace and joy flowed over me . . . I found myself crying, 'Oh Father! Oh Father!' . . . It was not a petition to the Father to reveal Himself but the ecstasy which had come to me because He had revealed Himself. So light and peace and joy continued to flow over me in successive waves.[19]

Geoffrey 'had preached on the Fatherhood many times. John's Gospel had always been a delight to me. I had often explained how the Father could not be known apart from the Son. Also, that the Holy Spirit had to show us both the things of the Father and of the Son.'[20] This was more than that:

Something unusual happened when I articulated that cry. It was as though *fatherhood* whether divine or human had been a concept. It may even have been a personal concept. Now it was a rich *reality*. What was more, I was relating richly to the Father. I kept crying out, 'Oh, Father! Oh, Father!' and each cry seemed to reinforce my understanding of Him, and my relationship with Him.[21]

'How long that period of experience lasted I do not know', Geoffrey says:

I could feel, so to speak, waves of light, waves of joy, and the flowing of serenity about me, enveloping me wholly. After a time I felt the intensity of what I can only describe as ecstasy was so rich that I could scarcely sustain it. I thought, 'I must get on to the bed, and back to normality' . . . The curious thing is that I could not physically feel the bed beneath me. It was as though I were in a cocoon of light, joy and serenity, and normal emotional feelings had been enhanced, yet also I could not feel the bed. The phrase kept mouthing itself, 'Oh Father!'[22]

Geoffrey had experienced the presence of God before, but this added something to it:

That He was Father was the new understanding. Nor was it simply an intellectual understanding . . . I suppose the word 'communion' is the only one which covers what was happening at that time.[23]

What are we to make of an experience of this kind?

Such experiences may be called subjective, but to me it was a rich apprehension of the objective, the reality of God's Fatherhood . . . It is not, of course, to say that one only knows the Fatherhood through ecstatic experience. All Godly knowledge is primarily by faith, but faith does not have to be exclusive of feelings.[24]

Should everyone have experiences like this?

The danger of recounting these happenings is that others may think they need to know God through similar visions or special states of awareness. That is not the case. All our knowledge is *by faith* and not *by sight*. At times, nevertheless, God visits in a way which is almost sight. Even so, it still requires faith to accept the 'sight' happening.[25]

This experience was not like a dream that fades, but a vision of reality from God that enters a person and becomes part of the fibre of his being—'it was an experience which is easily recalled. At this very moment of writing it is as vivid to me as it was on that night':[26]

> I knew it to be an experience of the ineffable, but one which had stamped itself upon my being in an interiority which would henceforth be inextinguishable.[27]

It stayed with him:

> For myself, the unusual experience was transforming. I have since carried indelibly in my spirit the notion and reality of Divine Fatherhood. It may not have altered the *form* of my theology but has transformed my understanding and living of it. It has given a different tone to my teaching and to my relationships with others.[28]

From that time, knowing God as Father became for Geoffrey the distinguishing mark of Christian faith, particularly 'in speaking to Moslems who do not know Allah as Father, and to Hindus whose all-embracing God is Ram, but far from that intimate, personal Father'[29] whom he now knew. Geoffrey tells the story of an encounter with a student in Pakistan who asked him what is distinctive about Christianity. Geoffrey replied, 'Christians know God as their Father'. The student said that in their religion this would be a terrible thing. Geoffrey asked, 'What do you call your own father?' The student replied proudly, 'I call him *abba*'—they still use the same word that Jesus used in Aramaic! Geoffrey said, 'That is how we know God'. The student looked puzzled, alarmed, and yet at the same time somewhat wistful.[30]

FATHERHOOD REVEALED
IN THE SON BY THE SPIRIT

When Geoffrey began to develop a theology of the Fatherhood of God,[31] he discovered *'how comparatively little material there is'* on this[32] in contrast to the materials on Christology (the person and work of Christ) and Pneumatology (the person and work of the Spirit). He coined a new term for it:

> Why is there not a discipline called Pateriology? If we have the person and work of the Son, why not the person and work of the Father? If we deal with the person and work of the Spirit (who is the Spirit of the Father and the Son, and that simultaneously), then why not, naturally, a similar theological treatment of the Father?[33]

While he teaches that 'Fatherhood must be at the core of the universe', he 'increasingly exults in the nature of the Triune God, and in the three discrete Persons Who constitute that Godhead of love and holiness':[34]

> Fatherhood cannot be known without Sonship, and these both cannot be known apart from the Holy Spirit.[35]

Geoffrey speaks of having had 'two other experiences equally powerful':

> ... one of the Lordship of Christ, and the other of the sovereignty and power of the Holy Spirit. Doubtless all Christians have had such, but I mean definitive experiences such as this one of the Father. Interestingly enough they were in the sequence order of the Spirit, the Son, and the Father.[36]

Geoffrey's experience of the Spirit we have spoken of in the previous chapter. His experience of the Son came also in Pakistan around this time:

> ... I was having my usual prayer-time, and suddenly a song began to come out of my mouth. As I sang—and I knew not what—I saw Christ hanging on the cross, and he had just died. Indeed, he

was being taken down from the cross, and placed in the tomb. I saw the women looking down at him, with loving pity. Then it seemed to be the time between the Friday and the Sunday, and he lay still but his eyes were open, and he rested peacefully. It must have then been the morning of Easter, for suddenly he stood up, through the grave-cloths, and he was most regal, his royal being standing and looking over all history as its eternal Lord. I sensed that Lordship deeply, and longed that the vision should not pass. In fact, it all passed into me, much to my joy, and even as I write it is no less real to me than when I first saw it. I think his Lordship has never ceased to reside within me, and to be the ruling factor of my life.[37]

Geoffrey makes much of Psalm 2—along with Psalms 45 and 110, much quoted or referred to in the New Testament—as a key to delineating the 'Messianic Sonship'[38] of Jesus at the centre of God's purpose for His creation, in the context of human sin and rebellion:

> I have set my king on Zion, my holy hill
> . . . You are my son;
>   today I have begotten you.[39]

Kingship is what keeps God's Fatherhood from being merely sentimental:

> . . . God has ever been the Father–King, but the Kingliness comes to the fore in the O.T., and whilst it does not recede in the N.T. the Father element becomes revealed in greater measure, and in wonderful fulness. At no point does His Fatherhood descend to the trivial or the banal, and certainly never to the sentimental. The fact that He is King preserves it from that. His Son Jesus is Lord which is, virtually, King. He too upholds the grandeur and the glory and the holiness of the Father, although in one sense that is unique to the Father.
>
>   All things, then, show that the Creator–King is the Father–King, is the Creator–Father, and that He will bring His creation to its ripeness and fullness, without pollution and without the triumph of evil. In all this the Father and the Son work together, and so show their love for their creation.[40]

Is God known as Father in the Old Testament? Geoffrey conducts an extensive review of Israel, as God's 'first-born son',[41] who can call out to their covenant-God as 'our Father; our Redeemer from of old',[42] and comes to the conclusion:

> Israel knew something of God as Father beyond that which was merely metaphorical. They expected no less of Him than of an earthly father, and much more. Likewise in their thinking, especially their prophetic thinking, begins to emerge the idea of a special Son. This is seen in such Psalms as 2 and 89, amongst others ... God having a special Son, who sometimes appears to be Israel, and sometimes Israel's Messiah, all goes to give a high view of God's Fatherhood.[43]

Even so, 'man's rebellion against God and his rejection of God as He is' means that no human person can clearly, fully see true human fatherhood, let alone true divine Fatherhood:

> After all, the only image of fatherhood men had was that of their own fathers ... to work from human fatherhood to divine Fatherhood ... would be most dangerous. All else that is spoken of about God in His law, holiness, justice and wrath would distort the image of God if approached from a human point of view. The Father would then be virtually demonic. On the other hand, to take the attributes of longsuffering, kindness and goodness would be to reduce the image to a benevolence without judgement and justice. It seems that the O.T. economy was not fitted to take a full revelation of the Fatherhood of God.[44]

'It awaited the coming of the true Son to bring full revelation':

> ... it needed a direct revelation of Fatherhood from the one who was truly the Son of God.[45]

This came with Jesus. Geoffrey comments on when Jesus says, 'I am the way, and the truth, and the life. No one comes to *the Father* except through me':[46]

> He is not simply the way to God, but the way to *God as Father*.[47]

As he is also the truth of the Father and the life of the Father:

> The simple way of showing His Fatherhood was for God to bring His Son to the world. The simple way for us to see that Sonship was for the Son (Jesus) just to walk, talk and live Sonship in the ordinary ways of life.[48]

Not only that:

> The Father sent the Son to be the saviour of the world. The Father set him forth as a propitiation. The Father raised him from the dead by His glory. The Father set him at His own right hand on high.[49]

Knowing God as Father comes no less by the agency of the Spirit, who is 'the Spirit of your Father' and 'the Spirit of his Son',[50] such that 'the Spirit . . . reveals the mystery of the Father–Son relationship':[51]

> The Holy Spirit is 'the promise of the Father'. The Father sent the Spirit of His Son into our hearts crying, 'Abba! Father!' He is the one God and Father of us all who is above all, and through all, and in all. Daily grace and peace come from him. He is the Father of all mercies and the God of all comfort. He is the Father from whom every family (or, the whole family) in heaven and on earth is named. From the Father comes every good giving and every perfect gift. He gives good things. He gives the Holy Spirit. He is God our Father who loved us and gave us eternal comfort and good hope through grace.[52]

While the Old Testament name of God is *Yahweh*—associated with the somewhat mysterious and inconclusive 'I AM WHO I AM'[53]—Geoffrey notes that in the New Testament:

> . . . the only name for God is 'Father',[54]

and concludes that this has been His true nature from eternity. Geoffrey will not abide any relativising of God's Fatherhood by making this out to be one image among many:

The insistence that this is merely metaphorical is obnoxious. Whoever cried 'Abba!' to an earthly metaphorical father, much less to the Heavenly Father, i.e. to 'your Father who is in heaven'? We must protest against this denigration of God's Fatherhood, i.e. making it simply figurative.[55]

It is not metaphorical, but is truly relational:

If God is only 'like a father' then man is only 'like a son'. He has no *essential* relationship with God as Father. He is only treated as a son. At best he is a creature of the creation, and if redeemed, a new creature. Even then God must be 'like a Father' to him. It is not actual sonship he has but metaphorical sonship—whatever that could be![56]

Does this leave motherhood out of the picture?

Feminists might be permitted their anger when we seem to place so much emphasis upon the Fatherhood of God. Some feminists speak of God as Mother. Whilst I think this is unwise I can understand it as a gesture . . . there is motherhood in God. A number of times God is referred to in such terms.[57]

Even so, that does not make God Mother and not Father. When the Genesis accounts show that God made man in His image and made them male and female, it certainly infers, if not insists, that male–female duality exists in God . . . God is One . . . Our problem is that we work back from man to God, and think that sexuality in man is parallel with sexuality in God, which is not the case . . . The male–female of God is called Father, given that God is often likened to a mother but is never as such called mother. Yet the word Father embraces both.[58]

KNOWING GOD AS FATHER THROUGH THE CROSS

We should not underestimate the barrier of sin, which prevents us from knowing God as Father:

What we find difficult to understand is that no one can, of himself, know the heavenly Father. The Fall made sure of that, and our 'having exchanged the truth of God for a lie' sealed the matter. We would never want to know Him. Hence Jesus once said, 'No one knows the Son save the Father, and no one knows the Father, save the Son, and he whom the Son is pleased to reveal him'. In the same vein he said, 'No man can come to me except the Father draw him'.[59]

'Sonship is really the actual impact of the work of the Cross and the Resurrection. By that we mean it is the receiving of total forgiveness, which comes through the Cross':[60]

> Apart from the Son, the way is blocked off to God *as Father*. That is the reason why Jesus had to die, his death reveals not simply the obedience of the Son, and the love of the Son for sinful humanity, but it primarily reveals the love of the Father. At the same time, it shows the nature of true Sonship, which leads us to true human sonship . . . Not only does Jesus' sonship indicate the Fatherhood of the Father, but he has removed the impediment of sin, which prevents us from coming to God. Because of the Cross, we have access to the Father.[61]

Not only that, but by the Father not withholding His own Son but giving him up for us all,[62] we are secured in the knowledge that the Father loves us no less than He loves His own beloved Son:

> When Jesus said on one occasion, 'My Father loves me because I lay down my life . . . this command have I received of my Father' (John 10:17–18), then he was telling us that in one sense the Father overleaps His love for his Son in His love for us. This is not strictly true, of course, but in a manner of speaking it is true.
>
> Man's guilt, sin, moral inferiority, and anger against God prevents him believing this most astounding fact, namely that God loves him. That is why Jesus prayed in his High-Priestly prayer, ' . . . that the world *may know* that thou has sent me and *hast loved them even as thou hast loved me*' (John 17:23) . . . It needs, then, the Cross to display the Fatherhood.[63]

'Even so, we must be careful to include the Resurrection in that work':

> ... Christ's Sonship is validated by the Resurrection.[64] In that sense his revelation of the Father is also validated. In addition, Romans 6:4 tells us 'he was raised from the dead *by the glory of the Father*'. Thus, in the Resurrection, Christ shows the glory of the Father.

Further, the Ascension validates and completes the Resurrection:

> When Jesus said he would convict the world of righteousness 'because I go to the Father',[65] he meant the Ascension validated him and his Sonship. It also showed his acceptance by the Father ... Hebrews 1:3–5 ... quotes Psalm 2:7 of the Ascension, in terms of Christ's Sonship. This must mean the Ascension also reveals the Fatherhood.[66]

'Whilst what we have said about the Ascension is true, we may miss the more intimate aspect of it, the one which is of great comfort to the true children of God':

> He is going to prepare a place for each of us in his Father's mansions ... He does not ascend, then, simply to authenticate himself in the eyes of the world. He goes there for a purpose. After all, it is the Father's home that matters! His brethren are to share that home.[67]

BRINGING MANY SONS TO GLORY[68]

Geoffrey asks the question: 'Have all men been created as sons, and are they sons, essentially?' He enumerates four different answers to this question:

> (i) All humans created by God have been created by Him who is essentially Father. Therefore they are sons. It follows that His Fatherhood will reject none of His sons. Hence, we can formulate the doctrine of the universal Fatherhood of God and the universal brotherhood of man.[69]

Geoffrey says this 'cannot be maintained in that form, for John 1:12 speaks of those receiving Christ as being given the authority to *become* the children of God. Galatians 3:26 speaks of men becoming sons of God by faith in Christ Jesus':[70]

> (ii) God has created no one as His son. However, He has planned, through certain processes, that men who have sinned shall become His sons. Only those who go through this process or processes [of redemption and ultimate glorification] will become sons of God. Such are His elect.[71]

This 'has quite a problem to solve since it speaks of man as never being, in any sense, a son. It must mean that through redemption man becomes what he never was, in any sense—a son':[72]

> (iii) All men were created to be sons of God, but in the Fall lost that sonship entirely. Only in Christ shall they regain their sonship.[73]

Geoffrey says that this 'seems reasonable', especially 'in the light of John 1:12 and Galatians 3:26' (see above). It does preserve against the 'universalistic' first view, which 'does not really meet the problems of God's holiness and His wrath in judgement' and 'infers that none can be lost, finally'.[74] But Geoffrey takes the fourth view:

> (iv) In Adam, who was created a son of God, were all men brought into sonship. In the fall of Adam they lost this sonship in the sense that they have rejected their relationship as sons with the Father, God. It was always God's intention that this sonship should be regained through Christ and the Spirit, and this sonship be brought to fullness by the end of the age. The word 'regained', however, does not do justice to the grace act of God, whereby in a sense they become even more sons than in creation. It is—as it were—that the potential for sonship is filled out and made complete.[75]

This 'believes that whilst in a real sense sonship is lost, yet it is not obliterated'. Geoffrey says that this view is best expressed by the statement, 'God is the Father of all men, but not all men are the children of God'. Our rebellion cannot stop God from being

Father. 'God goes on being Father as He wills, but man in rejecting his own sonship cannot make claims upon the Fatherhood of God.'[76] Nevertheless, the sonship of grace which comes to us through salvation is not something alien to our original creation.[77]

What is most telling is that the glory and nobility we see in the risen Son will belong to us no less in our human sonship. Geoffrey says of 'the People of God's Possession':

> We know this community is God's treasured possession . . . I have often asked myself—and others—'Why does God treasure it so? What does He lack that such a possession would supply it to Him?' My answer is a trembling in my body, tears in my eyes and a great sense of fear and awe. For I see that all Creation has been formed and ordered so that His Fatherhood might have a Family in which everyone is conformed to the image of His Son. There have been brought into being incredible creatures that—though being humans—have been brought to such glory that they have bodies of glory such as the risen Christ has. And their bodies are immortal by the power of Christ, the same power by which He is able to subdue all things unto Himself . . . This is the community by which God will express the truth of His Being, which is His glory throughout Eternity.[78]

RESTORED RELATIONSHIPS

Geoffrey says of his experience of God's Fatherhood in Calcutta:

> I suppose the most remarkable thing about the revelation of that night was that I saw all relationships are healed when once the matter of Divine Fatherhood is settled.[79]

This was true, first of all, for Geoffrey himself:

> I had thought that my view of my father in later years had been as good as a son could have, but seeing Divine Fatherhood melted any reserves of thought concerning him that I might have retained. In a few moments my understanding of my mother was also transformed and no less of my brothers and sisters. In fact it helped me

to experience affinity with all the human race, stretching back through the past and reaching forward to the future.[80]

Since then, he has sought through counselling to bring this release to many others:

I have seen countless transformations in human relationships when Divine Fatherhood is experienced. I have just spoken of the healing of the human spirit by that Fatherhood, and it is such healing I have seen innumerable times. It is the healing of relational rifts, the dissolving of anger and bitterness which have arisen from these rifts, and accompanying emancipation from lifelong heaviness of spirit which children—some of whom have grown to their three score years and ten—have been carrying without relief from the time of childhood.[81]

Geoffrey reckons with a key issue:

. . . the principle of Fatherhood and authority are closely linked. Man has a problem with authority, but when he understands the love of the Father and comes as a son to the Father he is then liberated from his former views concerning authority.[82]

Thus a person comes to full participation in the purpose and action of God in a way that is deeply satisfying:

When a person comes to the revelation of the Father through the Son, via the agency of the Holy Spirit, then—and only then—he is fulfilled. What he has needed becomes his gift. He has needed, always, to correlate with God in a contingent manner. This is what makes his creaturehood, sonship and servanthood whole and authentic, and so he becomes a true, viable person. He is no longer frustrated, thwarted, unfulfilled. Moreover, he can now—indeed he must now—relate to others. He relates through the Father via the Son and via the love-fellowship-unity gifts of the Spirit. *He has come into Family!*[83]

Geoffrey has seen this happen many times:

Hundreds of memories crowd into my mind at this present time. I see the faces of persons rapt with wonder, full of adoration and a sense of security as they have come to know God as Father. One woman said, 'You did not mention earthly fathers today, but your talk took away a hang-up I have had with my father for twenty-five years.' She would be representative of hundreds of others who have said similar things . . . Daughters who hated fathers because they were not strong and authoritative, mothers because they were, and sons who found it difficult to be strong husbands and fathers because of anger against one or both parents. In each case a revelation of the love of God as Father changed relational attitudes.[84]

Geoffrey sums up the practical theology that underlies this:

The theology I have come to hold tells me that man's deepest need is God, and especially God as Father. It teaches that all human creatures need to see God as Creator-Father, and Redeemer-Father, and draw from Him their emotional fulfilment. This they cannot do without the Son, who is the Way to the Father. The Spirit is the Spirit of both Father and Son and through him comes the revelation of both. Man thus comes to the Father and Son via the Spirit, and in particular through the Son himself. At this point man becomes merged in community, in the true family of God, and his personal and emotional needs are met.

I have never found this theology to fail.[85]

ALL IN ALL [86]

Geoffrey's final verdict on his special experience of God's Fatherhood is this:

I think the significance of this episode was that I now saw that everything—yes, everything—lies in the Fatherhood of God.[87]

This comes through in his vision-like rendition of the end of all things:

The mystery I cannot reveal. The revelation I cannot tell.

What I can tell, however, is what I saw, as the countless multitude, those of every tribe the earth has ever known, and every creature of every species which has ever been gave thunderous and unceasing praise . . . As the applause and the worship and the adoration, the crying and the shouting, the splendid music, and the throb of the new song came into being, the whole multitude of men and shining ones and creatures of sky and earth and sea lifted up their voices into one full-throated roar of ecstasy and knowledge.

In this great hour they had but one word, and it came in such unity as things on earth have never known, and that one word was the full truth of the mystery, which, if a man know, he need never know more, not in history-time or vision-time, for the one word to which they gave voice in their freedom, and their self-knowledge, and their knowledge of all things was this,

'ABBA!'*

* *Abba*: This is a word used in some Eastern languages for 'Father'.[88]

[1] 'Love's Wounds Never Fester', in *Twice-Conquering Love*, 73.

[2] David Hewetson, interview with John Dunn, 27 January 2009. David Hewetson and Reg Hanlon also went to the 'mission field' at that time.

[3] Marcus L. Loane, *These Happy Warriors*, 90.

4 'Story Number Three', unpublished manuscript, n.d.

[5] *Laurel's Story*, 56.

[6] *These Happy Warriors*, 90.

[7] One of them, Bashir Jiwan, became the first bishop of Hyderabad; *Laurel's Story*, 62.

[8] *Twice-Conquering Love*, 77.

[9] *Twice-Conquering Love*, 76–77.

[10] *Laurel's Story*, 83; also Geoffrey Bingham in 'The Opening of a Bible Institute', *Sind News Letter*, New Zealand Church Missionary Society, June 1960, p. 7. I am grateful to the Rev'd John Bales for copies of these Sind news letters; also to Heather McLeod of CMS Australia for copying this material and copies of the Bingham prayer letters from files at the NSW State Library. Marcus Loane in *These Happy Warriors*, 90, mistakenly gives the founding date as 1961.

[11] *Twice-Conquering Love*, 78.

[12] *Laurel's Story*, 83.

[13] Bingham Prayer Letter, 30th October 1963.

[14] *My Beloved Family*, 148–149.

[15] *These Happy Warriors*, 90–91.

[16] Bingham Prayer Letter, 12th June, 1963, p. 1.

[17] *My Beloved Family*, 150.

[18] *My Beloved Family*, 149.

[19] *My Beloved Family*, 149–150.

[20] *I Love the Father*, 4; see John 16:12–15.

[21] *I Love the Father*, 4.

[22] *I Love the Father*, 4–5.

[23] *My Beloved Family*, 150.

[24] *I Love the Father*, 5.

[25] *I Love the Father*, 6.

[26] *I Love the Father*, 5.

[27] *My Beloved Family*, 151.

[28] *My Beloved Family*, 153.

[29] *My Beloved Family*, 148.

[30] Personal recollection, Martin Bleby; there is a reference to this in the recorded study, *The Person and Work of the Father*, BSPF07 'God's Fatherhood and his Household', on NCTM MP3 disc 954 'God Our Father 1: Teaching on the Fatherhood of God'.

[31] The first edition of *I Love The Father* was published in 1974. In 1977 a more popular treatment of the subject was published under the title of *Father! My Father!* A systematic study, *The God and Father of Us All*, developed from earlier material on 'The Person and Work of the Father', was first published in book form in 1982. Geoffrey's teaching on God's Fatherhood comes across most dynamically in the spoken teaching, as on NCTM MP3 discs 954 and 955, 'God Our Father 1 and 2: Teaching on the Fatherhood of God'.

[32] Geoffrey found a notable exception in the writings of Karl Barth: 'Lately I have been reading a posthumously published essay of the theologian, Karl Barth. It is entitled, *The Children and their Father*. The gentle, simple words of this famous theologian brought tears to my eyes. Having read much of his *Church Dogmatics* I thought, "He has kept the good wine until last!" In this sixty-page treatment he shares what the Father means to him, and it is deeply moving. From the simple peasant then, to the erudite theologian, the human heart witnesses to restlessness until it finds the Father.' *Oh, Father! Our Father!*, viii.

[33] *I Love the Father*, xiv.

[34] *I Love the Father*, xviii.

[35] *I Love the Father*, 5.

[36] *I Love the Father*, 5.

[37] 'Lovefest Three', *Twice-Conquering Love*, 152. Also recounted in *3 Special Stories*, 43, and on a recording of NCTM Summer School 1990, 'Christ the Beloved Lord', SCH 33, available on NCTM DVD 614.

[38] *Father! My Father!* 52–66.

[39] Psalm 2:6, 7.

[40] *The God and Father of Us All*, 56–57.

[41] Exodus 4:22–23; compare Hosea 11:1; Isaiah 1:2–3; Romans 9:4.

[42] Isaiah 63:16.

[43] *The God and Father of Us All*, 15–16.

[44] *The God and Father of Us All*, 16, 22.

[45] *The God and Father of Us All*, 16.

[46] John 14:6.

[47] *The God and Father of Us All*, 90; hear also on NCTM MP3 disc 954 'God Our Father 1'.

[48] *Oh, Father! Our Father!* 20.

[49] *Christ's People in Today's World*, 74.

[50] Matthew 10:20; Galatians 4:6.

[51] *The Holy Spirit, Creation and Glory*, 129.

[52] *Christ's People in Today's World*, 74–75. References here are to 1 John 4:14; Romans 3:25; 6:4; Ephesians 1:20; 3:14–15; 4:6; Luke 11:13; 24:49; Galatians 4:6; 2 Corinthians 1:3; James 1:17; 2 Thessalonians 2:16.

[53] Exodus 3:13–15.

[54] *The God and Father of Us All*, 11.

[55] 'Truly Knowing God and Man', in *The Stranger in the Cemetery*, 59.

[56] *The God and Father of Us All*, 11.

[57] See Isaiah 66:13; Psalm 131:2; cf. Psalm 27:10.

[58] *I Love the Father*, 19–20; see also *Father! My Father!*, 100–101.

[59] *Christ's People in Today's World*, 78–79; see Matthew 11:27; John 6:45, 65.

[60] *Father! My Father!*, 49.

[61] *Christ's People in Today's World*, 79; see Ephesians 2:18.

[62] See Romans 8:32.

[63] *Christ's Cross over Man's Abyss*, 109.

[64] See Romans 1:4–5 and Acts 13:32–35.

[65] John 16:10.

[66] *Christ's Cross over Man's Abyss*, 110.

[67] *Christ's Cross over Man's Abyss*, 111.

[68] Hebrews 2:10.

[69] *I Love the Father*, 34.

[70] *I Love the Father*, 35.

[71] *I Love the Father*, 34–35.

[72] *I Love the Father*, 35.

[73] *I Love the Father*, 35.

[74] *I Love the Father*, 35.

[75] *I Love the Father*, 35.

[76] *I Love the Father*, 35–36. This position is by no means accepted by all. For example, the position taken by J. I. Packer in his book *Knowing God* (Hodder and Stoughton, London, 1973, 223) is, 'a Christian is one who has God for his Father. But cannot this be said of every man, Christian or not? Emphatically no! The idea that all men are children of God is not found in the Bible anywhere.' Geoffrey carefully argues against this in *I Love the Father*, 135–143, drawing on Luke 3:38, Acts 17:22–31, and other Scriptures.

[77] See *I Love the Father*, 137.

[78] *The Beautiful City of God*, 111–112.

[79] *My Beloved Family*, 152.

[80] *My Beloved Family*, 153.

[81] *My Beloved Family*, 152–153.

[82] *The God and Father of Us All*, x. See further: *The Authority and Submission of Love*.

[83] *I Love the Father*, 24.

[84] *I Love the Father*, 15–16, 18.

[85] *Christ's People in Today's World*, 204–205.

[86] See 1 Corinthians 15:24–28.

[87] *My Beloved Family*, 151.

[88] *Bright Bird and Shining Sails*, 121.

CHAPTER 10

GOD SENDS
Revival

Pakistan Bible Training
Institute Chapel

Family in 1966

SOMETHING QUITE WONDERFUL

IN MAY 1958, a report appeared in the *Sind News Letter* from CMS in West Pakistan:

> What would you think if after the preaching of the Word of God in your church one Sunday evening, people rose to their feet to pray for forgiveness of sin? If members of your congregation began seeking out others in the church fellowship to ask forgiveness for some wrong done? If the young people of the church began to come regularly and eagerly to a Bible Study every week, and offer themselves (hitherto so reluctant) for Sunday School work and other Christian service? If the barometer of giving rose steeply in a matter of weeks? What would you think? That the Spirit of God was at work? This is what has been happening in the Hyderabad congregation this winter as a result of two missions in the church under the ministry, through interpretation, of the Rev. Geoffrey Bingham, our new missionary from Australia.[1]

The second of these missions 'was to take three days—Friday to Sunday, with two meetings each day'.[2] It had been well prepared for:

> Leaflets were printed and for the first time folk visited every Christian home in the city. The first day of the Mission arrived and in the morning the Church was full when most should have been at work—they had obtained leave![3]

'Something quite wonderful was in the air, and, of course, the expectancy was high.'[4] Geoffrey recounts what happened after the Sunday night meeting:

> On the last night of the meetings the pastors walked to the door to shake hands with the people as they left the church. Only a few folk

did that, and even they hung around the door, as though anticipating something. I, who for years had dreamed and prayed and longed to see revival, had sensed God would do something even more wonderful than the things we had witnessed . . . Suddenly something happened. The whole congregation broke out in spontaneous singing. It was singing, yet singing like nothing I had ever heard. The songs were well known and were in both Urdu and Punjabi, and some even in Gujerati, but it was the beauty and the sweetness of the singing that was beyond description. Joy was flooding the whole congregation. Nothing was organised or led by the pastors or others.[5]

'Oh my friends', Geoffrey wrote at the time, 'I have never heard anything so sweet. It was sheer joy, the sort of thrilling music we will expect to hear around the Throne . . . How we worshipped!' What was happening? 'Because the pockets of darkness were cleansed from our hearts only pure light shone—Christ Himself.'[6] The theme of the messages during the Mission had been 'light and darkness, love and hatred, pollution and cleansing'.[7] Here it was happening in practice:

After some of the songs, some members of the congregation would rise and embrace others with tears of joyful reconciliation. Occasionally someone would stand and read a passage of Scripture so that some promise or encouragement would come to all. As the passages were read they would seem to fit the occasion, and seem to be adding one to the other on the themes of love, forgiveness, cleansing, fellowship and unity.[8]

At 9.15 pm the vicar suggested to the people that they should have some food before continuing in prayer. They did so, returning at 10 pm.[9] 'The meeting which was supposed to complete the teaching series went on and on, through midnight, and until the morning':

The congregation never seemed to weary. Here and there a person rose and went home, but on the whole no one wanted to miss what might happen next. Many stood before the congregation and shared what God had done in their lives over the months, and in particular, during the series of meetings, and even on that night.

186

Certainly love had come to the church—the pastors and the people.[10]

'The Mission officially ended on the Sunday but it had ceased to be a Mission':

> On Monday evening folk were meeting in groups in homes and on the compound. Men came to us—John Rawat [the vicar] and myself, and everyone wanted to be praying—all the time. Folk were hungry for teaching. On Tuesday night we were asked to go to one of the homes and there some forty folk were gathered for prayer and fellowship, which we had. For the remainder of the week we had meetings each night, and on the Friday evening many stood up and testified to having received Christ as Saviour. These included children, young men and women, folk middle aged and older. Some of the very respectable members of the community, who in one sense should have been a bit scandalised by the unusual proceeding were those who shared most of all.[11]

Individual persons were affected in different ways. There was healing:

> One of the Punjabi teachers came to me and said, 'For months I have had a running sore in one of my ears. I was extracting wax with a knitting needle when accidentally another teacher pushed against the needle and perforated the eardrum. The ear has been suppurating for months, and the hospital has been giving me some treatment. However, it never improved, but when you laid hands on me during these meetings—at my request—the ear healed overnight. I can hear with it now.'
> She smiled gently, and said, '*Dawai se nehie, sirf dua se, mang thik ho gaie,*' that is, 'Not by medicine, but by prayer, I have been healed.' The words *dawai* and *dua* sound similar in Urdu. Hers was a mild punning.[12]

There was conversion:

> A Muslim said he had been seeking God for years but could not find him in Islam, in spite of constant reading of the Koran, and

faithfulness in his prayer. Out in the desert he had had a vision of great water flowing, bringing life to the desert and to him, and a voice told him it was the water of life, and he would receive this in the city of Hyderabad. He had walked into the church—an unusual thing for a Muslim to do—and he had heard of Christ as being the water of life. The message of the Cross affected him deeply, and now he knew a fountain of life's water was springing up within him.[13]

Forgiveness flowing from the Cross brought powerful revelation:

> Often Muslims—though few in number—would come into the after-noon and evening meetings. Wide-eyed, they watched Christians asking forgiveness of one another. Such pure humility and recon-ciliation of this kind would have been unknown to Islam. This kind of brokenness requires the truth and power of the Cross of Christ to take place. Forgiveness—even of one another—is conditional upon forgiveness first known at the Cross, and then given in genuine love, the *agape* of God. When forgiveness was asked, I saw Muslims begin to weep. They could not control their feelings; they were witnessing a phenomenon previously unknown to them.[14]

Notably, there was a difference among the children:

> What was a new phenomenon was the comparative quietness of the children during the meetings. Generally they ran unchecked, shouting and playing and quarrelling, but in these meetings they seemed to be held supernaturally in a bond of quietness. It was true that mothers suckled their babies if they stirred, but for the most part there were few babies who cried. Both John and Emmanuel[15] marked this as a sign that God was present in the midst of the people. They had dreaded the noise the children might make.[16]

None of this was uncontested. 'Such a revived group will be more than ever subject to Satanic onslaught and so they must be taught to be "aware of Satan's devices"':[17]

> One member of the congregation had had a dream or a vision—he was not sure which it was—and he came to John, Emmanuel and me, and told us that two young men would come into the

188

congregation and try to disturb the meetings. He did not know who they were. He could not see them in the dream. Sure enough, the next evening two young men walked up to the front and attempted to address the congregation, saying that the unusual phenomena were not to be trusted, and with all due deference to our new missionary, this well-meaning foreigner was introducing elements that were not truly of the Pakistani Christian culture. The dream—or vision—had prepared Emmanuel, and he stood firmly in the chancel and rebuked the young men. He said that their very way of addressing the congregation was certainly not of their culture, but—even more—it was not of the Bible, nor of the early Christian pattern. He disposed of them very quickly.[18]

One significant outcome was the founding of the Bible School:

> ... this is the thrilling news that I almost forgot to tell—work has commenced on the building for the Bible Training Institute. The Church here in Sind has passed a resolution thanking God for Revival at Hyderabad, and proposing the Bible School, and has voted much money towards it.[19]

Geoffrey and Laurel themselves were impacted by all that happened:

> Each night when we returned to the compound we could hear folk singing in their own homes. We—my wife and I—would get out a hymn book and sing together, something we had not previously done. Music was in the air, singing kept wanting to express itself from the heart. Worship was as pure as I have ever known it anywhere. Teaching began to be the gift of some of the younger as well as the older men. Not long after that, we—as a family—had to return to the hills for the children's schooling and more language study for the parents. With reluctance we waved 'Good-bye' to the Christian crowd of people at the railway station. There were tears in their eyes and ours.[20]

Geoffrey wrote back to Australia: 'I felt to put some things on paper, would be almost to demean them. I can only say that *never* have I experienced such fullness and joy as I have over these past months, and what a mighty working of the Lord there has been ... the very simplicity of it all has taught me that when people truly believe God's Word, and are not bothered with the complexity and spiritual sophistication that we often have in Australia, then God can work.'[21]

BACKGROUND TO REVIVAL

This was in March 1958. It did not come out of nowhere. A movement had begun the previous year with the earlier 'Mission':

> In December 1957 we, without any preparation, commenced a Mission. The Mission lasted for three days, during which there were six studies, all on the Cross.

The studies were 'on the meaning of the Cross for salvation, surrender, discipleship and service'.[22] The pastor 'was delighted with the way in which people crowded into the church. He said it was unprecedented.'[23] Geoffrey himself 'was gratified and even amazed at the response which came':

> If I remember correctly, some forty members of the congregation came into a transforming experience of Christ, and something new began to grow in that congregation. Emmanuel was delighted beyond measure. We would spend hours a day discussing the truth of the Scriptures, which he insisted was a little less than marvellous, much of it being new even to him.[24]

'Those meetings ... were really a preliminary preparation for what was to take place in March of the next year.'[25] Solid teaching continued at Fellowship meetings on Saturday evenings, and in Bible exposition on Friday evenings and the Sunday morning service.[26] 'Shortly afterwards we began meeting each morning for prayer':[27]

> ... we began—about half a dozen of us—to meet at five in the morning for prayer. Emmanuel had the March meetings in his sights, and we trusted special things might take place during them—though just what sort of things we were not sure. Laurel, my wife, would come with us whilst the children slept on.[28]

Visits to other places, up to hundreds of miles away, generated 'a link of prayer' between them.[29] Supporters were also praying in Australia.[30] As the Mission in March approached:

> Morning after morning we prayed, and we noticed the number of our group begin to swell rapidly. Prior to the special meetings the number mounted to sixty. We decided to pray from the evening until dawn on the night prior to the special meetings. It happened that we prayed through until dawn on every night of the meetings.[31]

These prayer meetings in particular left an impression on Geoffrey:

> Perhaps it is the nights that I most remember. Prayer was not looked upon as a painful, drawn-out vigil. It was a time of great joy, of intermittent singing, and of intercession for those who attended, and those who did not. Then, as the teaching began to penetrate, a new note came into the praying. I well remember its rather curious nature. A kind of rhythm came into the personal praying. I could generally follow the meaning of the prayers, but was surprised to hear personal confession to God, as though the ones praying were suppliants for forgiveness and mercy.[32]

Geoffrey was also aware of much that had gone before. 'In those days there were Christian missionary compounds all over the Indian sub-continent.'[33] In the Christian cemetery 'you can see the names on the headstones of the graves—missionaries who refused to return to the countries of their birth':

> I can remember burying one of them who was well into her eighties, and who had been almost clothed with deity by the local folk who loved her—both Christian and non-Christian alike.[34]

When Geoffrey asked why the revival had come about, his answer was:

> Firstly, God promised me this in Australia. Yet long before this His servants here, and throughout the world, had prayed for what had happened. The Reidman sisters ... have been out here for thirty years, patiently praying for these things.[35]

There were also the national clergy:

> The vicar of the church on the compound was one of the most
> intelligent and capable men I have met in my life. As an interpreter
> of Urdu into English and English into Urdu he was brilliant. I doubt
> there ever was his equal. He was also a kindly man, organising us
> into good order, advising us, warning us of the cultural traps into
> which we could fall, and, on the whole, settling us into peace in our
> new home.[36]

Fellowship among the pastors was rich. Emmanuel and another
pastor 'were almost inseparable friends, life was good when the
two came together':

> They both had a rich sense of fun, and punning was their forte. It
> happened to be a weakness of mine.[37]

So teaching, prayer and good fellowship all contributed, but it
was not these which brought it about:

> The one thing that impressed me was that it was not in our hands.
> It was truly a work of the Holy Spirit, and therefore was authori-
> tative. It is this kind of authority that people respect—not the
> ability of a preacher, nor the good arrangements made. The other
> thing that was apparent was that there was a real core of solid
> believers, and so, if one may say so, it was 'safe' to have a revival.[38]

Hints also came through of the great need in the local church.
'I cannot tell you how deep a work is needed to be done in this
situation', Geoffrey would write, and 'There are some things
which cannot be told'.[39] Unbeknown to the missionaries, there
were deep divisions within the Christian community:

> To begin with, those who lived on the compound were always sus-
> pected of gaining advantages over those who did not. On the other
> hand, those who lived outside the compound had a certain courage
> in doing so. They had to learn to live with those in the community
> who were Muslims, Hindus and Parsees. Then there were other
> difficulties, namely the caste system, which although it was not sup-
> posed to exist within a Christian community still influenced the way

Christians saw one another. Some converts had come from various Hindu castes, and held on to the memory of being up the social scale from some of their brethren. It took a generation or more for those who had come into the Christian fold from Islam to be accepted by the congregation as genuine and not as calculating converts. These were some of the elements which caused social and communal rifts, and often spread their bitterness into the church services.[40]

It was these rifts that were being healed in the revival:

Confessions of an intimate kind were made—of previous hatred towards some, of anger and division, and those who prayed cried as though their hearts were breaking, as though they could no longer tolerate failure to be reconciled. It was only later that Emmanuel and John explained to me that feuds were dissolving, family differences were being resolved, and harmony was beginning to come to the congregation.[41]

Geoffrey wrote to his supporters:

...in Hyderabad, we all gathered. There was no denominational barrier.[42] We did not meet in order to 'get something out of it' for our particular group, which so often happens in other places. Oh, brethren, we say we want revival, but we would often be amazed if we knew what we were concealing, Yet light (the Light) cannot flood until darkness be cleansed. How much of secret ambition, jealousy, unbelief, fear, uncleansed sin, we conceal ... I am convinced that it is the clean hands and the pure heart—and they alone—which shall 'receive the blessing from the Lord'.[43]

There was also the problem there, 'as in evangelical circles at home', of 'easy believism' which is really:

...an inadequate view of sin, or to put it bluntly, the Gospel preached without the convicting power of the Holy Spirit.[44]

Geoffrey asks, 'What is revival?':

Is it something unusual? To be feared? Revival, as has often been said, is simply Jesus Christ. That is, Him in the midst. You and I laying down at the foot of the Cross ourselves—really and truly, our ambitions, our hatreds, our unforgiveness, our suspicions, our past darknesses never confessed to Him, our futures, our possessions, our *pride*. It is being prepared to have our brethren in Christ quietly and simply point to things which need to be rectified and brought into the light that the brethren might dwell together in unity. All darkness withers and loses its power when the Light of the World shines upon it. Revival is never to be feared. Only the darkness fears and hates the Light. The Light is kindly because He is love. Why fear then, to have the entire being flooded with light?[45]

Did it last? An eleven-year-old boy wrote a few months later: 'Some people have gone cold, but the keen ones still gather together for prayer, each day, and they are praying for these others'. Geoffrey comments:

Yes, the work is still going on, and if it takes a missionary to keep it stimulated, then I believe it was never a work of the Spirit of God. Pray for the pastors and leaders who are feeding their people, and for folk who are now going out in a team to win others in the villages.[46]

And also:

The revival that has come to the church is simply the Spirit cleansing and renewing His people that He may fit them to be the instrument of His glory. I am sure that so cleansed the church is being prepared for a time of such testing and opposition that has not been dreamed of. So pray, and pray without ceasing, whilst ever praising Him for the things He is doing.[47]

REVIVAL IN THE PUNJAB

Geoffrey and Laurel returned with their family to continue language study at Murree in the Himalayan hills.[48] Geoffrey needed to be ready to begin Bible College, lecturing in Urdu, in the next year:[49]

... I gave myself to some very deep study of the Word and also began a study of Islamics which has now cleared my mind. Bluntly put, I can see that we need, and only need, Spirit-filled men and women, who can be simple instruments of the same Spirit, wielding His Sword with cutting power.[50]

They stayed on for a while to be house parents at the Girls' Hostel of Murree Christian School. During this time Geoffrey was vicar of the Murree Holy Trinity Church and preached also at the Union Church.[51] Here on Easter Day 1959 Geoffrey preached his first sermon in Urdu:

... I abandoned the notes and spoke from my heart, and was amazed at how the language came, even though my wife and I had only had a year's study of it. Later a university professor said, 'I leant back during the message and I closed my eyes and thought, "This is not a missionary but a Pakistani speaking."'[52]

Here also 'For the last weeks of term the staff met nightly and entered into an experience of the fullness of the Spirit':[53]

Studies on the work of the Cross led to an experience of the inflowing of the Spirit of God in a quiet yet powerful way. So there was certainly love amongst us as a fellowship of missionaries. Those days remain memorable for their quiet love and their sharing, and the good family fun we had.[54]

Geoffrey also went to speak at Convention and Presbyterian Synod meetings at Daska and Gujranwala:

It was in this area, during the early days of the century, that the well-known missionary John Hyde, later known as 'Praying Hyde', had, with his fellow missionaries of the Reformed Presbyterian Missionary Society, been used by God in great revival. At that time the church held its first Sialkot Convention meetings—patterned after the style of the Keswick Convention in England—and Hyde was one of the speakers. A man of prayer, he was in his tent at the time of one of the meetings, and they could not awaken him out of what seemed to be a trance. Finally they managed to tell him he was due to speak, and he walked to the edge of the great meeting-tent, and said nothing but 'Oh, Father!' three times, first in Urdu, then in English, and some folk began weeping, others fell to the ground in worship, and others cried out in wonder and joy. Out of that ministry began a revival that swept through that part of the Punjab, and it was to the children of that revival that Gene [Glassman] and I were speaking.[55]

Here there had been longstanding differences and resentments between foreign missionaries and national Pakistani pastors:[56]

Then in July we had a never-to-be-forgotten Convention in which God wonderfully melted these differences, and for the most part has made us one in Him. I feel it is the beginning of a new era for the work in this land, and is an answer, as I am given to understand of many years of patient praying by older and spiritually minded missionaries, who have seen the great need, not only for keen evangelical workers, but for those who know the secrets of the Cross, and the power of the Holy Spirit.[57]

BUSINESS AS USUAL

While Geoffrey says, 'This "revived" condition should not be regarded as phenomenal but simply the natural and right condition of the church',[58] it would be a mistake to think that life was made up of extraordinary happenings all the time. Much of the Binghams' time in Pakistan was getting on with the business of living and teaching. 'Domestic things often so keep our eyes downward that we do not lift them above.'[59] Once the Bible Institute was opened in February 1960, there was the daily routine with the students:

Their programme commences at 5 a.m. and continues to 10 p.m. Lectures commence at 7.30 a.m. after chapel and continue until 12.30. From 4 p.m. to 5 p.m. is compulsory study, followed by an hour's sport, then worship, supper, another hour of study, and then free time. Studies are from Tuesday to Saturday inclusive, with Monday as a rest day.

Our course has covered the following subjects: detailed studies of Genesis, Isaiah 1–40, and full Bible synthesis of Genesis to Daniel, detailed study of Luke, Romans, Ephesians, Acts, Philippians and I and II Timothy, Biblical Principles of Evangelism and Bible Teaching ... Worship consists in a half hour's service in the morning, led by the Principal, and an hour or so in the evening which is shared by all.[60]

Geoffrey gave 25 lectures a week while not away elsewhere, with help from others.[61] It was 'a work requiring much patience':

Much of it consists in patiently weeding and taking out stones from the soil. Yet it must never be perspiration without inspiration. Nor can ministries such as these be assessed—no one can see what the end will be, nor should we so demand to see.[62]

There were issues to address:

... after a few weeks had passed it became clear that we had to dismiss two students. It was after much investigation and prayer that we did so, and although this was a difficult thing to have to do, immediately the atmosphere of the Institute changed, and we have made rapid progress from that time.[63]

Laurel was no less occupied:

Laurel is kept busy with talking students out of imaginary sicknesses or treating them for real ones. She teaches Elizabeth, Ruth and Mary daily. Her Sunday School at the time of service on Sunday evenings is quite large.[64]

Laurel's own writing about this period focuses almost entirely on family issues—her own giving birth in Lahore, and major surgery in Rawalpindi; the children's playmates, illnesses, and broken legs; shopping in the bazaar; housing, water supply, laundry and toilet conditions—and family separations:

... we had to leave the three older children in boarding school as we went to the plains ... I felt helpless to alter the situation ... we knew Dick wasn't coping at MCS ... On fifteenth January [1960] Dick went home to Sydney to what we thought was the best boarding school ... I felt so sad to see him go ... he looked so forlorn in his huge greatcoat ... My Mum took him in hand and bought all his uniform etc. and had studio photos taken and sent to us. They tore my heart.[65]

After furlough in Australia in 1962, the two older girls also remained there. Geoffrey wrote:

Laurel and the three girls here are well. Dick, Carol and Anne tell us how kind folk are to them in Australia. How that warms our hearts.[66]

Through all this, God was working:

Our meetings on Friday night at the house when Laurel supplies tea and home-made buns, are grand evenings. You would tingle to hear some of the testimonies. One student, once actually sentenced to death, at another time a height jumper in a circus and then a severe ascetic (sat with only a loin cloth for nine months day and night exposed to the elements) speaks of the joy of grace. Another, also a sadhu, would not wear shoes or sleep on a bed because he deemed this worldly, confesses to the snapping of law's chains, and the adornment of the joy of grace. Others have less dramatic, but none the less impressive testimonies of this receiving of life at the Institute.[67]

Geoffrey was convinced that the Bible Training Institute was 'part of God's plan for His people in Pakistan':

Anyone can open a B.T.I.—but let him not dare to say it is God's will until he has been led to do so. B.T.I. is not just part of an over-all technique for evangelism or church-extension. We know it to be His will. We cannot believe the vast amount of support would have flowed so easily—if this were not so.[68]

Students, used to learning and repeating by rote, acknowledged that 'this is new, different teaching':

It is impossible to describe the sense of astonishment with which the students have received teaching ... I am sure it is not simply because we endeavour to use the 'inductive' method as far as possible, but because we are trying to emphasise the living truth more than the academic. I hasten to add I am not criticising the academic, nor consider it to be either destructive or opposed to what I would call 'living'. Yet we have often missed the living substance of truth when our approach is that of absorbing a number of given facts. We sense the great volume of prayer that is ascending and to this we attribute results at this very early stage.[69]

Yet the teaching given was not new:

It has not always been understood that B.T.I. does not have a 'new teaching' but indeed a very old one. It is that of the Scriptures. The great truths of grace and forgiveness, justification by faith, life not lived in the tension of justifying works, but in the impulse and motivation of love inpoured through the recognition and acceptance of the Cross—these things are the basis of our teaching. These do not cut across church discipline but enliven it. Nor does our teaching end here. We speak of the new life born of the Spirit and lived in the Spirit—a life of prayer, of reading the Word, of fellowship lived in light and sensitivity.[70]

It went on from there:

We speak of the power of the Spirit to awake the dead spirits of men through the work of proclamation. It is a life of evangelistic ministry drawing its strength from the engifted worshipping body—the Church. We believe the out-going evangelising church is the only one that has vivid life—albeit its problems may exceed those of others. In this context the meaning of the Word and Sacraments (ordinances) becomes vital. The Gospel is of itself realistic and dynamic, needing only the Spirit to communicate it.[71]

The perils of 'strong denominationalism as such, separatist spirit, hardness-in-orthodoxy, planning for group extension' which stand in the way of revival[72] were eschewed:

We have sought to fight the perils of professionalism and abject submission to some patterns which are not in the ethos of apostolic Christianity. Whilst drawing our students from every denomination, we have never experienced division on the group level. Appreciation of various disciplines has been inculcated and suspicion of other groups dissolved. Fellowship has been maintained at a high level.[73]

'The aim of BTI was primarily to train laymen so that they might return to their lay occupations, and whilst assisting the local church might prove to be flames to light the fires of revival.'[74]

The students were active in ministry:

> Students have taken part in the selling of literature in the bazaar. They run the Christian Book Shop in Jacob Road and take services in the local church and various basties. Many of these meetings they have created themselves. They have had a number of personal contacts with enquirers. The Institute also conducts the Correspondence Course in Urdu and English for Sind. This has been mainly carried on by one student. The students take a very personal and active part in the life of the local church.[75]

In addition to the daily worship, which 'have been times of spiritual enrichment', Geoffrey wrote, 'We have quiet days for prayer when we feel the necessity of special refreshment. On two or three occasions we have had such blessing that for this we can use only one word—revival.'[76]

REVIVAL AT THORNLEIGH, 1962

When Geoffrey came back to Australia on furlough (missionary leave) in 1962, he brought revival with him: 'what happened in Pakistan in those early days of the revival fired Geoff in his ministry back here in 1962'.[77] His powerful preaching impacted the lives of many:

> This began at the CMS Summer School in January that year. He gave the morning Bible studies on Romans. These had a huge impact on people. Many lives were changed as a result of Geoff opening up the great theme of God's righteousness, and of the grace that comes in the work of the cross to bring entire liberation from guilt.[78]

Stuart Piggin writes:

> Bingham's spirituality preceded that of the main influence of the Charismatic movement, and was a genuinely indigenous revitalisation movement of a type rarely experienced in Australian history.

Perhaps his greatest work in Australia was in local church missions where revival was often experienced. The addresses he gave at these missions were Bible messages on the bondage of man to sin and Satan and the powers of darkness and of flesh and the world, and the true freedom which Christ gives from such powers. This biblical and cross-centred teaching often revived the heart.[79]

In August 1962 Geoffrey led a week-long mission in St Luke's Church at Thornleigh, where he had been catechist ten years earlier. Margaret Rush writes in her history of the parish:

> In 1962 Geoff Bingham had a teaching mission which brought great blessing to the Parish. The church was full to overflowing and many have since recalled this occasion as being a spiritual highlight of the time.[80]

The Reverend John Cornford said of that mission: 'It was a powerful time, because basically it was all about agape love. For me it was especially dynamic as it introduced me to the work of the Holy Spirit in a way I had not known before.'[81] Stuart Piggin writes: 'it was during that teaching mission, taken by Geoff Bingham, in August 1962 that Revival came to Thornleigh Anglican Church'. He recounts one incident that happened in the home of Fred George:

> During the Thornleigh mission, a prayer meeting of about thirty people was held in a private home. Bingham read from Psalm 24, 'Who shall ascend to the hill of the Lord? He who has clean hands and a pure heart.' And then he suggested that those present should come to the Lord and ask him to reveal himself to them. They all knelt down in a circle, and then someone began to weep, and a great conviction came over all of them. Some tried to pray, but dissolved in sobs. And then there came over one present an incredible sense of his own depravity in the sight of God. He saw something extraordinary. It was as if he were standing outside himself, looking at himself. And he wanted to flee from himself as fast and as far as he could because of the horrific sight he had of his own sin. He was crushed and broke down and sobbed convulsively, and the others around him were prostrate on the floor,

broken hearted. Then a gentle quietness came over the whole group, and then a wonderful sense of God's total forgiveness. Then they sang and sang until they were hoarse. The singing and intercession just went on and on, until someone said, 'It's half past four in the morning'. Everyone was staggered that so much time had elapsed.[82]

The effects of the mission were profound and lasting. 'What happened in all of this—and I cannot emphasise this enough—Geoff's teaching brought about an incredible sense of unity and love at St Luke's Thornleigh, to the extent that when Geoff was to leave, people wept openly.'[83] 'I know it was a very inspirational time because I recall the young people's group being very strong after that mission.'[84] This was a group established by John Dunn, Geoff Duffy, John Yeo and others in the late 1950s:

It had Anglicans, Baptists, Congregationalists and Presbyterians in it, and it met every Saturday night for 10 years, and between 30 and 50 packed into the Dunn's lounge room for the fellowship, the singing and, perhaps especially the teaching. John would teach one week and Geoff Duffy the alternate. Geoff was a quite brilliant Bible expositor and subsequently went to New Zealand where he became Professor of Chemical Engineering. Geoff Bingham had put John Dunn in touch with Robin Bird who was the Australian representative of Banner of Truth, and so the great foundational truths of redemption and reformed theology were laid at the same time as they studied the Scriptures together. After Geoff Bingham in August 1962 held a mission in the Parish, the tapes of his addresses were played over and over again, and his astonishing teaching on the holiness and love of the Father in the efficacy of the cross became the regular diet. Scores were converted and many went into the mission field or the ministry.[85]

'He also spoke at a number of meetings at St Mark's Picton which was one of his sending churches (under CMS). Barry Schofield was rector.'[86] Of another parish mission taken by Geoffrey, also in 1962, one reported:

Geoff Bingham came to our church in 1962 and I have never forgotten how he wept in the pulpit while delivering his sermon. I don't think I had ever seen a man cry in my 16 years of life . . . My heart never forgot him, his word made such an impression on me . . . I wonder . . . how many other people, like me, felt the impact of that word and came under a personal revival from the Lord which radically changed my life! I have never forgotten the awesomeness of that encounter with God, nor could I ever turn from Him. Hell was real—but it was the Lord's wrath which terrified me—not fear of hell, but of He, [sic] who could send me to hell.[87]

Thus Geoffrey was instrumental in a movement that was to have wider ramifications in his homeland: 'Nourished by the experience of its missionaries in the East African and Pakistan revivals, a number of Sydney clergy followed Bingham's lead and forged a unity of Keswick-inspired spirituality with Reformed theology. From this highly combustible compound, the fires of revival began to smoulder in a number of Sydney parishes.'[88]

LOVEFEST THREE

At the end of his time in Pakistan, Geoffrey experienced revival again in ways he had not known before. 'I know what happened in the years of 1965 and 1966 in Pakistan was a genuine and wonderful work of God. It has indelibly left its imprint on many lives, and certainly on my own':

> In 1965 a number of us from the Pakistan Bible Training Institute . . . went on our yearly visit to the Rahim Yar Khan area, where we had ministered for quite some years. Some ten or more of our graduates were now pastors in that district, and all of them were competent shepherds of the flock.[89]

Here 'something strange happened':

> . . . in the last meeting some members in the congregation saw flashes of light come over the meeting, and some saw light shining from me. There were also some visions. I was preaching on the event recorded in Acts chapter 4 where the house in which believers

were praying was shaken and the Holy Spirit fell on all who were present. I felt a strange power in the preaching, and said that God could do that very thing with us in this very meeting.[90]

Geoffrey describes the setting:

We were under a large *shamiana*—a meeting-tent held up by tall poles. It sheltered us from the intense sunlight. We were in a compound bounded by the walls of two houses, and with two more walls which helped to form the protected courtyard. Outside the square the Christian cooks were preparing our next meal.[91]

Here is what happened:

At the end of my talk we sat and sang prayerfully a song in Hindi which pleaded with God to pour out His Spirit upon us. As we sang, something began to happen. The whole courtyard shook, as though an earthquake was happening. I have been in the heavy tremors of earthquakes, but this was different. I saw the *shamiana* poles sway, and felt the heaving of the ground.

My first thought was, 'I have been preaching too intensely!' . . . All had immediate human explanations, but after a few moments we realised that what had happened in the Book of the Acts was happening to us. Many rose to their feet and cried happily, 'He is here! He is here! The Lord is here!' Others shouted, 'We have been filled with His Spirit!'[92]

Interestingly, 'Outside, the cooks felt nothing, absolutely nothing. Missionaries living some hundreds of yards away felt nothing.' Geoffrey writes:

I had the most tremendous sense of faith—as it were—almost becoming sight. Certainly there was the palpable presence of the Lord, and my life was greatly enriched. From that point onwards, quite unusual things began to happen to folk in the church, mainly womenfolk. Some months later, at a retreat for present and past students at our Bible Institute, the pastors told stories of dull Christians suddenly coming alive with the infilling of the Holy Spirit. Their whole community was changing.[93]

'Even so, the passing event of the shaking of the place did not provide what I increasingly felt I needed—a new power of love and spiritual fire in my life and ministry.' Geoffrey spoke with the third-year students, 'who itinerated in ministry, taking their tents and cooking gear with them', and suggested 'they needed to be those who set off the fires of revival, rather than simply be evangelists in the modern mode'. Their respectful answer was: 'I suppose that if the father cannot light a fire then the sons will not be able to do so':

> What they said struck me deeply. They meant, of course, that I, being the father, could not fire them sufficiently to light the fire of revival. My own theology has always taught me that revival is a sovereign work of God, but that since revival is simply the church living at its true pitch—that is, in full life—then we should never be satisfied when it is not in full life.[94]

One morning Geoffrey in tears told the students and staff, 'Long ago, in Australia, I was sure that God promised us there would be revival in Pakistan. It is not long before we are going home, and as yet I have not known the love that I ought to have known. I have not lived in true love to you, and to others.' It was not feelings that Geoffrey sought, but rather 'the reality of Christ as the living Lord'.[95] This was when Geoffrey was given his vision of the risen Christ, described in Chapter Nine. Something of this transferred to the other missionaries, and to the third-year students:

> From then onwards was a stream of happenings, phenomena which often attend revivals. Given in what we would call supernatural happenings, and accepting these phenomena, the greatest of them all was the love which came upon the whole group.[96]

Some of the best was kept for Geoffrey's final days in Pakistan:

> About that time the Bible Institute closed as we had our Graduation Service. In all, there were about five hundred people in the meeting,

as the local church was bidding us farewell officially. At the end of that service a very beautiful Urdu song began to well up within me, and I sang it . . . I did not know what words were coming next—but they came! When it was finished there was scarcely a dry eye. Some of the folk rushed forward, asking me excitedly, 'Where did you learn that song? Where did you get it? It is the sort of song that is like our old folk-songs—from a thousand years ago!' Certainly it was a strange and beautiful song, like a saga of salvation, and a cavalcade of love.[97]

Even more remarkable was what happened shortly afterwards. Geoffrey paid a final two-day visit to Rahim Yar Khan, and spoke at four meetings. The final one lasted for six hours:

When I finished my address, which had gone on for at least a couple of hours (nobody at all disturbed by that!), I was about to give the blessing when suddenly the song I had sung at Hyderabad, and whose words and lines I had forgotten, began afresh, of itself, so to speak. Again I did not know what the next words would be, but they came. Even more wonderfully than that, the whole crowd joined with me, and sang with me, and not one of them had heard it before.

It was then that I knew fully what Luke recorded when he said, 'They lifted their voices *together* to God,' and 'Now the company of those who believed *were of one heart and soul*, and no one said that any of the things which he possessed was his own, but they had everything in common.' It was then I knew the utter oneness of the unity of the Spirit, and sheer fullness of love—God's love.[98]

One who was present at this time, 19–20th May 1966, reports that one 'notable factor in the work' in that region was that 'the workers and one ordained minister were trained at the Bible Training Institute at Hyderabad under the Principalship of the Rev. Geoffrey Bingham':

These men returned to their fields with new experience of the Holy Spirit, the Lordship of Jesus Christ and the vision of their work . . . Mr Bingham came to Pakistan with a vision to see fire kindled in the churches. Just before he left, God let him see the movement of the Holy Spirit in his students and in their ministry. His labours in the

Bible Training and Evangelism has at last shown the fruit. He left with joy and a thankful heart.[99]

BACK IN AUSTRALIA

Experience of revival in Pakistan in some ways spoiled Geoffrey for subsequent ministry elsewhere. He was always on the lookout for revival, and could never be wholly satisfied with anything less. Yet because of this he was able to give powerful witness:

> Revival is not merely a sudden outbreak of joy, a new surge of vitality, a refreshing of the saints, and a renewing of old and broken relationships. It is all these things, but much more. It is at once the judgement of God upon the dryness, apathy and lassitude of the earth. It is a sudden sensitising to evil, to a new and almost terrifying discernment of the depths into which the church and the land has sunk. The great truth of God bears down upon many who are unsuspecting of its arrival. Just as sudden flash floods overwhelm careless travellers, or fires break and explode in dry places, and as waters swill across lowland and rise to inundate all, so too revival comes as the most critical of God's gifts. It is irresistible in its impact; no one can gainsay it . . . When revival comes men and women wonder what kind of lives they had been living. They see how far the land and nation had receded from its former godliness. The spirit of immorality, inordinate desire for pleasure, consumption of drugs and alcohol, addiction to gambling and other expressions of evil suddenly are unmasked, and a true fear strikes where it should. This discernment is one of the forerunners and fruits of revival. When renewal comes it is strong and deep and lasting.[100]

Geoffrey characteristically sets his understanding of revival in the over-all plan and purpose of God. 'Re-vival' presupposes an original gift of 'vival' which has suffered from 'de-vival'. It is 'giving life where there had been life previously but this life has been lost, stultified or neglected . . . living in given (created and covenantal) life is *vival*, and having it restored is *revival*':[101]

Revival then—in its widest meaning—is the restoring to, or renewing of, the life which God gave to man.[102]

'*Revival comes when the Gospel is preached in prophetic power by men filled with the Spirit of God.*'[103] The day of Pentecost (Acts 2) is 'the Greatest Revival on Earth':

> ...in one sense Pentecost remains the source of power, life, truth and witness, and in another sense its action goes on continually, i.e. God is always pouring out His Spirit.[104]

What follows from this needs to be continuous 'vival' or 'revival':

> *It is waiting upon God for the resource that is needed at any particular moment*...The basic principle of vival and revival is to have faith in God, i.e. to rise up to the level of grace by faith-response. Faith is knowledge of God, but it is also trust in Him. At its fullest it is obedience because it believes God and acts upon His word, i.e. His promises, His gifts and His commands. If we can ever talk about the key to revival, then this is it...the resources of God are always at hand when the church is in need. It is not that God refuses to supply the resources. It is that He *is* supplying them, but we are poor in faith.[105]

Can we do this for ourselves? When 'we see the immense cost of atoning and redemptive love—in the Cross', then 'we realise the utter impossibility of a human being bringing himself back from death to life'.[106] Revival, then, is necessarily a sovereign act of God. But it is 'not something which is done over the heads of careless and unseeking persons, or something which is dropped upon a careless and indifferent church':

> God will awaken the sense of need. When revival comes, we will give Him the glory, but will also have immense gratitude that we wrought, worked and prayed for this end, because He had put this desire into our hearts. We would have been *unnatural* not to have such yearning and consequent seeking.[107]

While open to and glad of 'signs and wonders', Geoffrey always kept his theological bearings. He writes systematically of 'the subsidiary ministry which works, deeds, gifts, and signs and wonders play in the overall scheme of the Gospel. Their place is important, but they must not be emphasized out of proportion.' He shows that 'what is primary in life is the word of God, His communication to us', and advocates 'Living in the power of the word of the Cross by the power and ministry—to us—of the Holy Spirit'.[108]

WUDINNA, SOUTH AUSTRALIA, 1969

Hence, when invited by Methodist minister Deane Meatheringham to lead a mission on the west coast of South Australia, 'Bingham came to Wudinna not to give revival messages, but to simply preach from the Bible':

> The messages were straight-out solid teaching on the bondage of man to sin and Satan and the powers of darkness and the flesh and the world and so on; and the true freedom which Christ gives from such powers.[109]

Deane Meatheringham had begun in his first appointment there in 1967 'by preaching the simple truths and basic doctrines of the Christian faith':

> By October 1967, the numbers attending Sunday services were actually down to about 9 or 10 people, and most of those were reluctant even to speak of 'spiritual' matters.[110]

A sermon preached in November 1967, to which Meatheringham invited a formal response, 'marked the beginning of an outbreak of groups in which many people expressed an unprecedented desire to learn and grow in their faith . . . A continual stream of people found their lives renewed as they happily put their trust in Jesus Christ.'[111]

'The mission was planned for 24–31 August, 1969 . . . entitled "FREE INDEED" . . . The Rev. Geoffrey Bingham came to Wudinna with a team of 11 students from ABI.[112] They played an active and significant part in the worship services and shared their own personal testimonies with the locals.'[113] A surprisingly large crowd of about 150 locals turned out to the first meeting, swelling later in the week to 200–300. Many were impacted by life-changing conversions.[114] These extended even to one who did not attend:

> A farmer who had not been coming to the meetings, although his wife was, was out on his tractor, when great conviction came upon him and he got down in the dust and gave his life to the Lord.

There were healings:

> A woman believed she was healed of a kidney complaint in one of the meetings, and tests at the hospital the next day showed that there was no longer any problem with the kidney.

'There was also great opposition. Some shouted back or walked out as Geoff was preaching.' Nor was the opposition only human:

> On the Monday night at Kyancutta as Bingham was preaching, he could hear strange noises going on during the meeting. He had been fighting to get his words out . . . he said, 'Satan, in Christ's name we rebuke you, and command you to leave this meeting'. There was a loud bang. People sat there a little bit astonished at what had happened, but the whole place was absolutely quiet. People later remarked that up until that point they had felt their minds were very scrambled and they couldn't hear what the preacher was saying. It had not made sense, people couldn't hear rationally. But at once, everything changed and the preaching was full of power. Many people remained behind after this meeting and refused to go home until they had spoken with someone about becoming converted to Christ.[115]

'The reality of God's Presence and the singing in the meetings was quite extraordinary . . . Of the final night Bingham said "like a great rain of beauty and silence and joy, it just descended on the whole congregation . . . I'd have called it a very gentle but a very powerful outpouring of the Holy Spirit."'[116]

'In the weeks, months and years that followed the mission, God continued to reveal his love to his people at Wudinna':

> The mission had been no seven day wonder, but folk continued to be converted to Christ ... Meatheringham was untiring in his efforts to nurture his people ... As a Pastor he moved well among the community and encouraged people to continue in their faith. In all there were 61 confirmees during his 5 year term at Wudinna. Pastoral letters were written to teach, exhort and encourage people. The instruction given was clear and simple. People were enjoined to accept their salvation joyfully, live by faith in Christ, read the Bible diligently, pray earnestly and worship regularly.[117]

The effects went out from there, in witness and service:

> One of the leaders, when praying during the mission 'saw' a large heap of leaves and a strong gust of wind scattering them all over what seemed a map of Australia. This was interpreted as lots of people touched by God would be moved on into many parts of this land ... Many people moved in later years to Western Australia, Victoria, Queensland and other parts of South Australia.[118]

When asked at the Annual Methodist Conference what techniques had been used, Deane Meatheringham replied, 'We organised a mission and God got out of hand'![119]

HOLY TRANSFORMATION

Geoffrey never ceased to pray, desire and work for true revival. From one of his novels:

> It was the hour of true power and love, and none of it was of man's making. No sooner had Balwone ceased from singing his song than another broke out, and then another. All were singing in unison, but at the same time cries were breaking forth from different persons. Here a man stood with great joy, lifting his arms in praise, on the one hand almost inarticulate and on the other allowing cascades of joy and delight to break over those around him. Little children were as vocal, and here and there an aged person would

struggle to his or her feet and begin thanking the Most High for the multitudinous blessings of life they had now come to realise had been from him.[120]

[1] *Sind News Letter*, May 1958, p. 8.

[2] Bingham Prayer Letter, May 1958, p. 4. It was 14–16 March; *Sind News Letter*, August 1958, p. 5.

[3] Bingham Prayer Letter, May 1958, p. 1.

[4] 'Love-Fest One', in *Twice-Conquering Love*, 132.

[5] *Twice-Conquering Love*, 135–136.

[6] Bingham Prayer Letter, May 1958, p. 1.

[7] *Twice-Conquering Love*, 133.

[8] *Twice-Conquering Love*, 136.

[9] Bingham Prayer Letter, May 1958, p. 4.

[10] *Twice-Conquering Love*, 136.

[11] Bingham Prayer Letter, May 1958, p. 4.

[12] *Twice-Conquering Love*, 134–135.

[13] *Twice-Conquering Love*, 135.

[14] *Twice-Conquering Love*, 133.

[15] See *Twice-Conquering Love*, 129. The Rev. Emmanuel Mall came with his staff from Mirpurkhas to help, particularly with interpreting; see The Rev. J. B. Rawat, Vicar of Hyderabad, 'A National Padre Greets You', *Sind News Letter*, August 1958, p. 5.

[16] *Twice-Conquering Love*, 132.

[17] Bingham Prayer Letter, May 1958, p. 5.

[18] *Twice-Conquering Love*, 134.

[19] Bingham Prayer Letter, May 1958, p. 3.

[20] *Twice-Conquering Love*, 137.

[21] Bingham Prayer Letter, May 1958, p. 2.

[22] Bingham Prayer Letter, May 1958, p. 3.

[23] *Twice-Conquering Love*, 128.

[24] *Twice-Conquering Love*, 130.

[25] *Twice-Conquering Love*, 130–131.

[26] Bingham Prayer Letter, May 1958, p. 3.

[27] Bingham Prayer Letter, May 1958, p. 1.

[28] *Twice-Conquering Love*, 131.

[29] Bingham Prayer Letter, May 1958, p. 1.

[30] Bingham Prayer Letter, May 1958, p. 2.

[31] *Twice-Conquering Love*, 131–132.

[32] *Twice-Conquering Love*, 132–133.

[33] *Twice-Conquering Love*, 127.

[34] *Twice-Conquering Love*, 126–127.

[35] Bingham Prayer Letter, May 1958, p. 2.

[36] *Twice-Conquering Love*, 127.

[37] *Twice-Conquering Love*, 131.

[38] Bingham Prayer Letter, May 1958, p. 4.

[39] *Sind News Letter*, July 1959, p. 6, and November 1959, p. 6.

[40] *Twice-Conquering Love*, 129.

[41] *Twice-Conquering Love*, 133.

[42] John Rawat reported: 'The Methodists and the Salvation Army co-operated with us'; *Sind News Letter*, August 1958, p. 5.

[43] Bingham Prayer Letter, May 1958, p. 2.

[44] *Sind News Letter*, November 1959, p. 5.

[45] Bingham Prayer Letter, May 1958, pp. 4–5.

[46] Bingham Prayer Letter, May 1958, p. 5.

[47] *Sind News Letter*, July 1959, p. 7.

[48] *Sind News Letter*, July 1959, p. 4.

[49] Bingham Prayer Letter, August 1959(?), p. 2.

[50] *Sind News Letter*, July 1959, p. 4.

[51] *Sind News Letter*, July 1959, p. 7.

[52] 'Lovefest Two', *Twice-Conquering Love*, 139.

[53] *Sind News Letter*, July 1959, p. 6.

[54] *Twice-Conquering Love*, 138–139.

[55] *Twice-Conquering Love*, 141, 143–144.

[56] *Twice-Conquering Love*, 139–140.

[57] Bingham Prayer Letter, August 1959(?), p. 1.

[58] Bingham Prayer Letter, May 1958, p. 5.

[59] Bingham Prayer Letter, August 1959(?), p. 1.

[60] *Sind News Letter*, April 1961, pp. 12–13.

[61] Bingham Prayer Letter, 30th October 1963, p. 1. The others included John Greenslade of New Zealand CMS, and Geoffrey's former language teacher, converted while staying in his house, now the Rev. (later bishop) Bashir Jivan, assisted in parish ministry by Makhzan Ullah.

[62] Bingham Prayer Letter, 6th March 1963, p. 1.

[63] Bingham Prayer Letter, 6th March 1963, p. 1.

[64] Bingham Prayer Letter, 30th October 1963, p. 2.

65 *Laurel's Story*, pp. 65, 77.

66 Bingham Prayer Letter, 12th June 1963, p. 2.

67 Bingham Prayer Letter, 30th October 1963, p. 1.

68 *Sind News Letter*, August 1966, p. 7.

69 *Sind News Letter*, June 1960, p. 9.

70 *Sind News Letter*, August 1966, pp. 7–8.

71 *Sind News Letter*, August 1966, p. 8.

72 *Sind News Letter*, August 1966, p. 8.

73 *Sind News Letter*, August 1966, p. 6.

74 *Sind News Letter*, August 1966, p. 5.

75 *Sind News Letter*, April 1961, p. 13. From Bingham Prayer Letter, 14th December 1962, p. 2: 'Our Correspondence Course is really having a good ministry. In answer to newspaper advertisements we have so many applications they are difficult to handle.'

76 *Sind News Letter*, April 1961, p. 13.

77 John Dunn, email to Martin Bleby 14 April 2012.

78 John Dunn, email to Martin Bleby 14 April 2012.

79 Stuart Piggin, email to John Dunn, April 2012.

80 Margaret Rush, *St Luke's Anglican Church since 1909*, 1984.

81 John Cornford to John Dunn, 7 April 2012, in email to Martin Bleby, 14 April 2012.

82 Stuart Piggin, email to John Dunn, April 2012. Also recounted first hand in Interview with John Dunn, 9 September 2008.

83 Interview with John Dunn, 9 September 2008.

84 Margaret Rush to John Dunn, 7 April 2012.

85 Stuart Piggin, email to John Dunn, April 2012.

86 John Dunn, email to Martin Bleby 14 April 2012.

87 Ruth Goozeff to Stuart Piggin, undated letter, September 2004, Stuart Piggin, email to John Dunn, April 2012.

88 Stuart Piggin, email to John Dunn, April 2012.

89 'Lovefest Three', *Twice-Conquering Love*, 147.

90 *Twice-Conquering Love*, 148.

91 *Twice-Conquering Love*, 148.

92 *Twice-Conquering Love*, 148–149.

93 *Twice-Conquering Love*, 149.

94 *Twice-Conquering Love*, 149–150.

[95] *Twice-Conquering Love*, 150, 151.

[96] *Twice-Conquering Love*, 155.

[97] *Twice-Conquering Love*, 155–156.

[98] *Twice-Conquering Love*, 158.

[99] A paper entitled 'Pakistan Revival', by John Rowel, All Saints Church House, Badin, West Pakistan, pp. 1, 6. Undated, it reads as a detailed diary of events written at that time.

[100] 'The Descent of Stephen Stylites', *3 Special Stories*, 66.

[101] *God Sends Revival*, 2, 10; see also *Dry Bones Dancing!* 85.

[102] *Dry Bones Dancing!* 8.

[103] *Dry Bones Dancing!* 109.

[104] *Dry Bones Dancing!* 25.

[105] *Dry Bones Dancing!* 74, 75, 76.

[106] *Dry Bones Dancing!* 52.

[107] *Dry Bones Dancing!* 90.

[108] *God and Man in Signs and Wonders*, 213, 212.

[109] Trevor R. Faggotter, *Sparks of Revival! An Episode of Christian Life at Wudinna, South Australia*, paper prepared for BTh. studies (1992), 2007, p. 5.

[110] Faggotter, p. 2.

[111] Faggotter, p. 2.

[112] Adelaide Bible Institute.

[113] Faggotter, pp. 3, 4.

[114] Faggotter, pp. 5, 6.

[115] Faggotter, p. 6.

[116] Faggotter, pp. 6, 9.

[117] Faggotter, p. 9.

[118] Faggotter, p. 10.

[119] Faggotter, p. 11.

[120] *Beyond Mortal Love*, 291

CHAPTER 11

THE
HEAVENLY
Battle

Adelaide Bible Institute
Principal Bingham

LEAVING PAKISTAN

SUMMER IN 1965 saw the Binghams at Ziarat on the North West Frontier, near Pakistan's border with Afghanistan. They didn't go to Murree that year, as they did not have any of their children at the school, and 'it had become full time counselling etc. and no rest for Geoff'. This was supposed to be a holiday:

> It was a good time only Geoff felt he had to write for the first four hours of the morning then we could go out together. I think Geoff has never ever learnt to totally relax. He always has the gospel foremost in his heart and that is him.[1]

While Laurel was keen on sightseeing, Geoff had no interest in being a tourist. Laurel had her way around that, and had been in contact with missionary friends in Afghanistan:

> Earlier I had written to the Kabul folk to invite Geoff officially, so we went there via Peshawar ... we had ten glorious days and Geoff preached well and we saw much. Even up to the Russian border to buy slippers and I wish I had bought more.[2]

Family matters back in Australia began to impinge during this time:

> Sometime during our last year [Geoff's] father died but he didn't get his Mum's letter for nearly two months as she had sent it to India. The students sat around Geoff's bed where he rested from the shock, and were very sympathetic as they sat in silence then quietly sang and prayed, it was a great comfort and witness.[3]

More disturbing news reached them while they were away. Geoff was at Quetta when he heard that their son Richard was in trouble back in Australia, and that they needed to come back and provide a home residence for him. Laurel started packing once again, and they returned to Hyderabad to be ready to leave.[4]

Even so, Geoff's mind was still also on present and future ministry, with a keen eye for the latest communication technology:

> Geoff was onto another meeting and came home with a confounded big tape recorder, a heavy old American one, that meant I had to adjust our luggage and toss some out. We had to get a transformer in Australia. Having been so long away I guess we didn't realise there were better ones at home.[5]

That 'confounded big tape recorder' was the beginning of an extensive recording ministry, from reel-to-reel and cassette tapes through to MP3 CDs, video cassettes and DVDs, of many thousands of hours of gospel teaching over the next forty years.

So it happened that 'After nine years of outstanding service in West Pakistan, the Rev. Geoffrey and Mrs Bingham have returned to Australia where for family reasons they will be setting up their home'. They arrived back in June 1966—though in July Geoffrey 'visited N. Borneo for a ten-day Convention ministry', where it was his prayer 'that if it be God's will such a ministry to different churches in Asia may open before him in days to come'. Bishop Woolmer of Lahore in his Diocesan Letter registered his appreciation of Geoffrey's time in Pakistan:

> There can be few missionaries who, in such a comparatively short period, have made such a mark for God in their time overseas.[6]

Marcus Loane concurs:

> It is given only to a few who begin their work in a Muslim country when in their late thirties to leave so deep a mark for God among fellow missionaries and national converts alike.[7]

Many years later, the name and ministry of Geoffrey Bingham was still being spoken of appreciatively among Pakistani Christians.[8]

A COLD RECEPTION

'He came home on a high-crested wave. His face shone, his eyes sparkled, his whole being was vibrant.'[9] On his return, Geoffrey was to report back to those who had been supporting him. 'I knew that they too had been praying for revival and would be glad of the news of its happenings.'[10] He was 'expecting to be able to build on that and work from it':

> Just before they were to come back, he sent a prayer letter to the representatives in Sydney; and in that he documented all that had happened in Pakistan in the latter part of that time when there was this great movement of the Spirit—there were lots of conversions, there were great miracles, there were great evidences of God being present . . . and he had put this in this prayer letter . . . He sent off this prayer letter to the prayer secretary here in Sydney, but the prayer secretary in Sydney decided that this was unsuitable material for Sydney Diocese Anglicans, and expunged it all from the prayer letter.[11]

Geoffrey speaks of 'the report he had sent back to his friends earlier, before he had returned from the revival area':

> His own promotional secretary had refused to send it out. She knew the effect it would have.
> 'This letter will close every door you had ever had opened to you,' she said.[12]

He 'was utterly devastated to discover that . . . not a soul here knew anything about what had been happening in Pakistan . . . He was . . . terribly distressed.'[13] Geoffrey gives an account of his reporting back on arrival:

> I can remember speaking to this listening group when I came back to my original country . . . It was a kind of 'reporting to the church', just as Paul and his companions would do when they returned to the sending church of Antioch. So I told them, in an unvarnished account, what had happened. I imagined they would rise and express their joy, perhaps in words, perhaps in praise, and even in spontaneous singing such as I had heard in those wonderful days.

The response was far from that:

> To be honest I do not know to this day what was in their hearts. I
> realised as the report proceeded that some eyes were puzzled,
> others suspicious, and some coldly indifferent. Some looked
> shocked, some held disbelief, and some were angry. The atmos-
> phere was cold. Finally I knew the despair of someone who has glad
> news which is not seen that way, but rather as the ravings of an
> unsettled mind. I suppose I finally stopped before I had told all. It
> was pointless in continuing.
>
> After the report there were a few other items of business and
> somehow my report was lost in it all. Folks chatted a trifle and
> gradually the group melted away. No one talked to me about what I
> had said. Things had returned to normal. The revival was as though
> it had never been.[14]

Geoffrey was actively discouraged from pressing it further:

> In the days that followed, the message was conveyed to me that I
> had better not dwell too much on the events in which I had been
> involved. It would be more helpful if I would use the gifts of
> teaching and preaching as I had used them in past days. This was
> what audiences expected of me. Otherwise, my friends would feel
> that I had let them down.
>
> One night we were invited to dinner by one of the leaders, and the
> meal was indeed very tasty. That man of wisdom talked to me in a
> gentle way. He admitted that there could have been a lot which was
> significant in the revival itself, but pointed out that our culture was so
> different, and our lifestyle of another kind. What he conveyed to me
> was that I must not subject people *here* to the events that had
> happened *there*. We left that home with a cold feeling in our hearts.[15]

Geoffrey later could see some of the reasons for this. There was
the tradition, that he himself had been brought up in, 'that such
gifts had been for the initial launching of the church but had
passed away as the need for them also ceased'.[16] Apart from that,
things had changed since 1957. These were now the swinging
sixties:

> New movements were beginning to appear in many churches.
> Different views of marriage, divorce, social living and morality had

emerged from 'the new theology' and the 'new morality'. The world had become a 'swinging' society and this had greatly affected the church. Television had caused evening church services to dwindle in numbers and dedication. The sincerity of leaders was being put to rigorous tests. Life was changing everywhere. The old guard was bewildered for the most part.[17]

For them, Geoffrey 'represented just another movement which was confronting the traditional faith and its practice. In fact this was not the case; but it seemed to be.'[18]

Geoffrey, as 'a man who had always been sensitive . . . over-reacted to the non-acceptance of his friends, as also the opposition of his enemies':[19]

> I was in a horrible state of darkness. Had I been wrong? Were all the happenings explainable on psychical and social grounds? Were they the sudden upthrusting of generations of emotional need, and other elements which are beyond our Western understanding? These, and many similar thoughts would go through my mind, torturing me. Why should I think these matters right when my closest friends looked upon them as unreal and unscriptural? Why would these friends withdraw from me, when once we had such friendship and such theological and spiritual affinity?[20]

Geoffrey longed to be able to get back with people to where he had been before:

> Now I was in a lonely situation, and at times my thinking was bewildered. I must be wrong. If only I would return to my former humility things would change. Friends would forgive the temporary aberrations. Life would resume its normal patterns again.[21]

'One thing kept me from returning to what they chose to call sanity':

> It was the brilliant memory of a change in my life, my wife's life and the life of the children who had been with us. I could remember the tremendous joy of those who had been released from their former manner of living. Some who had had little peace because of demon possession, others who had been healed, and many who had

discovered a lasting joy—all of these gave the 'No!' to those who would not accept my report and my message.[22]

In addition there was the response of ordinary people to Geoffrey's deputation ministry with CMS, which lasted until January 1967.[23] John Dunn drove Geoffrey to most of these meetings and recorded them on reel-to-reel tape: 'every one of those meetings were occasions when Geoffrey would simply just open up the Scriptures and preach'. Rather than just talking about CMS as such, 'he was there to preach, to proclaim, to teach, and so on':[24]

> Churches were filled; the lives of many changed. I had letters, 'phone calls, and visits from those who had caught a new dimension not hitherto seen or felt by them. These things encouraged me.[25]

A more widespread ministry was opening up: 'Then different people started to ask him to take teaching missions[26] . . . he then started coming to our Saturday evening cottage meetings in Thornleigh and Pennant Hills'. John Dunn cannot remember Geoffrey 'talking publicly about what happened in Pakistan'. But 'it was in the car that he started to tell me what had been happening in Pakistan . . . here was a man telling me that all that stuff in Acts is all still true—it all still happens! . . . It's all just as valid today as it ever was . . . all these stories that Geoff was telling me in the car were so life-changing that all I wanted was to be in that, and now to be moving forward in that way.'[27]

Even though he did not speak publicly much about the revival in Pakistan, Geoffrey began to be 'labelled as a Pente[costal] on the basis of what was now filtering through'. As a result, 'he was basically locked out of having a parish here in Sydney'. Before he left, there was a token offer of a minimum amount of parish work, to free him for wider ministry, but he did not accept it:[28]

> When it was time to go, it was mainly in silence that he was farewelled, he and his wife and children. The lasting impression was of the blandness of old friends, the things they did not say, the apparent relief on faces at the departure.[29]

Geoffrey admits that he did not respond well to this. He likens his reaction to setting himself apart from the world on top of a pole, like Simon Stylites of old,[30] except that in his own case it was 'a cunning platform for instant retreat'[31] from unacknowledged 'inner hurts':

> The hurt and the wounding I had received was driven more deeply down, covered over with the busyness of life and the passage of the years . . . Of course I never lived on a literal pole, but the pole was no less a reality . . . I realise now that in the midst of my business of serving I had kept my distance from people, even the people who have loved me most. I had reared a pole in my mind, and had constructed a platform on it. It was—so to speak—my ivory castle. At any second I could be withdrawn into it, and at the same time retain my identity as a spectator. I believed my special world was the universe of theology and my participation a ministry of service. These two things protected me against new hurts and dangerous involvements.[32]

Even though Geoffrey knew that 'for a genuine believer, all hurts and wounds are redundant', and that 'one need not keep or cultivate such hurts, but see them borne in Christ's immense and personal suffering on the Cross',[33] for him the hurts were deep enough to remain hidden. It would be some years before he could acknowledge them fully and climb down from the pole.

THE CLASH OF THE KINGDOMS

Throughout his ministry, Geoffrey was no stranger to opposition, which 'all too often sprang from nothing more than hearsay',[34] and to the polarisation that comes with the proclaiming of the gospel. Part of that was because, as 'a renewer of the truth as it had always been', he never settled for 'the stereotypes of belief and worship' that for many were 'established and therefore good'.[35] Geoffrey was cheered when he heard by accident that someone whom he held in high regard had said of him:

'Don't worry about him. He will never be a heretic; his theology is too good for that. It is just that he is always on the frontier of things. He is always looking to see what God is doing, and to hear what He is saying. That's why he'll always be misunderstood.' That remark—overheard by chance—often comforted him in times when he was fiercely opposed.[36]

Geoffrey was also orthodox enough to know that in all these things 'our struggle is not against enemies of blood and flesh, but against the rulers, against the authorities, against the cosmic powers of this present darkness, against the spiritual forces of evil in the heavenly places', and that forgiveness must come 'so that we may not be outwitted by Satan; for we are not ignorant of his designs'.[37] Geoffrey was surprised to find standard missiology texts that had little or no mention of the devil in the index,[38] and he wrote authoritatively on the subject.[39]

His teaching is, as always, simply a setting-forth of what the Scriptures say. Once, in Pakistan, Geoffrey announced to the students that the next day he would tell them about the demons. The students inwardly scoffed: 'What can this Westerner know about the demons? *We* know about the demons!' The next day Geoffrey simply set forth everything the Bible says about Satan and the evil powers. The students were amazed: '*This man knows about the demons!* Not only so, but he knows how to be free of them.'[40]

SATAN AND EVIL

Geoffrey is careful not to put evil on the same level of reality as God and His goodness:

> The rebellion of supernatural powers against God is described in the Scriptures, as also is the rebellion of man against God . . . since evil did not exist in creation prior to these acts of rebellion, then evil cannot be said to have an ontological origin. It had an *apparent* origin, but not an *essential* one . . . We must conclude, then, that a word such as origin will be used in regard to evil, but not *properly* so.[41]

Geoffrey is concerned not to accredit to evil a reality that does not belong to it:

> What we mean is that sin has no ontological reality, but that it is 'a reality' in that we recognize it as a force and power ... we can biblically argue that in 'the regeneration of the world' there will be a heaven and earth in which no evil will exist. This being the case we can argue eschatologically that sin and evil have never had ontological reality. They have always been perversions of reality but never true expressions of it ... Indeed, we must always see [evil] as an attack on reality, i.e. the essential goodness of God as expressed in His true creation. This reality is often known as 'the truth'.[42]

Geoffrey shows how Satan, a 'once glorious creature', driven by irrational pride, hatred, anger and ambition, set himself an unachievable goal:

> ... his goal is to equal or supersede God. To do this he must gain control of supernatural beings, and capture mankind. Impossible as this task appears to be by the very nature of the case, he nevertheless persists. If we fail to see this, and remain 'ignorant of his designs' (II Cor. 2:11) then we may perish with him, or at least sustain great damage.[43]

Having no independent reality of his own, all Satan can do is work on what is given in God's good creation, by attacking it and attempting to usurp and subvert it to his own unjustified ends:

> Satan must virtually use for his purposes that which God structured to be used for His—i.e., certain powers which we call supernatural, certain powers which we call natural, and angelic and human powers. He must be a father (John 8:44, I John 3:10f) and have a family (Ephesians 2:2-3, John 8:44, I John 3:10f). He must have an incarnate son (II Thessalonians 2:3), and be worshipped (Revelation 13:4, II Thessalonians 2:3-4) and men must be sealed (Revelation 13:17f, cf. Ephesians 1:13, 4:30). He must have a spirit who is equivalent to the Spirit (Revelation 16:13) and prophecy—because it is the dynamic of the true faith—must be headed up by a special prophet (Revelation 16:13, 19:20). As God energises His children

(Philippians 2:12–13) so must Satan energise his (Ephesians 2:2–3). As God has His system—the Kingdom of God—so Satan must have his. The true family (the Church) and the true city are opposed by the evil Babylon, the worldly people who oppose God, and the city which is unholy.[44]

This is the 'key to all Satanic operation':

> It is the key to understanding the patterns of evil which infest the created world, and it takes us away from a dissociated under-standing of what Satan is about. It is no wonder then that Satan is able to—and must—transform himself into an angel of light, and his servants into seeming to be the very apostles of Christ, see II Corinthians 11:12–15. Nor is persecution to be wondered at since Satan must ever be (a) destroying what God is building up, and (b) seeking to build up for himself what he has sought to destroy of God's plan. As we say, this understanding is the key to the whole purposes and operations of evil and we must steadily see these things in this way.[45]

In these ways, Satan has gained power over the human race:

> John said, 'The whole world lies in the evil one'. Satan is both the prince and god of his world. Jesus did not deny that Satan had authority over the world's kingdoms. We are told clearly that man is in the actual power of Satan. That he does not think he is, is a testimony to the shrewdness and deceit of Satan.[46]

How does Satan gain and maintain this control?

> The clue to his power comes in Hebrews 2:11–15. We are told he has 'the might of death'. Men and women, through fear of death, are all their lifetime subject to his (the Devil's) bondage. How is this?
>
> I John 4:18 states that 'fear has to do with punishment'. In other words man fears death because of the judgement, that is because of his guilt. When Jesus said, 'Satan has nothing in me', He was suggesting that Satan certainly has something in sinful man, or, because man is guilty, has something on him. Remember that he is the accuser, and remember that accusation is very powerful and even bitter. Guilt and accusation have a most hurtful sting.[47]

Geoffrey concludes, 'The key to man's bondage is his guilt, and *guilt is the powerful weapon which all evil uses against man*':[48]

Guilt, then, is the power which Satan wields over man. Guilt, the fear of death, and the fear of judgement are all, really, the one.[49]

The machinations of this guilt are convoluted:

Guilt holds man in a state and sense of rejection by God, even rejection by others and himself, and makes him feel alienated, and so sets up the condition for further sin, failure and guilt. In this, man develops habits which are sinful and destructive, until sin becomes an invader, as it were, of his very biological realms. His thought-life becomes engrossed in sin and failure. Often he compensates by pleasure seeking, and is easily a candidate for investigating the occult. Increasingly he is gripped by the power of sin. Sin's power lies in its guilt, its penalty, its pollution, and its habits.[50]

Idolatry compounds the guilt, and the bondage:

Idolatry is the giving to anything or person that worship which is due to God as Creator and Father. Satan increases his grip on man when he is led into idolatry. The drive in man to worship and to relate deeply to an object [of] worship makes him a prey to idolatry. It may be worship of a person, a system, or a thing, but whatever it is it will be most powerful. God, if ever He were acceptable to the person, will now become more distasteful. He will have no attraction. In fact the guilty one will try to judge and criticise Him, and demean Him. He will not wish to retain the knowledge of God in his memory (Romans 1:21, 28; 3:11). The alternatives to knowing and obeying God are deliberate indifference, idolatry, the works of the flesh. As a theologian once said, 'Satan only tempts where there is innocence. Where there is guilt he has already gained control'.[51]

Geoffrey has no illusions as to the depths to which human evil can descend. Made in the image of God in a way that even angels are not, when that image is reversed we can fall further than the fallen angels:

The evil of man can—in a manner of speaking—even outclass the symptoms of derangement that a demon might induce.[52]

'It is so easy to see as demonic, that which in fact is part of the action of our mind and will.'[53]

THE KINGDOM OF GOD

Over all this, sovereign and inviolable, is the reign of God:

> Though fallen angels and men may seek to build another kingdom, or each of us his own kingdom, yet there is one kingdom, namely the reign and rule of God over all things. Not only is this the biblical reality, but if it is not the basic reality of history, then everything is a chaos.[54]

The fullness and victory of that kingdom is not at all lessened by the vast force of angels and humankind opposed to God:

> When it is remembered that angels and men are only creatures, and that their natural-given powers are from God and not, innately, from themselves—all rebellion to the contrary. In fact, that rebellion was incorporated in God's plan of grace. God is not caught unprepared. Nor is He as one caught, but yet able to create an expedient to meet this painful exigency. Far from it. He has His purpose in the evil which arises from the pride of Satan, angelic creatures, and man.
>
> What we are saying, in other terms is that God's Kingdom always prevails, even though we cannot see this fact through our natural eyes.[55]

How, then, do we come to know this?

> That men might know and experience the triumph of His Kingdom, God has sent His King, His Messiah-Son, the Mediator-Creator, the Eternal Word, Him whom we know as Jesus. Preceded by John the Baptist who announced the Kingdom, Jesus Himself also announced the Kingdom, and then proceeded both to demonstrate its powers, and fulfil its authority . . . what He accomplished on the Cross is being outworked in history, and is the means whereby the ultimate

defeat of evil is fully effected. By this we do not mean that He saved the Kingdom, or that He added something to it, but that He simply expressed its powers and was the agent of effecting its designs.[56]

If guilt is the one thing by which Satan holds humanity in subjection, then 'Something had to happen in the Cross to destroy the guilt of man, and set him free from his enemies':[57]

For one to destroy guilt would be the masterstroke which would release man, and take away from evil its power to dominate the universe. Somehow make a man pure and Satan's grip would fall away from him.[58]

'Against holy redeeming love no evil power can stand.'[59] Geoffrey takes his cue from Luke 22:53—'this is your hour, and the power of darkness':

Soon there would be the scaffold, the pain, and the depthless suffering.

We have been told that the whole of the things of evil knew in a trice that they had triumphed. Smarting from their recent bruisings, and enriched in their ancient cruelty they came from every corner. Out from under covers they crawled. They hurried like compulsive lemmings to the central place of meeting. They flew up high like some vast carrion crew. They swarmed over the earth like some mocking mites of a plague. The high and haughty ones came with lofty scorning, but the anger beneath burst out into sulphurous expression. Around the glorious head swirled and moved and flocked the unspeakable pollution, and the ribald mirth, and the obscene utterances and accusations. The stinging hatred, and excruciating perversion of the truth bore in upon him in the great suffering . . . After the mocking and the screaming hate, and the deafening ribaldry came the quietness. The glaring evil could not penetrate the iron wall of holiness about him and the deep pity of its love. They could draw no answer from him, no response equivalent to their hurting. It was not that he did not hear it, and that every accusation was not a barb, nor every vituperation an excruciating sting—it was! It was that his holy love opened its arms, as indeed those arms were pinned wide, and in them he embraced the filth and pollution, the suppurating evil of it, from men and fiends, from foes and friends, and took it to himself to both hug and destroy.

None could rescue it from him. It was as though a great maw opened within him and into it was poured the stain and the shame, the guilt and the degradation, the convulsions of sorrow, and it disappeared and was covered over.

As I have said, even the vilest thing fell silent, baffled and defeated by this unspeakable power, this simplicity of love, this tenderness of acceptance, this gentle glory of wounding . . . The whole enormous world of evil fell into that maw of love, and was taken to its exhaustion, its destruction, its extinction. Even while it pitted its blows against him, and battered at the inner citadel of his pure mind and conscience, he let the strong pure waves of his love flow across it and still it for ever.[60]

SPIRITUAL WARFARE

This sets the tone and pattern for the church's engagement in spiritual warfare:

> . . . Christ accomplishes his victories over evil through his people . . . The world—the evil age—uses all kinds of methods to win the battle, but the new age is one of righteousness, goodness, holiness, love and truth. It must—and does—confine itself to such weapons. It cannot use the stratagems, techniques or weapons that the kingdom of darkness employs. For this reason the believer has to live in the tension of the two ages. His own flesh cries out to use similar weapons—to defeat evil by political might, by surpassing the power techniques of worldliness, but he may not. He must use the seemingly mediocre weapons and armoury of love, joy, peace, faith, hope and humility. Even so, this tension is most beneficial. On the one hand it teaches him the effectiveness of these spiritual elements and on the other continues to train him, and by such discipline to bring him into moral and spiritual maturity—the true maturity of character . . . How frustrating and infuriating for the powers of darkness to see people of faith rest in the work of God, and *not* seek—in panic, fear and attempted self-justification—to defeat them by special acts of supernatural overcoming. Simply to rest in Christ in his victory, is angering to the creatures of God's wrath—the denizens of the kingdom of darkness.[61]

This is powerful in its effects:

> The fight is the fight of faith. When the Church has faith in the complete work of the Cross; when it dispels the guilt of men and women, and sets them free, then are the forces of darkness defeated. When it shows the love of God so that men are motivated to obey from love, then is evil defeated. When darkness and impurity become abhorrent to the people of God; then is darkness defeated. When love and humility clothe the members of Christ; then is Satan overcome. When the accusations of the enemy are countered by the justification of the Cross; then is evil rendered powerless.[62]

ADELAIDE BIBLE INSTITUTE

Geoffrey's disappointment at the cool reception he received in Sydney coincided with an opening for being considered as Principal of the Adelaide Bible Institute at Victor Harbor in South Australia. He went over there in late 1966 and was interviewed by the Council:

> He warned the institution of the new negative stance that had been taken against him by many, for this might militate against those who would engage him for teaching. To make sure that his prospective employers understood, he sent them a copy of the report he had sent back to his friends earlier, before he had returned from the revival area . . . the new group could read it and if they did not like it he would not come.
>
> They liked it. 'Sounds just like the days of the early church, as though it were pages from the book of the Acts,' they told him, and he and his family prepared to leave for their new ministry.[63]

Geoffrey wrote: 'At first we were not easily convinced that this was God's will, but it became very clear that the call to A.B.I. was just as truly a call as had been our former one to Pakistan':[64]

> Geoff's experience in Pakistan was splendid preparation for the kind of work which lay before him. He was forty-eight years old, and six years were to be spent in this field of service. There were ninety or so students when he came; there would be one hundred and

twenty when he left. The Institute cast its net over much wider waters than the students in residence. There was a fresh outreach in Correspondence Courses; there were Monday night classes in Adelaide with more than a hundred in attendance;[65] and there was an Easter Convention at Victor Harbor.[66]

There was also a Summer School to which many came to taste the life of a student for a week each January.

A 21-year-old student at ABI in 1968, Ian Pennicook later recalls:

> Lectures were interesting. Dominating the scene was Geoff Bingham, 'The Boss' . . . The revival in Pakistan in 1965 was evident in his ministry in Sydney in 1966 and was just as much in evidence in his lectures in 1968. It was not the style or even the formal content which conveyed it. The style was doctrinaire and authoritarian. Woe to a student who appeared to be less than attentive . . . The content was determined by the course outlines, generally, I presume, set by the MCD.[67] But the quality of the man and the immediacy he knew with God and the way that affected his use of the Scriptures was amazing . . . His theology was alive.[68]

Another student remembers, 'The week before Easter 1967 was foundational for me':

> At chapel each morning the Boss taught the total victory gained by Jesus on the cross.[69] I realised that just as I had accepted Jesus as Saviour, I could accept by faith that His defeat of all evil liberated me from guilt. His victory enabled me to be free to serve Him without fear of being unaccepted. The kingdom of God had broken into our fallen world. During the three years it was wonderful to me when 'full forgiveness' would be experienced by a student, and many would share their understanding of the cross.
>
> The Boss was not afraid to show emotion—none of us could miss his 'shout' of Christ's cry of desolation from the cross. He expressed his awe of the holiness of God by thundering 'Holy, holy, holy!'—we felt we were there with Isaiah! His telling of his experiences in Pakistan gave me the impression that part of his preaching style was an 'echo' of Pakistan. He was gripped by the holy love and majesty of the Father, and the wonder of grace—he couldn't understand

how we could sit there unmoved—his appeal, 'Well, come on!!' demanded a response from us, at least a nod of agreement!...

There was no doubt about his teaching on God's holiness, His being Father, man's rebellion, the Cross in time and eternity, Scripture as revelation, relating to each other in the Family, the Holy Spirit—these themes he developed in his teaching and preaching.

We marvelled at his knowledge of the Scriptures. He replied that we could become competent too—by reading it seriously for years. The Boss didn't believe in short cuts or quick fire methods. He assured us that substantial Kingdom growth only came by the Holy Spirit, with the proclamation of the Cross and resurrection.[70]

Of course through the students in subsequent years the ministry went far and wide:

We can certainly thank God for our three years at ABI—they were wonderfully formative and influential years, and God used you to enrich our lives considerably, and we have always been grateful for that.

As I look back, I think the most significant section of teaching for us at ABI was the series you gave on God, Man, Sin and Salvation. I still have the notes, and I am convinced that this has been the basic platform of our ministry over the years, both in our cross cultural years and then in our 'church' years.

You may know that we spent many years amongst the Warlpiri, Gurinji and Alyawarra people of Central Australia, and our task was to teach the basics of the faith, to foster indigenous leadership, and to help aboriginal Christians to be confident in their relationship with the Father.

'Father' is a term with a rich meaning in the Central Australian tribes, and they have no hesitation in addressing God as Father. The concept of God as Father was something that your teaching helped us to grasp, and that was significant for our ministry.[71]

One student who had gone to church all his life thought one year at college in 1971 would be enough to 'polish up':

How wrong I was. God had other plans. I didn't even understand what liberal theology was and the Lord had far more to teach us than could be done in twelve months. So as you know we stayed for three years, and it was only in the third year that it all started to fit together. Of course Geoff Bingham played a major part in that, but I guess it was really the total impact of all the lectures, study and assignments that sorted us out and put us on the right track. Geoff certainly encouraged us to stay on and study for the extra couple of years.

What I do know for sure is that we would have been certain missionary casualties if we had headed off overseas without completing the three years. So ABI played a major pivotal roll in our lives without which I'm sure we would not be still here with Wycliffe 34 years later.[72]

John Dunn, who visited ABI in 1969, gives us some of the inside story. For a time he stayed with the Bingham family in their home. He was housed 'downstairs on a camp bed in the back corner of the garage', and Geoffrey's study was a little room off the garage. John would see Geoffrey go in there every morning at 5.00 am and remain there until breakfast at 7.30 am.[73]

Geoffrey was keen 'to get the students out of the College doing things'. Hence the missions to, among other places, Wudinna in 1969,[74] and to Darwin in 1973, when 'twenty-six students travelled by bus from Victor Harbor'[75] for some 'volatile' meetings where there were 'a lot of people converted'.[76]

One of the students travelling to the Darwin mission, experiencing for the first time the vastness of Australia's wide open spaces and sensing Jesus' lordship even over all of that, was a young student from Japan, Kazuo Sekine.[77] One of his fellow students was Lionel, a former prisoner-of-war with Geoffrey in Changi, now living in Victor Harbor, whose 'hatred for the Japanese' had been 'melted away by the love of Christ' through Geoffrey's ministry.[78] Geoffrey remembers welcoming Kazuo:

He was the first Japanese student we had received into training, and it was a test both to Lionel and me as to whether our love for the Japanese was genuine . . . I felt no trace of hostility for him. In fact I was delighted to have him at the College.[79]

Geoffrey's acceptance and encouragement of Kazuo, especially in the early days when he was still learning English and was not able to gain high grades, gave Kazuo his 'first experience of grace', and of being highly valued as a human being, in contrast to the competitive expectations he had felt placed on him in Japan.[80] 'He was enormously moved by the doctrine of forgiveness . . . Kazuo himself is [now] recognized as a dynamic preacher and teacher.'[81]

Highly significant also for Geoffrey and others from these years was the death from cancer of another of the students, Vicki Randall:

> She had the most beautiful equipoise of will that I have ever seen. She was alive to God and dead to all else. She had a serenity and freedom that I have rarely seen in human beings . . . One night she had a beautiful vision of heaven and saw the Father in His love. It greatly affected her, but even so she did not wish to have her earthly life quickly terminated. The students who visited her—and generally at her request—had an impression indelibly printed upon them that I doubt they could ever erase, even if they had wanted to do so. She gave a pure witness to that wonderful relationship which a child of the Father can have with Him. Her visitors went away most thoughtfully, and in her dying days she had more effect than the most brilliant theologian could have upon his disciples.[82]

Vicki had 'an incredible effect' on Geoffrey that helped in his recovery from the rejection in Sydney:

> I began to sense again the freedom that had once been mine, and there was a loss of care, of fear of others, of the desire to prove myself in any way.[83]

At ABI Geoffrey also sought 'to introduce the students to the various . . . ways of communicating the gospel via media—through writing, tapes, videos, etc.'[84] A recording studio was built and fitted out on a shoestring budget. Lectures were recorded, duplicated, and sent to places across the state and around the world.[85] The ministry at ABI extended well beyond the college bounds:

I remember the football matches ... The Friday evening meal was a wonderful occasion to bring friends, many of whom were not Christians ... I remember the Friday night trial worship and sermon events and the crowds of friend[s] who attended them. Also the crits which followed the preaching and our changing of this particular pattern. The relaxed Friday nights were a joy ... I remember the Open Air meetings we had in the first year or two and which we relinquished appropriately. I remember the annual visitation of all homes in Victor Harbor and its good effects, the good Thursday Study Nights we had with folk from outside and how many of these came to Christ through our contacts. Quite marvellous was the introduction of an annual week's mission in various places, led by Staff members. I think it was a good part of our training.[86]

The shared fellowship is also warmly remembered:

A number of things stand out especially in my mind; the building of special friendships with students and Staff; the yearly intake of overseas students and our life with them; the Annual Graduation nights with the College choir; the morning chapels and their intimate teaching of the great eternities ... and the last six months of my Principalship when we gathered for voluntary prayer meetings at 5 a.m., sang from the new Scripture in Song music books of that era and shared personal testimonies ... I remember with a certain joy the body of truth we taught and held together, with the good outcome of results both in the College curriculum and the MCD external diplomas and degrees.[87]

Even so, 'I don't think Geoff ever really had the freedom to speak as I'm sure he maybe wished he could at ABI'. As well as 'various constraints that he was feeling ... he was locked in to the various academic courses that ABI was offering, and so all the lectures were geared to that. So the times when he was the freest were in the chapels and the workshops ... and the missions.'[88] Geoffrey explains, 'the tug of ministry in conventions, missions and world-wide requests made me realise I could not fulfil this wider ministry within the bounds of a College Campus':[89]

Geoff had gone to the World Congress on Evangelism at Berlin in 1966; and he went to the South-East Asia Congress at Singapore in 1968. Invitations for teaching and evangelistic missions with College students during vacations poured in from all over Australia, and in course of time he was to visit every State for such a mission, with the exception of Tasmania. He was also called upon to engage in a Convention ministry in various countries of South-East Asia.[90]

So the time came when Geoffrey and Laurel 'felt [that] they should launch out into yet another ministry of truth, and they were freed to do so'[91]—a story told in the next chapter.

DOWN FROM THE POLE

It was after this time that Geoffrey's formerly hidden hurts and anger came to the fore:

Then one night a revelation came to him which left him stunned.

He had awakened after midnight, and lay, unable to sleep. The old uneasiness had returned. He tried to reason the puzzling reversion to this state of mind, and in the midst of his thinking, the faces of many who had been his friends but who had rejected him rose up before him. With them were others who had made it clear that they regarded him as being a heretic and not a man of faith. Whilst he had rejected the accusations, he had always had to fight the hurtful things which had been said to him and spoken about him. He felt a warm anger rising up within him. With a sickening sense in his heart, he recognised that he was in a state of hatred, but hatred which he tried to tell himself was justified. He was feeling the bitterness of injustice. Had he—in those earlier days—taught untruth, or had lived immorally, he could have understood their opposition. He remembered the warnings he had been given—not to speak out. All the unwanted memories that he had once thought were gone, flooded him afresh. Almost in a panic he prayed, but his prayer was a protest.

'Lord,' he said, 'You know I have forgiven them all. How does it happen then that they are here again, as though I had never forgiven them?'

It seemed that the answer to him was, 'Quite so. You never did forgive them.'

He protested. 'Lord, you know I have forgiven them—many times.'

'Ah yes, many times,' was the reply, 'but once—had it been total—would have been enough. I have forgiven you, once for all, so you should have forgiven, once for all.'

This seemed so hard . . . 'If I forgave,' he asked, 'then why should I have to do it again?'

The answer was surprising, but its truth was clear. 'You forgave as a legalist forgives. The Gospel demands you forgive, so you forgave. It was easier for your conscience when you did so, but you see, you cannot forgive apart from love. I, your God, love and so forgive. You forgave, but never loved. Now you must love. Then you will truly forgive and it will be "*once* for all".'[92]

'As he lay there, the anger ebbed away. The hurt was quietly gone. A love for those who had neglected him came with ease':

> Freshly he understood Jesus' own cry at the Cross, 'Father, forgive them for *they know not what they do.*' He realised that Jesus had understood what had triggered his persecutors to kill him. He had understood their reasons and had not condemned them.[93]

Geoffrey came to terms with the fact that if they had not caught the ring of truth in what he had said, then they had not. He prayed:

> My friends and my enemies (so-called) I love and forgive you. My Father above, I ask Your forgiveness for retaining these hurts and angers over the years. They are my sins and I need Your forgiveness. All this time I should have loved. Indeed I was sure I did, but what has been hidden all these years has now been exposed. I am free from these attitudes as my friends and enemies are free from me.[94]

Truly, forgiveness comes 'so that we may not be outwitted by Satan'.[95] In the years that followed, Geoffrey was able wisely to comfort others 'with the comfort with which we ourselves are comforted by God':[96]

When I was with him in Adelaide, speaking one-to-one as we often did . . . we were talking about my own experience of life, and how I had been rejected . . . the hurts that I had experienced in life . . . and he suddenly said to me, 'Stuart, you don't have to feel this way'; and he gathered me in his arms and he hugged me. And what he said was that when Christ died on the cross, he died to take that pain away from you—he'd been there in your place; he'd taken all that upon himself—so there is no need for you to feel that way any longer. Now I didn't understand that mentally or intellectually. I understood it psychologically—it made a huge impact on me, I can tell you! As all the contacts with Geoff did. Every contact with Geoff was meaningful. A bit like Jesus, really—whenever Jesus had contact with anybody, it was always a meaningful contact. Jesus never just sort of passed the time with anybody. I don't think Geoff ever did either; it was always a significant act of time when I was with him. So there are those personal things that are very important to me as I remember him.[97]

[1] *Laurel's Story*, 99.

[2] *Laurel's Story*, 101.

[3] *Laurel's Story*, 100.

[4] *Laurel's Story*, 100, 105.

[5] *Laurel's Story*, 102.

[6] West Pakistan News, NZ CMS, August 1966, p. 5.

[7] Loane, *These Happy Warriors*, 91.

[8] John Thew, Federal Secretary of Church Missionary Society Australia and former missionary in Pakistan, in conversation with Martin Bleby, 29th October 2011.

[9] 'The Descent of Stephen Stylites', in 3 *Special Stories*, 41.

[10] 3 *Special Stories*, 47–48.

[11] Interview with John Dunn, recorded 9th September 2008.

[12] 3 *Special Stories*, 50.

[13] John Dunn, 2008.

[14] 3 *Special Stories*, 47–48.

[15] 3 *Special Stories*, 48.

[16] 3 *Special Stories*, 47. This teaching is associated particularly with B. B. Warfield, professor of theology at Princeton Seminary 1887–1921.

[17] 3 *Special Stories*, 50–51.

[18] 3 *Special Stories*, 51. This apparent marginalisation and disparagement of Geoffrey's ministry appears to be perpetuated in a history of the Anglican Diocese of Sydney: 'Bingham soon went to Pakistan as a missionary, taking revival with him and, although he remained an Anglican clergyman, upon his return he established New Creation Teaching Ministries in South Australia as a vehicle for his revivalist ministry' (Stephen Judd, Kenneth Cable, *Sydney Anglicans: A History of the Diocese*, Anglican Information Office, Sydney, 2000, 258). No mention is made here of his principalship of Adelaide Bible Institute.

[19] 3 *Special Stories*, 60.

[20] 3 *Special Stories*, 49.

[21] 3 *Special Stories*, 49.

[22] 3 *Special Stories*, 49.

[23] Loane, *These Happy Warriors*, 91.

[24] John Dunn, 2008.

[25] 3 *Special Stories*, 49.

[26] Ashbury, where Ray Wheeler was the rector, is one place that was mentioned, and there were others.

[27] John Dunn, 2008.

[28] John Dunn, 2008.

[29] 3 Special Stories, 50.

[30] Or Simeon Stylites, c. 390–459 AD, near Antioch in Syria, an influential Christian ascetic who lived on a platform at the top of a pillar for 39 years.

[31] 3 Special Stories, 59.

[32] 3 Special Stories, 58.

[33] 3 Special Stories, 58.

[34] Loane, These Happy Warriors, 89.

[35] 3 Special Stories, 40.

[36] 3 Special Stories, 40–41.

[37] Ephesians 6:12; 2 Corinthians 2:11.

[38] Martin Bleby, personal recollection.

[39] The Dominion of Darkness and the Victory of God, 1977; The Clash of the Kingdoms, 1989. Also a paper in connection with studies in the book of Daniel, 'The Battle of God and Satan—of the Nations—from Eden to the New Eden', 2004; as well as references in commentaries on the book of the Revelation: Revelation: A Commentary (undated); The Revelation of St John the Divine: Commentary and Essays on the Book of the Revelation, 1993.

[40] Geoffrey Bingham in conversation, personal recollection by Martin Bleby.

[41] The Clash of the Kingdoms, 15–16.

[42] The Clash of the Kingdoms, 16. Geoffrey devoted an entire book to the setting-forth of 'the truth': Truth the Golden Girdle, 1983.

[43] The Clash of the Kingdoms, 29–30.

[44] The Dominion of Darkness and the Victory of God, 29–30.

[45] The Dominion of Darkness and the Victory of God, 30.

[46] The Dominion of Darkness and the Victory of God, 32.

[47] The Dominion of Darkness and the Victory of God, 32–33.

[48] The Clash of the Kingdoms, 54.

[49] The Dominion of Darkness and the Victory of God, 33.

[50] The Dominion of Darkness and the Victory of God, 33–34.

[51] The Dominion of Darkness and the Victory of God, 34. See further, Dear Darling Idols: lords and gods piffling and appalling.

[52] The Clash of the Kingdoms, 77.

[53] The Dominion of Darkness and the Victory of God, 59.

[54] The Clash of the Kingdoms, 79–80.

55 *The Dominion of Darkness and the Victory of God*, 36–37.

56 *The Dominion of Darkness and the Victory of God*, 37.

57 *The Clash of the Kingdoms*, 126.

58 *The Dominion of Darkness and the Victory of God*, 41.

59 *The Clash of the Kingdoms*, 119.

60 *Bright Bird and Shining Sails*, 47–48.

61 *The Clash of the Kingdoms*, 189, 195, 246.

62 *The Dominion of Darkness and the Victory of God*, 51.

63 *3 Special Stories*, 50. See also John Dunn, 2008.

64 'The Principal's Page', A.B.I. Newsletter 1967 ('this first letter', written in Christchurch, New Zealand, whilst taking a Parish Mission at Bryndwr).

65 By 1970, 'Our A.B.I. Monday Night lecture class has rarely dropped below the 200 mark this year', A.B.I. Newsletter 1970. In 1999 Geoffrey recalled 'the Monday Night lectures in Adelaide which grew to over 300 per night', Mount Breckan Reunion Dinner, 1st May 1999, 'Reminiscenses to All Past Students and ABI Staff of My Years of Principalship'.

66 Loane, *These Happy Warriors*, 91.

67 Melbourne College of Divinity; see 'Geoffrey C. Bingham: A Short Biography, 1919–2003'.

68 'A Brief Reminiscence of ABI'.

69 Notes from the time indicate that it was again about the defeat of the 'enemies' through the removal of guilt.

70 John Letcher, 'Being a student at ABI 1967–69', in personal correspondence with Martin Bleby, 9 February 2011.

71 Jan and John Whitbourn, letter to Geoffrey Bingham, 2 May 2007.

72 Email to John Dunn from Len and Peg Whalley, 28 October 2008.

73 John Dunn, 2008.

74 See previous chapter.

75 Loane, *These Happy Warriors*, 92.

76 John Dunn, 2008.

77 Kazuo Sekine interview with John Dunn, 4 December 2008.

78 'Lionel', in *The Vandal*, 219.

79 'Lionel', in *The Vandal*, 218.

80 Kazuo Sekine, 2008.

81 'Lionel', in *The Vandal*, 218, 219.

82 *3 Special Stories*, 54. The full story is told in 'Vicki the Gentle Teacher' in the same volume.

[83] *3 Special Stories*, 54.

[84] John Dunn, 2008.

[85] Mount Breckan Reunion, 1999, John Dunn 2008.

[86] Mount Breckan Reunion, 1999.

[87] Mount Breckan Reunion, 1999.

[88] John Dunn, 2008.

[89] Mount Breckan Reunion, 1999.

[90] Loane, *These Happy Warriors*, 91–92.

[91] *3 Special Stories*, 55.

[92] *3 Special Stories*, 55–56.

[93] *3 Special Stories*, 56.

[94] *3 Special Stories*, 56–57.

[95] 2 Corinthians 2:11.

[96] 2 Corinthians 1:4.

[97] Dr Stuart Piggin, Senior Research Fellow in the Department of Modern History, Macquarie University, NSW, interview with John Dunn, 5 December 2008.

CHAPTER 12

THE *Quiet Revival* SPREADS

With Ian Pennicook

Martin Bleby,
Andrew Klynsmith,
Deane Meatheringham

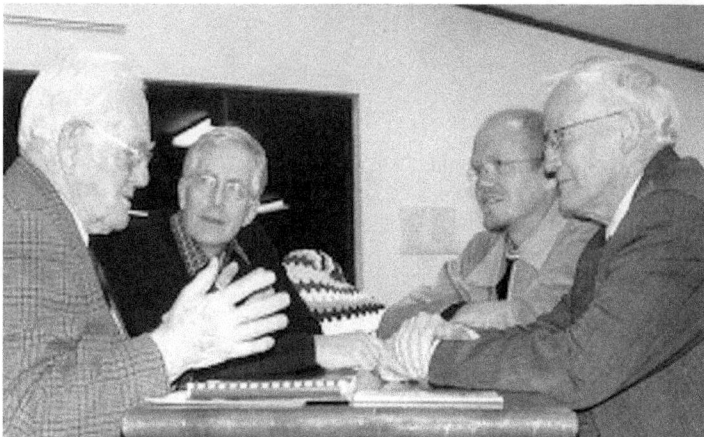

'AN UNMISTAKABLE VISION OF A WIDE COMMUNICATION OF THE GOSPEL'[1]

'I HAVE HAD few direct times of unmistakable special guidance. This was one of them.'[2]

The year was 1970 and Geoffrey Bingham as Principal of the Adelaide Bible Institute was on 'a strategic two months visit to South-East Asia':[3]

> I was in the World Vision building in Malang, Indonesia. There I met a retired New Zealander and his wife who were busy trying to meet the demands for recorded cassettes and tapes to fill the need in villages, churches and even Christian radio stations, for recorded messages and music. It was a very moving event . . . I believed I was given a vision of a wide communication of the Gospel in Australia. I was sure I had to go back to the Bible College where I was Principal and set up a Studio for teaching students to record, use radio and television, and also—through the same studio—send out a flow of evangelistic and teaching materials to the church in Australia and the lands beyond.[4]

'The idea of revival burned in my heart and I wondered how it could happen in a Bible Institute, longing that it should.'[5] Geoffrey set about trying to convince the ABI Council of the need for 'a thorough change'.[6]

A MOVEMENT

Geoffrey set out for the Council his vision of what a Bible Institute should be. First it was:

(i) <u>Residential training</u> of men and women for the mission field, and home, as pastors, teachers, evangelists, workers, effective lay persons. The training is primarily in the Scriptures, but with that which assists them to communicate what they know.[7]

Geoffrey was greatly concerned that training be actional and not just propositional. He noted criticism of the Melbourne College of Divinity course as 'too academic'. He referred to 'an upgraded internal Biblical course, which itself leaves much to be desired', and tabulated the students' increasing preference for this over the M.C.D. course. Geoffrey earlier had made 'recommendations for a "pre-Institute Institute" where teaching is for a short term, in relaxed (non-academic) atmosphere' and cited 'L'Abri' as an example of this on another level. Geoffrey observed that 'traditional patterns are being isolated by the growth of movements which are outside the church', and urged Council members to read *Jesus Kids* by R. C. Palms, *That New-Time Religion* by E. Jorstad, and *The Jesus Revolution* by Billy Graham:

> These movements are touching us now. Students entering, having been in actional participation in evangelism, are stunned by the immediate change to the <u>propositional</u> training, as against the former actional participation ... Propositional training tends to create propositional teachers, pastors etc. where, in fact, more involvement in action, will produce actional people.[8]

Geoffrey saw this as placing a requirement on staff:

> Hence lecturers will have to lead in more involvement. In fact students learn more by seeing their lecturers in action. For this reason practical opportunities will have to be sought for evangelistic and pastoral situations. Such will have to relate to actual churches, and planned evangelistic occasions. Nor must this be considered a week-end action. The use of missions and ventures into unevangelised areas will have to be considered. There will have to be involvement in work amongst alcoholics, drug addicts, drop-outs as well as in the conventional church situations. Work in remand homes and the like will not be an optional extra.

Geoffrey added for the benefit of Council members, 'Incidentally this will enhance the "image" of the College'.[9]

Just as important to Geoffrey was the need 'to take the College to the people':[10]

> (ii) <u>Training for those outside the Institute</u>. This may be done by 'Theological Training by Extension', by the media of correspondence, tapes, literature, and personal extension ministry in missions, schools and team ministries. It should also include bringing on to the ABI premises for short periods of teaching, those who are not internal students for Summer Schools, Conventions, and other situations.[11]

For this, 'Present facilities should be maintained and extended':

> . . . for <u>Monday Night Lectures</u>, always shaping the courses to be practical, and relevant to contemporary issues and problems; whilst retaining Biblical exposition. <u>Correspondence Courses</u>. This form of training should be greatly extended by the provision of a facility . . . It should extend its variety of courses, enlist a team of assistants, and be promoted. Its courses should include practical series. <u>Tape Ministry</u> should now receive its rightful place alongside the <u>paper ministry</u> of the Corres. Courses. The studio should introduce video-taping with a view to rapid production of video-cassettes before they are current in Australia. Production of Bible Studies for Groups should be extended. <u>Easter Convention</u> should be over-hauled with a view to a training programme (in evangelism, house groups etc) being incorporated, and a stronger Youth Programme. <u>Summer Schools</u> to continue, but be re-examined as to the practicality of the subjects. <u>Winter Schools</u> to be considered but <u>regionally</u>. <u>Missions</u> to be sought in various areas of the State. <u>Production of literature</u> to be introduced, covering all subjects of interest, being abstracted from the courses already prepared. An offset press is required for Corres. Courses, literature and promotional materials.[12]

Geoffrey was prepared to be at the forefront of embracing new technologies of communication:

> Related to all this is the <u>media</u> of communication. Most people live in a moving vitalistic world of radio, T.V., films, racily written

easily-read papers, journals etc. Most impressions come to people through these media. The teaching of vital Biblical truth must come through such media; hence the need of a developed communication centre with a view to participation in the media.[13]

In this he was mindful of *The Story of the Moody Bible Institute* by G. A. Getz—'a "must" for Council members':

> Instituted in 1889 its Corres. Courses commenced in 1901. Present annual enrolment is 40,000. 1926 opened their radio station. Moody Press etc. 1941. Institute of Science 1945 ('Fact and Faith Films'). Miss. Tech. Course 1949. Christian Booksellers' Assoc. 1950. Evangelical Literature Overseas 1963.

This is thinking big.

In this Geoffrey expected much of the Council of the Adelaide Bible Institute. Geoffrey proposed that he become 'President' of ABI with the 'present function of Principal' but 'able to be more mobile' as a kind of 'Extension Officer',[14] who 'should represent the College to the public and churches in his capacity of teaching and preaching'. He should also 'examine current trends in training, and the movements with the churches and the community with a view to adaptation and curriculum and training changes'. The day-to-day administration would be vested in a newly appointed Principal and a Registrar. The present Council was 'to be dissolved to form an Advisory Board (without executive power)', including 'men and women of missionary societies and similar bodies' and 'ministers of various denominations' to meet three times a year. The new Council of 'no more than eight men' who 'understand and support these aims' would meet monthly and work with the new Principal:[15]

> In this Council should not only be with him in intention, but action, They should regard themselves as a spiritual team working with him, and for this reason should take every opportunity to be in the events which he leads, i.e. conventions, Summer Schools, Missions and similar events. More particularly they should seek to have time with him in actual prayer, fellowship and personal sharing. They should seek to keep in contact with all that relates to a Bible

College, such as contemporary movements, missionary patterns and action, world evangelism and the like. This will mean that ABI has first priority in service and participation for Council members, and will not be just another Christian activity.

'The point of all these observations', Geoffrey concluded most significantly, 'is that ABI should be regarded as a movement rather than as a static academic training centre'.[16]

Whether or not this was workable, and whether or not Geoffrey presented it well, the Council did not accept the proposal. 'Had they agreed with this then all the NCTM ministry would today be within BCSA.'[17] Geoffrey later wrote of his return from the South East Asian trip:

When I returned to the College I found it difficult to communicate this vision. At first I felt the College Council did not understand, although some members really grasped the matter clearly. However —whilst we built the studio and set up a Christian Communications Course—the graft did not fully take.

Geoffrey later admitted, 'It was not to be at the College but in another ministry outside it':

Today when I am lecturing at the same College—which now, incidentally, has no studio—I can smile, knowing that what was in His mind was the New Creation Team and the ministry it could give which no college could hope to contain within its structure.[18]

'GOD'S WILL FOR US IN 1973'

'The Council had not agreed to my being an Extension Officer and I felt, because of many things related to ministry among people outside the campus, that I should resign':

In October 1972 I resigned from ABI, my resignation being effective from the 31st May 1973. My relationships with the Council were warm, ABI was really at a peak in its ministry, and we were warmly farewelled. I am sure the Council appreciated what burned in my heart but naturally they wished to carry on the Bible Institute after the well-known pattern it had always had.

'Hearing of my resignation some pastors and lay folk came to talk to me, and to pray for me. Some twenty of these met with Laurel and me for a weekend in January following our ABI Summer School.'[19] Geoffrey had been involved with some of them in 'Faith Advance', a Methodist-based 'ministry of evangelism and teaching in the churches'.[20] One who was there wrote an account of what happened:[21]

> At the beginning of January Malcolm Wilson wrote a letter to a number of interested people suggesting a mini-Conference at Victor Harbor where, around God's Word and prayer we might share together what we believe to be God's will for us in 1973.
> Sixteen persons comprising 5 ladies and 11 men (seven of whom were ministers) shared a memorable two and half days in the home of the Rev. and Mrs. Geoff Bingham.
> There was no prepared agenda nor any concrete objective to set before the group so we began by going round the company and asking each one to share what they believe God was saying to him/her through their recent experiences.

'Before we were a third of the way round the company it was evident beyond any reasonable doubt that our very varied experiences and gifts were a clear indication from God that He wanted us involved in some kind of team activity.'

Geoffrey's contribution was in teaching from the Scriptures:

> Our conversation was interlaced with Biblical expositions and we were equally convinced that the Holy Spirit was speaking to us through Geoff Bingham as Scripture was related to action.

What came through was Geoffrey's concern that teaching and living be 'actional' and not just propositional:

> Arising from this we recognised that there were certain lines of action which God was obviously blessing today as compared with other church-related activities. Amongst these we listed Home

Fellowship Groups, Adult Camps for training in Leadership and Witnessing, Lay Evangelism, teaching Missions, Literature, and the Tape Ministry.

In the group we had persons with extensive experience in one, or more, of these ministries. We were under the conviction that God was pointing us to some kind of corporate activity in these matters.[22]

Geoffrey later wrote: 'At the time Laurel and I supported the idea but didn't see ourselves as being other than minor contributors to such a ministry. I felt this strong desire to preach the holiness of God, grace, love and revival, to people where they were.'[23] Meanwhile some definite plans were shaped up:

It was difficult for us to see such a team ministry working apart from some centre from which to operate. However, on the matter of property and location we received no clear guidance, except that we were reasonably convinced it ought to be within about 10 miles of Adelaide . . .

Our concept, at the moment, is of a permanent (though fluid) core of full time men and women, lay and ministerial, living in such a Centre and being mainly responsible for the activities . . . Probably about eight persons who, for one year or more, would voluntarily undertake some Franciscan vow of poverty.[24]

There would be 'a wider group of "resource" people on whom to draw for part-time leadership activities', and then 'a much wider group of "friends of the Centre" who would support with their prayers, assist in making the Centre known, and seek God's guidance in the matter of financial involvement'. It was hoped that the Centre could be 'independent of any particular denomination yet open to all persons from any church to receive practical training'[25]—'we should not be tied up to any current trends in theology, strategies, structures (or experiences) but should be sympathetic to all movements or endeavours which are manifestly extending Christ's kingdom', while remaining 'open to the leading of the Spirit to pioneer new ways if He should indicate them'.[26] There was a further hope:

... that the work of the Centre might eventually so commend itself to the various established Churches that they will see the practical value of directing their ministers-in-training to the Centre for a period of six months, or a year, that they might work alongside experienced people and gain practical skills for which neither College nor University can presently cater.[27]

Geoffrey later wrote: 'New Creation Teaching Ministry virtually began with that meeting at ABI in January 1973, but it did not formulate itself until a little later'.[28] Here is how he saw this meeting:

... we were given a clear vision of a teaching centre equipped to produce teaching materials such as books, study leaflets, and audio and video cassettes. It was to be a centre with a library, a studio and production facilities, and motel-type chalets in which folk who desired to write, study and rest could have a temporary retreat opportunity. The centre was to be related to the life and ministry of churches and in no way to supersede them or draw money and personnel from them. Also it was to continue the kind of ministry given previously by Faith Advance.

He added: 'Whilst in some way it was to be related to my ministry, yet this was not the focal idea of the weekend'.[29]

Geoffrey's time at the Adelaide Bible Institute concluded after the mission to Darwin in May 1973:[30]

Immediately on leaving the Bible College I was occupied in fulfilling requested ministry in New Zealand, the U.S.A., Guatemala, Mexico and Panama. On returning I began more teaching missions in different states of Australia, and New Guinea.[31]

During this time a number of pastors, teachers, church leaders and others continued to meet, but for some months 'the practical direction was not wholly clear'.[32] Some were moving towards forming what was to have been called the 'Cherith Community', and by the end of the year had determined to sell their homes and buy a place for this community at Ironbank in the Adelaide Hills. Geoffrey and Laurel said they did not want to be a part of that; another of those involved was called away to a different ministry, and the sudden death at the end of the year of one of the major participants brought that scheme to an end.[33]

NEW CREATION TEACHING MINISTRY

'I resigned from the Principalship, and in May 1973 our family moved to Mount Compass, where we occupied a farmhouse provided for us by Peter Leane. We lived there for two and a half years whilst our daughters finished their high school courses.'[34] Peter Leane, one of the congregation at the local Church of Christ, had recently been able to get a lease on the farm next door:

> He said we could have the house rent free for this year and as it was we never did pay any. It was so neglected they were going to demolish it. He and his wife painted the rooms that had deep red or purple ceilings and lots of grease on the walls and around the light switches and repaired it where it was too bad while we scrubbed and cleaned it up.[35]

'During this time we had rigged up a studio (of sorts) and were recording messages for cassettes. The equipment was very rudimentary.'[36] Mattresses up against the sleep-out wall were not sufficient to keep out sounds of the many birds in the pine trees outside from impinging on the recordings that Geoffrey was making and copying there.[37] 'In addition we began writing some Christian Teaching Series booklets.[38] Also I was writing the first full book, *I Love the Father*.'[39] A slightly different group began to gather:

> About that time a number of pastors—some of whom were previous students of mine—began preparing to run training courses for young people. I became involved with them, with the leaders of the Jesus People movement, and others. South Australia at that time was in a spiritual ferment, and they were days of expectancy. Towards the end of 1973 a group of four couples met at Mount Compass, and the first meeting of New Creation Publications met on January 10th 1974 to draw up a constitution and become an

incorporated body. The name 'New Creation' came out of a meeting of pastors which had been held previously.[40]

'The objective of the group was to provide simple, sound, biblically based teaching to those who needed it . . . on a non-profit basis . . . The teaching of the group should not be partisan to any particular creed, but to be non-controversial and constructive.'[41] Thus, 'The work of New Creation Teaching Ministry began with a second-hand duplicator in a borrowed farmhouse near Mount Compass, South Australia':[42]

> The new Council met monthly. Meetings with pastors and leaders took place on various occasions . . . a group of folk who wished to share in teaching missions formed a pool of available leaders and helpers, and missions were conducted in many places and States. I continued to have certain overseas ministry. Books began to be printed and equipment was purchased to produce better materials. However, the equipment was still quite primitive; for example, a duplicator was made up of three others! We copied cassettes on five players linked up to one tape-deck, taking an hour to copy five recordings! And so on.
>
> These were days of great anticipation. A stream of people needing help and giving help made the trip to Mount Compass.[43]

The work had its drawbacks:

> Sadly enough incorrect rumours—which always seem to bedevil any work of God—became rife. Some thought I had been ejected from A.B.I., some that we were seeking to found a new Bible College, and the usual terms of 'Pentecostal', 'Arminian', 'Calvinistic', and the like were regularly heard. Just a few detected some new heresy! One has had to weather such storms over many years, and we weathered, even if—at times—a little sadly.[44]

It also had its rewards:

> The small Council that we had, and the groups of pastors, leaders and teachers, all combined to make a rich supportive ministry. The high expectation of the impact that teaching could make all helped when we conducted our various missions, had ministry in

universities and Colleges of Advanced Education, opportunity in students' groups, and churches of many different denominations.[45]

REMARKABLE PROVISION

'It was remarkable how the finance for the work came in, I not being on a salary and the work being committed to nil promotion and nil solicitation of help.'[46] One particular instance of this was soon to happen:

> We had left A.B.I. with only our monthly salary and a very modest superannuation cheque in hand, plus a motor vehicle and a small amount of furniture. We had nothing else, and no foreseeable income. The heavenly Father met our needs in His quiet way.[47]

Geoffrey and Laurel knew that when their daughters had all completed their Matriculation they would need to have a home for them in Adelaide. 'By the end of 1974 and the beginning of '75 our family situation had suddenly changed':

> One of our daughters—Ruth—was killed in a car accident in Melbourne (where she had been studying), and two others—Carol and Elizabeth—had married.[48] Our last daughter—Mary-Grace— would finish her Matriculation course in November of 1975.[49]

'Early in the year Laurel and I talked about coming to Adelaide, and the place Coromandel Valley was in her mind':

> One day I received a phone call from Western Australia and talked to a man whom we had known years before, and in fact whose wedding I had conducted. He had been given some of my cassettes by a former A.B.I. student and he immediately got in touch with us —this after some 25 years! He was passing through Adelaide shortly afterwards and volunteered to help us in the matter of a home. He and his wife came a little later to a Mission I conducted with the Church of Christ at Victor Harbor, and both said they had been enriched by it.
>
> The outcome of our meeting after so many years was that this couple helped us to obtain a home with six acres of wooded country in Coromandel East.[50]

'The man was interested in the work, but said the place was to be a surety for our old age.' It passed to Geoffrey and Laurel when he died.[51] A two-storey house on the property provided for the family. Laurel, with housework in mind, later wrote, 'I hated the idea of a two storey place at any price, but Geoff was in love at first sight. Afterwards he told me he always wanted a big home like that.'[52] A further provision from Geoffrey's family helped the work to proceed at the new site:

> My mother died at that time and a legacy gift enabled us to add a room onto the double garage. The garage itself we turned into a Recording Studio for meetings. The new room was for everything; office work, duplication of notes, accounts, and a place to pray and fellowship.[53]

The studio later housed the offset presses and became the print room, and the other became the staff room.

John and Beryl Skewes bought the five-acre block next door when they joined the team in 1977. On it they built their own home, and a Resource Centre housing 'below, a workroom for duplicating cassettes and notes and sending out the mail orders' and a top section which originally housed the library and was used for larger meetings, but was later 'utilised to the full, with offices and a Computer Room which has a bank of electronic machines for producing books, study notes and other materials'.[54] By 1983:

> We decided the Studio was too small for our monthly Saturday Morning 'Living Faith Studies', and planned to build an auditorium on the property. It was thrilling to build this great building without solicitation for finance. It all happened in wonderful ways, so many folk contributing labour and other help . . . We soon realised the Auditorium was not large enough and in a few months we extended it . . . Because we needed more and more of the Resource Centre space, in 1991 we opened a beautiful new building for the Library.[55]

Thus came about what Geoffrey could later describe as 'a Centre of eleven acres with good functional buildings which cater for teaching classes, library work, production of books (with typesetters, computers, scanners, printers and printing press), teaching materials, audio, music and video cassettes, correspondence course (with personal tutors), training courses, counselling—and the like'.[56] All of this came by the timely provision of God, through the unsolicited gifts of His people. The vision, rooted in Geoffrey's experiences of the Pakistan and Adelaide Bible Institutes and elsewhere, driven by his 'strong desire to preach the holiness of God, grace, love and revival, to people where they were', and formulated at the meeting in January 1973, had come to fruition:

> At this point [1996] I can say that all which constitutes the vision we were given as a group that January has been fulfilled, with one exception, by what we now know as NCTM and NCPI. The one exception is that we [do not] have motel-type chalets on the property for folk to rest, meditate and, if wishing to do so, use the teaching and study facilities of the Centre. We are not allowed by Government and Local Council regulations to have more than one house on the property, so this yet awaits fulfilment, even though this ministry has been somewhat fulfilled as folk have made use of the Skewes's flat.[57]

THE WIDENING WORK

The work began to have a significant impact in Adelaide and beyond. 'This was a time of great spiritual ferment—charismatic and otherwise':[58]

> During 1975 the group of pastors and teachers conducted a memorable series of training–teaching sessions called 'Friday Night Course'. This was held at the Epworth Methodist Church in Young Street, Parkside. It was thrilling to see over 300 people (75% of them young) gather for these meetings. After some worship and sharing a 50-minute in-depth study would be given by me, and then we would break into groups led by the large team of pastors and teachers. We had teaching materials for them and for the others, and 50 to 60 minutes was spent in trying to apply the study to the local church situation and to our lives. The impact of this

series on 'The Unity of All Things', 'The People of God', 'The Kingdom of God', and 'Christian Basics' cannot be assessed, but we have had reverberations from them over the years following. Some of the meeting leaders said it was this course which 'fixed' their ministries, gave them understanding, and set strong direction for the future.[59]

'It seemed to me that all were enthusiastic and there was a groundswell in those receiving the word of the Cross and the message of "great grace".'[60]

Comprehensive systematic teaching followed. 'In December 1975 we began Masters Classes (later called *Living Faith Studies*) in our new Studio.'[61] Fifty of these studies were given and recorded over five years, amounting to 1,125 typed A4 pages, ranging widely over such diverse themes as 'The Nature and Meaning of Love', 'Prophecy: Its Meaning, Scope and Significance', 'The Christian Doctrine of the Atonement', 'Praise and Music in the Scriptures', 'The Doctrine of the Last Things (Eschatology)', and 'The Glory of God, Man and Creation':

> The materials contained in these studies have been ferreted out from the Scriptures with the usual aids of concordance, Bible Dictionaries and encyclopaedia . . . The writer has researched some of these themes over many years and so has added his own thought to those of accepted authorities. Basically, of course, the Scriptures are the general foundation for all themes . . . The writer then has sought to provide gathered material for preachers, teachers and leaders, from which they may draw, and on which they may care to build.[62]

Geoffrey admits, 'No claim is made that the studies are the fullest coverage available'. But he adds, rightly, 'Few, however, have complained about the shortage of material'! Many have gone to them to begin their own investigation of a theme, and have come away enriched. A good number of the studies have been translated into Russian. It has been found that they transfer well across cultures, because they do not attempt to go beyond the Scriptures. Many of them have since been published as separate books. While a number of the themes have been developed into other volumes, this series of studies gives mature and foundational expression to the massive scope of Geoffrey's theological concerns.

'In 1976 we began Short Term Bible Schools':

> The first one was attended by well over a hundred people, and the subsequent ones settled down to the fifties and forties, but they were demanding courses. A number of pastors and teachers led the different subjects. In every (six-weeks) course there were thirty-two lectures given. This involved a weekend away at a conference venue ... Many of the leaders of courses put in considerable time with preparation [of] materials and these materials are now invaluable, covering as they do introductions to every book of the Bible, the background, history and geography of Old and New Testaments, the exegesis of a number of the important books of the Bible. The series given on Christian Basics was a useful course, whilst topics such as the Person and Work of the Father, of the Son, and of the Holy Spirit were invaluable as doctrinal studies.[63]

Study books of lasting value and use, such as *Salvation History* and *The Knowledge of God*, came from these Bible Schools.

From 1977 the Bible Schools, along with Winter Schools, and a Christian Writers' Course, were run in conjunction with the former ABI, now known as the Bible College of South Australia. The 1982–1984 Summer Schools at Victor Harbor were also linked with the Bible College. After that these Schools were run solely by the New Creation Teaching Ministry, and continued to grow each year. The Summer School in particular became a major event, changing in character to become more like a great family camp, helping to raise a whole new generation in vibrant faith and active ministry. Summer School topics ranged from *God Sends Revival*, through *The Power and Preaching of the Cross*, to *All Cry, 'Glory!'* Whatever the theme, invariably they traced 'the whole counsel of God'[64] from creation, and fall, through the history of Israel, to the cross, resurrection and the coming of the Spirit, and on to the new creation, with practical application to living in the church and in the world. The Summer Schools continued to grow after Geoffrey handed over the leadership in 2001, and after he died in 2009. Around six hundred people attended the 2012 Summer School, with over two hundred in the youth and children's program.

While in the early days Geoffrey himself did the bulk of the teaching, he readily enlisted other younger men to teach alongside him. He trusted the Spirit by largely giving them a free hand and allowing them to make their own mistakes, while keeping a strict eye on the content and character of their presentations. Occasionally he would take them away on a retreat with no set agenda—these proved to be powerful and transformative times. In 1986 Geoffrey began monthly Pastors' Studies on Monday mornings. These were later opened to others on Saturday mornings and renamed Monthly Ministry Studies. They were also recorded and posted out to many. In these Geoffrey would trace a theme over a number of months, producing ten or so pages of notes each time. Many found these a lifeline in ministry—like being taken from the smog below out into the strong, clear, pure mountain air, with a sharp focus.[65] Geoffrey continued these Ministry Studies every year until June 2006, when they were taken up by others. The year 1990 saw the first of many annual Pastors' Schools (also later changed to Ministry Schools) held in South Australia, Victoria and Western Australia, which spread the benefits more widely. These were geared pastorally to those with some theological training. They called upon speakers and participants to do some more thorough and profound exegetical and theological work. Topics included *The Liberated Pastor and His People, Trinitarian Theology: Human Unity and Relationships,* and *Christ's Living Church Today—One, Holy, Catholic and Apostolic.*[66]

Here is the impact that Geoffrey had on one such person in pastoral ministry—one of many:

I had left the tape sitting on my desk for several weeks. After all what more was there for a young pastor to know about the forgiveness of sins? I had kept 'short accounts with God' and was teaching the people in my first congregation to do the same. It had taken just over a year for the reality to set in that I was not scratching where people were itching, and what was worse, I had deep itches that began to inflame my conscience and stifle my heart and voice. Choices made whilst growing up within a Christian home and the Christian community had delivered me into a legal, contractual form of 'Christianity': one in which fear still dominated, and the most effective means of moving myself, and now the congregation I had been given, was guilt. It was not true that I knew nothing of God's love for in His mercy He broke through my fire-walls and keen evangelical ignorance, and on occasions I knew fleeting assurance, comfort and a sense of destiny. However, it was 'Cross-less' really. As Geoffrey would say I had used the cross merely as a handy rinse. Its powerful revelation of love had never broken through.

Late one Saturday evening, struggling to find the right challenge for the congregation on the following day I started listening to the tape by Geoffrey. As I listened, a whole new world, the world of God's love as grace began to envelop my heart and mind. It was as if God pushed a huge vacuum cleaner into my study and sucked off layers of sin's guilt, fear, the morass of corrupted images of God, my shame and pain and the terrible legacy they had left in my heart. I recall hearing words flooding up from my depth, words I had often used but never cried out from my belly, 'Father!' 'Oh Father!' I was home at last and the Father's arms were around me. I ran from the study telling Dorothy, 'I think I have just become a Believer!'

The following morning I couldn't wait to be with the people, even if it meant telling them to forget most of what I had been saying. Father's grace had gripped me, killed me and resurrected me. I thought that the whole world would fall about in joy as I had done. The sinners, the itchy ones began to do so, but those who had invested much in religion simply got mad and left. Thus for forty years the grace that gripped me that day has got richer and deeper, and the battle against it has never let up, from within and without. The older I get the more I am stunned by the mercy of God upon me. 'Oh dear Father, thank You!'[67]

Another younger man in pastoral ministry wrote after Geoffrey had come to his parish for a teaching mission in 1982, 'I feel like Timothy who has just had a visit from St Paul!'[68]

OUT AND ABOUT

Geoffrey resolved to go and preach and teach wherever he was called to do so, no matter how large or small the place or the number of people. This took Geoffrey, and later those who joined him, to every state in Australia, often at the invitation of former students. In one year there could be up to twenty local missions, over a weekend, or lasting one or two weeks.[69] Always with a team, they generally consisted of house meetings and larger gatherings.[70] The following gives a flavour of this on-the-road ministry, both in its preparation and delivery. It relates to one of the annual Spring Schools in New South Wales, which began after Ian and Zara Pennicook joined the Ministry there in 1986, held at St Paul's Anglican Church, Chatswood. Geoffrey's account begins at his home in the Adelaide Hills one September morning in 1992:[71]

> It is early in the morning. Three a.m. in fact. I get up and go to renew the slow-burning wood fire . . .
>
> It is time for me to go to the study. Today I am going to prepare some talks on revival. When I think about them I have inner quavers of my spirit. How can I talk about such things—I who have seen such things, but know they are beyond the mind to understand? . . .
>
> Even so I sit at the desk, bound to compose nine studies on the theme. The quavering goes on but I command my computer to make a document and then I give it a heading . . .
>
> My trouble is that doing such structured essays in my study is somewhat unreal. I have to imagine I have an audience, and that they are hearing me. I tremble again because they may not understand me. In fact I have to compose things on the screen with the idea in mind that they may protest. They may say, 'We don't understand you'. Therefore I have to be simpler, so that they will understand . . .
>
> Always at the computer I am preaching to the puzzled, and sometimes to the indifferent. Even so, I press on. I love them in my heart, though they may not see this love on my face. That is why my words must be very powerful, my declamations filled with the same astonishment and wonder that I know even before I begin composing. After a time I have the first study finished, and I go back,

adding in bits and pieces and taking out other elements that do not quite fit.[72]

Geoffrey goes out into the dawn where the magpies are carolling. He comes back inside and takes Laurel breakfast in bed. He returns to his preparation:

> ...I have yet much to do to fill in this whole day and before the plane wings me off tomorrow to the city of Sydney, where most of my boyhood memories will come alive as we touch down on the vast tarmac.[73]

By now Geoffrey is not alone:

> Members of the team are assembling in the staff room, and I go across to be with them for a short time. We exchange our day's happenings, and then our anticipations for the meetings in Sydney. Three of them will be leaving early next morning in the heavily loaded Valiant station wagon—heading towards Sydney. I will be flying later in the same day. Somehow the meetings ahead seem a trifle unreal, but behind the seeming unreality is the fact of selling our books, recording the messages and copying them. For years we have been doing this, and the mystery of proclaiming truth never palls in its action. There is always the pleasant anticipation that some will hear and respond. Others will read the books, be surprised, resonate to the words and the sentences and to the uttered ideas and—in some cases—have a transformation of life.
>
> The day is now well in motion. The typographers are at work, the books are shaping in the printing room. Mail-orders are being wrapped, and phone calls answered. Today I am being protected from the latter, otherwise I will lose the time I need to complete some of the studies.[74]

Geoffrey goes back to the studies:

> Slowly they mount up. They are interrupted by lunch and the mail, and by matters which have to be discussed with the team. We need to talk about this and that, especially about what will happen in my absence.

I want to walk about the place, but the grass is still wet, and the day is cold—hail, wind and rain being forecast. So I switch on the heater in the study, and then cover my knees with a rug. I forget all but the studies. Even so, they are not easy to devise . . .

Messages seem unreal in the privacy of my den because they are to be lived out with some passion in the pulpit . . . If events of the past did not encourage such teachers as me, then the present moment would be dismal indeed.[75]

More interruptions come later:

Some of the team come to wish us well for the days ahead. John, Beryl and Kay also come to chat over last preparation details and to pack in my extra luggage. Others come to show their love, and their assurance that it will be a grand time. I think of the prepared studies and am not sure. After the coming weekend Spring School there will be more studies to give to a Community[76] and these I will not be able to prepare before going eastward. I have quavers of trepidations, but cover them over. What is grace for, if not for such occasions? I become calm, and our farewells are affectionate. I go back from the good interruptions to muster up more messages. In the late afternoon I wander through the misty September rain, and have the thinking that comes in the quiet of these hills.[77]

After the evening meal, and the TV news and current affairs:

I finish the studies. Now I have to get all my papers together, along with the books I may need 'over there'. I pack my clothes, making sure I remember all garments and toiletries. The trouble is I do not know whether it will be warm or cold 'over there'.[78]

'In the new dawn I am heartened':

My battles at the computer are finished. My brief case carries the fruits of those labours. I go out into the dawn and see it promise a high day . . .

I watch silently whilst Kay drives her small car to John and Beryl's house, and I see them pack in her things, and after reversing the Valiant John glides out of the drive, the vehicle loaded to the gunnels. They will have a good time on the long two-day drive to

Sydney. There will be joking and teasing and chiacking, and stops for coffee and meals, and they will like the rare luxury of the motel for the night. Tomorrow we will meet, and they will be tired but cheerful. We will be thinking in hope about the first meeting on the Friday evening.[79]

They are reunited the next day, after Geoffrey has flown over and been met by John Dunn:

There is good fun and laughter as we talk about the long journey from Adelaide to Sydney. We have done this sort of travelling many times, but there is also much that is new, even on the long run from Balranald to Hay. Our fellowship is strong, tougher than tempered steel. We have been dealing in the substance of rich teaching and varied humanity over many years. Nothing can break the unspoken compact. We talk about the coming meetings with assurance but no pride. After coffee and biscuits they depart to set up the equipment for the meetings. We will meet in the evening.[80]

The first night of the meetings arrives, with 'more than a touch of fear, a smidgen of apprehension, a surge of excitement, an anticipation of responses and reactions':[81]

Ian is at the lectern. He is welcoming folk who have come from many places. I think how fine he looks, and how quickly we are moving into good worship. Here there will be no 'hype', no manipulation, no false note. Soon we are singing a hymn that we all know, and the throb of life is in the worship. God is in the midst. The Son of Man is with us. His Holy Spirit is already giving us sensings of ourselves as His people.[82]

As Geoffrey begins his first study, on 'The Revival We Need', he is mindful of 'the great men of my youth', who had preached at this same location—mostly Anglicans, also Methodists, Presbyterians, and Baptists—with 'their grip of truth . . . their zeal . . . the fire in their bones':

Those men had taught the truth which came back to many of us in war days, and which set the shape of theology and life for us for all our lives. Here now was I—white-haired and in my seventies—

much the same as they had been. Long before us there had been others. It was this faith we wanted to see freshened in our city and our land. We wanted outbreaks of living water, gushing across our parched community. Material things we possess in plenty, but the riches of true wisdom are not guiding the counsels of our political and social leaders. Strange things are happening in our land. This is why we are talking before God and Man of revival.[83]

Geoffrey starts with Habakkuk, who called on God to renew His work and in wrath to remember mercy. He goes back, through Moses, to old Jacob in Genesis, then on to Samson, Elijah and Elisha, and Nehemiah: revival means 'coming to life out of death'.[84] At the end of the message there are two more songs:

> Then there is the closing prayer, and after it a silence that is like a long gentle sigh, and finally people begin drifting out of the church. Some are standing about, talking softly. There are smiles and quiet affection. In the hall there is the chatter of those who seek coffee and tea to drink. Beryl is standing at the bookstall, and folk are browsing or wanting to buy, selecting from the vast range of good writing. Kay joins Beryl and John begins to run off the recording of the meeting.
>
> In all the conversation, the meeting and greeting, the reality of love is palpably present. I move to greet old friends with joy, and some speak of what God has been saying to them, not only in this meeting but prior to it. Some desire long and earnest conversations. We are moving in the communion of saints. We are living in the marvel of His church. Nowhere on earth is there anything like this: nowhere. Of course what is here is also in many places—many, many places. That is the substance of the miracle, the reality of the gathered people of God.[85]

Many who have been part of these occasions, occurring many times in various ways in many different places, will recognise the flavour.

Some groups Geoffrey came back to again and again. One such was the Redeemer Baptist Community at Castle Hill, later at North Parramatta, over a period of twenty-seven years from 1979[86]—'a church I visit almost annually and share the new insights the Lord has given me over the past twelve months, or the truths that were green for me many decades ago'.[87] Geoffrey both encouraged and stretched them:

> Geoff has been foundational in my understanding of theology and all that we believe. He has also always given us all practical encouragement in applying truth to our lives—'truthing it', as he says. His godly counsel was particularly instrumental in helping me out of a black hole in my life a few years ago. He constantly reminds us of the bigger picture.

> Geoff is not an easy man in the sense that he doesn't leave foolish statements unchallenged and is 'prickly' although less so over the years. I believe he is a prophet and they aren't nice but they are very solid and when something is burning in their soul it has to be said . . . Geoff's visits are always anticipated as an occasion when God will reveal something important.

> The biggest impact of Geoff on my life has been the man himself: his walk with the Lord throughout his long life; his obedience to the ministry God has given him; and the urgency with which he longs to enrich others with the truths that the Holy Spirit has revealed to him . . . All his teaching has been based on the Scriptures. He is a man of great integrity and the love of God flows from him.[88]

Powerful and effective as the short-term missions were, a realisation of people's need to be established in ongoing teaching was part of the decision to build the Teaching Centre on the Coromandel East property, and to hold regular weekly classes there and in other venues around Adelaide.[89] For thirty years or more, up to a dozen or so such classes were held each week, using many different speakers,[90] attended by a total of two to three hundred people over each year. They covered a wide range of Biblical themes, and most books in the Bible, along with series on Church history, Christian living, and pastoral ministry. Practically all sessions were recorded for ongoing listening and study, amounting to thousands of recorded talks. A number of these classes were made available as Correspondence Subjects, in which students received notes and recordings, and responded with assignments to personal tutors. A Christian Workers' Course, using the weekly classes and other materials, attracted numbers of students, some of whom went on to further theological training and ministry through other institutions.

Geoffrey, Deane Meatheringham and others continued to lecture from time to time in Bible Colleges,[91] and the New Creation Teaching Ministry itself retained some Bible College-like features, but the temptation to revert to being a Bible College, and to acquire government accreditation and funding, was consistently rejected. While this placed New Creation outside the mainstream of theological education, it gave the Ministry freedom to range over subjects and materials that were considered timely and appropriate. It also kept the Ministry in closer touch with people at the grass roots, and more directly reliant upon the direction and provision of almighty God.

Worshipful singing was always a part of the teaching occasions. Kay Robinson (later Carney), who joined the team in 1976, began writing and recording songs that arose from and gave succinct expression to the teaching she was hearing from Geoffrey.[92] Others wrote as well. In 1991, after some earlier collections, the first volume of the *New Creation Hymn Book* was launched: 'a collection mainly distilled from the great heritage of older public domain hymns and from hymns composed by people associated with the New Creation Teaching Ministry'.[93] Over the years this collection has been extended to include four hundred and thirty-six songs and hymns, of which seventy-three are by Geoffrey.[94]

As befits a man who had prayed, 'Let me go to all the nations of the earth',[95] Geoffrey in Australia made ready contact with people of different ethnic origins. Pastor Jack Braeside speaks of the formation of the Aboriginal Evangelical Fellowship in 1967: 'Rev. Dr Geoffrey Bingham' was among their advisers.[96] At the first Port Augusta Convention in 1970–1971, 'Geoff Bingham, principal of the Adelaide Bible Institute, was the study leader'.[97] Muriel Olsson writes:

A father of faith—one who has encouraged pastors and laymen alike in learning and understanding Kingdom principles.

As an Aboriginal Christian woman of the Yankuntjatjara tribe from the north-west corner of South Australia—Geoffrey Bingham gave me the opportunity to speak of my experiences as one of the 'stolen generation' at a National Pastors' Conference in Adelaide.

He believed that I had something of importance to speak into the Christian community. I no longer see myself as part of the 'stolen generation' but by God's grace—a part of the 'chosen generation'.[98]

Geoffrey also was a speaker for a time at the annual Katherine Convention of indigenous Christians in the Northern Territory.[99]

In 1976 a number of Chinese graduates in Adelaide felt called to form a church to reach out to people of their ethnic group, and Geoffrey encouraged them. At his suggestion they called it the 'Austral–Asian Church'. From that time until they engaged a full-time minister in 1985, Geoffrey did more than one-third of the regular preaching there, along with Lutheran Vic Pfitzner and Pentecostal Barry Chant.[100]

During his latter days at Kingswood, Geoffrey's contact with a local picture framer led to his regular preaching in a Greek Evangelical congregation.[101]

These initiatives, together with his cross-cultural work at the Pakistan Bible Training Institute, and his enlisting of overseas students at the Adelaide Bible Institute, led to part of Geoffrey's Order of Australia award being for 'encouraging cross-cultural theological education'.

FAR AND WIDE

'The first Christians used the resources of human speech, human actions, travel, and writing. Doubtless they would be the first to use whatever media present themselves were they with us today. Media of themselves are neither good nor bad. It is the use to which they are put that decides their true value.'[102] Geoffrey always sought to make good use of whatever media came to hand. Yet his use of these was never gimmicky or showy, but simple, substantial and direct. Given his ready use of media to communicate the word, he still considered the human body, face and hands to be the most effective visual aid.[103] As well as the setting up of recording studios, and extensive use of audiocassettes, he made sure that the Ministry also obtained one of the first high-quality video-recording cameras. He later encouraged the transferring of these resources to MP3 and DVD technology, and the construction of the website, as these innovations came along, and as helpers readily offered considerable time and skills to do the massive amount of work that this entailed. Electric typewriters were replaced with computers and continually upgraded. Geoffrey personally utilised the latest in computers, printers and photocopiers.

One participant speaks of the impact of song and message. She quotes a song of Geoffrey's that includes the verse:

> I was not proof against that love;
> The hands I saw were scarred with nails;
> The eyes—that once were filled with pain—
> Spoke love to me that never fails.
> I gladly bowed to conquering love
> Of Father, Son and Holy Dove.[104]

So, in a 1992 Thursday morning class at New Creation Teaching Ministry, in this song of love, God Himself convicted me of sin, of righteousness and of judgement. His Kingdom was opened up to me and I could not stop hearing—in relationship with the living God as Father—speaking to me, reassuring me of who He is and of His reign and rule. His story came in Truth.

I became an undistracted learner, and an avid 'tape listener' which almost drove my husband and two young children mad! (Not literally.) Tapes, tapes, tapes—they were like lollies in the lolly shop—and I loved sharing them with others to hear Truth too. I learnt quickly to copy tapes in the work room.[105]

People would often listen to tapes and CDs while driving:

I have spent the trip from Sydney to Wollongong (also the distance it takes to listen to a Christian Workers Correspondence School tape) with blurred vision as God continues to reveal Himself to me through the ministry He has so graciously given all of you.

It is beyond words how much God has spoken to me through New Creation over my 21 years, and I am amazed with God that He should choose to bless me so much with such deep teaching, and that He continues to do so.[106]

It was particularly through his gift and love of writing that Geoffrey communicated widely. In all he wrote a little over two hundred books. These range from simple booklets such as the 'Comprehending' and 'Christian Teaching' series to major theological works such as *The Day of the Spirit* and *The Law of Eternal Delight*. There are books that give a wide-ranging overview of Christian faith, such as *Salvation History* and *The Things We Firmly Believe*. There are biblical commentaries, notably those on Galatians, Ephesians, and the Book of Revelation. Books like *I Love the Father, Christ's Cross over Man's Abyss*, and *Spirit-Baptism: Spirit-Living* speak powerfully of the triune God in action. There are books with a more devotional bent, such as *The Everlasting Presence* and *The Spirit's Harvest*. Pastorally helpful books, such as *Angry Heart or Tranquil Mind?*, *The Wounding and the Healing* and *The Cleansing of the Memories* have proved life-changing for many, while *The Wisdom of God and the Healing of Man* is a significant work among books on biblical counselling. Issues of marriage in particular are dealt with in *God's Glory, Man's Sexuality* and *The Profound Mystery*, among others. Geoffrey wrote much on the life and ministry of the church in such books as *Christ's People in Today's World* and *The Beautiful City of God*. The task of evangelisation is addressed in *Proclaiming Christ's Gospel in Today's World*. Along with these are a range of novels, poetry, essays and short story collections, such as *Tall Grow the Tallowwoods* and *Mr Hicken's Pears*, which give a unique perspective on living in God's creation.[107]

After the first ten years of New Creation Publications Geoffrey could say:

> The main surge of distribution has taken place in the last five years, e.g. the average sales of books is 6,000 per year, but the twelve months of 1982–83 will be well over 12,000. Cassettes reached a peak of 10,000 in 1980–81, but average 6,000 per year.[108]

Nor were these all just by Geoffrey. At that same time he lists twenty-three other authors and writers and twenty-eight other speakers.[109] New Creation went on to publish and reissue works by a number of other authors, such as Marcus Loane, P. T. Forsyth, Adrio König, and Geoffrey's missionary colleague from Pakistan days Jens Christensen.

Marcus Loane makes this assessment of Geoffrey's writing:

> Geoff himself was a prolific author, and New Creation Publications proved a perfect outlet for his work, with its high standard in technique and an economic price for the bookselling market . . . All his books have the same stamp of reverence for truth, loyalty to the Bible, and love for the Saviour. There is imagination in his handling of well-worn themes and sometimes they map out a highly original line of approach . . . his books show how his mind teemed with ideas. When he struck the anvil, sparks flew off on all sides . . . Geoff's sheer literary output was the product of his untouched reserves of thought and of spiritual fervour, and was due to the consuming eagerness with which he wrote. He could never write fast enough for the ideas that were ever welling up in his mind . . . Would he have done better to have written fewer books and to have written those few better? Who can say? What one can say is that no one can safely censure either books or author unless he were to take into account the glowing spirit that inspired them both.[110]

Geoffrey gives this account of his own output, particularly in the literary genre:

> By the 1960s my writing had a new beginning. Two books were published, one—*Cross Without Velvet*—by Moody Press in the USA, and another—*Liberating Love*—by The Christian Book House in Lahore, Pakistan. Even so it was not until the 1970s that my writing began in earnest. Then, in the eighties it accelerated and I wrote volumes of short stories and a novel. Two of these books in the 1990s—*Tall Grow the Tallowwoods* and *Laughing Gunner*—received The Australian Christian Literature Award for years 1992 and 1993. A new type of book was created, namely one with stories, essays and poems in the same volume. These were published along with theological and devotional books. In 1980 Angus and Robertson published *To Command the Cats* with a foreword by the author and poet Douglas Stewart who was the Literary Editor of the *Sydney Bulletin* . . . The *Reader's Digest* published a story of mine 'The Day I fought Kelly' in their *Great Short Stories of Australia and New Zealand*.[111]

Whether writing literary, devotional or theological works, Geoffrey was proclaiming the gospel of God. Part of the citation for Geoffrey's appointment as a Member in the General Division of the Order of Australia was 'as an author'. It was:

> ... an attestation of persistence in seeking to communicate through writing what we have quoted as 'flowing out the issues of life'. Preaching, teaching, writing and books, hymns and poetry have all been the means of my communicating, so that thinking and wisdom have not been limited to a theological circle of readers but have been used to communicate 'the whole counsel of God' insofar as this person has been able to so do. As we have been taught, we are God's means of proclaiming the truth as He has chosen us to be. In this case we use the means He provided us so that we can proclaim what He proclaims through us.[112]

Prolific as Geoffrey's writing is, it was a product of and subservient to the spoken word. When Geoffrey spoke of his 'greatest delight' it was 'preaching, teaching, writing and grandchildren—in that order!'[113]

Over time practically all of Geoffrey's published writing, along with material written by others, has been made available for free download from the website.[114] Arrangements were made for another website to host and freely make available quantities of audio and video recorded teaching.[115] After Geoffrey was no longer on the scene, the embracing of new technology continued. In the month of January 2012 there were over 2,200 downloads of teaching sessions from the SermonAudio site— about 75 each day (one every 20 minutes). During the previous year downloads had occurred in over 70 different countries around the world, including many where Christian ministry is very difficult. A Facebook page with a daily portion of Scripture and brief meditation[116] reached over 7,200 members—only 107 of these from within Australia, more than 1,800 in Pakistan, with lots of interest from Asian and African countries—and saw an average of 30 new people signing on each day. Many of these were from other faiths, especially Muslims, Buddhists and secularists, but without wanting to be argumentative.[117] This is a wide audience indeed!

THE TEAM

The New Creation team began with just Geoffrey and Laurel:

> In the Mount Compass days Laurel had duplicated the notes for
> studies, especially for the Friday Night meetings, and had looked
> after cassette copying . . . Just when Laurel could scarcely cope (we
> found later she had a really bad heart), folk who were interested in
> the work came to the rescue. Friends had helped us to build the
> annexe, to do typing, correcting and proof-reading for books and
> study materials, and later even some of the printing, when we had
> bought a table offset machine. Even so the work was still too much.
> That was why we were glad to welcome Kay (Robinson) from New
> South Wales in October 1976.[118]

Kay writes:

> In June 1974, at a youth camp where John Dunn was leading studies
> on Prayer, I came to know the Father. I was changed from being a
> God-fearer to a Father-lover, as I discovered His great love for me
> (I John 4:16–19). Later that year, while helping with the music at a
> teaching mission at St Paul's, Chatswood, I heard the good news of
> the love of Father, Son, and Spirit in the action of the Cross, as Geoff
> Bingham opened up the Scriptures. I was overwhelmed by the Word
> of the Cross, the truth that had set me free, and wanted to support a
> teaching ministry that would do this for other Christians who, like
> me, 'served' God in fear, but without love—not to mention those
> outside the church who needed this good news, too.[119]

She was confused when she spoke to Geoffrey about it, only to
be told that 'there was no need of help in SA, but that I should
serve the Lord where I was'. A year or so later:

> . . . in July 1976, while visiting SA for the Christies Beach mission,
> the Lord spoke to me again. I had just gone to bed, when a voice
> spoke to me, saying, 'Now is the time; there is nothing to hinder
> you; I want you to come over and help in this ministry'. The voice
> was so clear that I had no doubt it was the Lord, so I just said, 'OK,
> Lord', and rolled over and went to sleep. It was a day or so later
> before I had opportunity to speak to Geoff, but when the

opportunity came, during morning tea at a women's meeting, I told him that the Lord had told me to come and help in the work. Geoff said to me, 'You're sure it's the Lord, now?' and without hesitation I answered 'Yes'. He then told me that this was an answer to prayer, because the work had grown so much that he and Laurel (who was unwell at the time) could not handle it on their own any more.

'I returned home to Sydney to tell my family, to give notice from my position at Parramatta City Council, and to prepare to move interstate. When the time came, in October 1976, Laurel travelled over to Sydney especially to accompany me on the long drive to Coromandel Valley, SA, and this was just the beginning of a new adventure for me, in knowing our Father's great faithfulness as He calls and provides for His children in all things—praise His name.'[120] Geoffrey says: 'she gave us many years of wonderful service in Missions, in producing books, in singing, music and secretarial work'. Kay left the work when she married in 1993.[121]

'John and Beryl Skewes joined not long after Kay, in early 1977':[122]

At a Mission at Karoonda in November 1970 the Lord met Beryl through the ministry of Geoffrey Bingham and revealed His love and grace to her. During Summer School 1971 John also was led into grace by Geoff.[123]

'John and Beryl are man and wife. John was a Mallee farmer and came to work with us at the bidding of God.'[124] Even so, their coming onto the team was neither immediate nor straight-forward:

During 1974 we attempted to sell the properties because we sensed that the Lord was calling us into His service in a new area, although not knowing where that would be. The Lord prevented the sale of the land and so we believed that we were to stay at Karoonda.[125]

It was not until 1976 that things fell into place when, just after they had visited Geoffrey and Laurel at their new property, 'On Thursday April 29th a neighbour came and offered to purchase both Karoonda properties':

We asked the Lord to show us His will by May 22nd when we had arranged to go to Adelaide to talk to Geoff . . .

On Friday May 21st John woke with the words 'Kiriath-Jearim' in his mind. He told Beryl and they looked up a Concordance, Bible references and the Bible Dictionary. Kiriath-Jearim . . . means 'city of woods or of forests' and was of a high elevation. We knew this referred to the property next to Binghams— woodlands and on a high ridge. We knew we were to move to Coromandel East and participate in what the Lord was doing through New Creation Teaching Ministry in the way the Lord would open up to us and the Holy Spirit confirmed this to us. We told the children and they also knew that was what we needed to do as a family.

On Saturday May 22nd we visited Geoff and Laurel and told them of our decision. Geoff was not surprised . . . We moved to Coromandel East on January 21st 1977 after travelling to Darwin where we bought a caravan and lived in that for 10 months while our house was being built.[126]

'John became the printer as well as helping with building projects and general maintenance, while Beryl began to form the Library and then became involved in the production of books and other materials.'[127] After Geoffrey handed over the leadership in 2001, John as General Manager co-led the work with the Director of Ministry.

'The next to join us were the Meatheringhams—Deane, Rosslyn and their two children. This was at the beginning of 1980.' They came after 'a most distinctive ministry in Wudinna, Bordertown and Broken Hill':[128]

Our joining New Creation Teaching Ministry grew out of effective missions that Geoff and teams of evangelists had given to each of the parishes where we had been called by Christ to minister. This was initially so in the mission at Wudinna in Aug. 1969 where a close fellowship in the gospel of God's grace commenced. Already I knew that I was who I was by the sheer goodness of God revealed in the atoning death of Christ. But following the mission at Wudinna I began to expand in this transforming message of freedom and took time to understand and teach what I learned from Geoff.[129]

'Deane and Rosslyn were two of those who had gathered at our original meeting in January 1973, and Deane, a Uniting Church minister, was closest to me of any of the pastors, sharing the whole vision very warmly.'[130] Geoffrey and Deane had discussed the possibilities of Deane being on the team when Deane had 'travelled by train from Bordertown to Parkside each Friday to lead a small group after the studies on the "Unity of all things".' Nevertheless Deane and Rosslyn 'obeyed a call to Broken Hill in Jan 1976'. In this instance the call to join the team came quite directly:

> ...it was while we engaged in fruitful ministry in the Silver City that Geoff phoned me to tell me that the right time had come to join the team. Prayerfully we tested this and believing that this call was of God we arranged to find a home at Eden Hills. The change was demanding but the sense of believing that we were in the right place sustained us for an adventure that we could not have imagined.[131]

Geoffrey's affectionate and robust relationship with Deane and Rosslyn is perceptively depicted in one of Geoffrey's more whimsical short stories, 'Fair Waved the Corn', which has elements of rivalry in the vegetable garden as to who can produce the better onions and sweet corn. It includes this appreciation:

> You might have called him a dreamer, or a hoper, but then he was more than that. He was a visionary, but a visionary who sought to carry out the visions which came to him. Mostly he succeeded. You could see the aims of his heart in his two pale-blue eyes. In the pulpit they could be strong and stern, even fierce, but there was humour which relieved the intensity and told you the man was human. If he felt life too deeply, then he compensated by living it richly. He was human in an ordinary way, a way that had to do with food and fun, with exercise, and with action. That was why people did not mind being closeted with him in the study. They could open their hearts, tell their troubles, and receive the comfort and healing that he conveyed to them.[132]

The Meatheringhams spent twelve years on the team, 'Deane teaching and taking Missions, and Rosslyn making a contribution through her gifts of music'.[133] Deane took over leadership of the work when Geoffrey resigned (for a time) as Executive Director on his 70th birthday in 1989.[134] They left the team in July 1992 to commence pastoral ministry at Coromandel Valley Uniting Church. Deane says, 'We thank our Heavenly Father for faithfully keeping us, leading us and giving us ministry in the gospel of his Son'.[135]

Peter and Helen Farmer 'First heard the liberating Word of the Cross in 1967 when Geoffrey Bingham took ABI Monday night lectures at Mead Hall in Adelaide':

> Our lives were changed that year and from that time on the desire to hear and to bring others to hear that liberating word was given to us.[136]

Peter went to the Short Term Bible Schools in 1978 and soon became Registrar for those schools. They joined the New Creation Council and became more involved in other aspects of the Ministry, such as tape copying, sending out books and organising Winter Schools and Summer Schools. After a large Summer School at Victor Harbor in 1980 Peter began to sense a call, for some time in the future, to leave his work in surveying to join the team at NCTM full time. During these years Helen was working two days a week in the Work Room and helping Peter with organising meals at Winter Schools and also doing Children's Ministry at Summer Schools:

> . . . in November 1982 Peter resigned from Telecom (Telstra) and we became part of the growing full time Team at NCTM. This meant knowing the blessing of living by faith and seeing the gracious faithfulness of God providing for our daily needs.[137]

They left the team in 2001 when Peter resigned as Registrar, and remained on as helpers. At that time Celia and Bill Carter were called onto the team to take up the position of Registrar for the Schools. Bill Carter died in 2002, and Celia stayed on as Registrar.

Ian Pennicook with his wife Zara and four children joined the New Creation team in January 1986. They sensed they 'should not move to South Australia but stay in New South Wales', where they bought a property at Bowral. Prior to that Ian had been rector of St John's Anglican Church in Keiraville. Ian had first heard Geoffrey give a study in 1966, 'when the gospel I had known from childhood was amazingly "filled out" in my mind and conscience':

> At that point I knew that I wanted to preach a gospel with the same content, though I was prepared to leave the form that my ministry might take to the Lord.[138]

Ian studied under Geoffrey at ABI in 1968, and the Pennicooks first attended the Summer School in 1984:

> The 1984 experience, which confirmed to my mind the direction we should go, was seeing John Skewes working behind the scenes at the Summer School. His evident freedom in serving was deeply impressive and I felt that here was a team with which I could more than happily ally myself. Shortly after that we started discussions with the team to be clear in our minds that this really was the direction we should go.[139]

As well as preaching and teaching opportunities, 'which have been far less than I would wish', with participation in the New Creation Schools, and writing of books, Ian took a role in the foundation of Tabor College in Sydney and in its ongoing development over the fifteen years from 1992. Later contact with some local leaders resulted in his travelling overseas to teach and preach.[140] Geoffrey gives this shrewd assessment:

> Tall substantial Ian arrives ... He is competent, an astute thinker, a thoughtful speaker. I look at him affectionately because although brusque at times, he is a valuable person. He is like a son or a younger brother, but he has within him great depths.[141]

Over the years others came on the team for shorter or longer periods of time:

> John and Lauraine Octoman came [in 1980]. John was our Business Manager, taught in the classes and visited the book

shops to promote our books, and Lauraine helped with the typesetting... Douglas and Mavis Schultz, at the end of 1983... Doug superintending the building and maintenance, and Mavis helping with the proofreading. Grant and Chris Thorpe joined the Team in 1987; Grant taking up some of the teaching and having ministry in student work, Chris helping with the bookkeeping. Kelvin Nicolle joined the team in mid-1987 to use his computer skills in the typesetting area of the work... Peter and Margaret McEntee and Alison Carroll joined the team in early 1989: Peter as Business Manager and Margaret, who had run our cassette library for years, began to superintend the Correspondence Courses. Alison contributed to the work in the typesetting area and the production of books, etc. Glynis Bensley joined the team in late 1990, helping in the Library and in the proofreading area.[142]

The Octomans, Schultzes and Thorpes left the team for other ministries in 1992; Kelvin Nicolle in 1990; Alison Carroll and Glynis Bensley in 1993. Others not mentioned here or elsewhere include Danielle Whittlesea, 1989; David Maegraith, who developed the website, 2000–2003; Keith and Lol Bettany, assisting Martin Bleby, 2004–2007, and Bob and Robin Pickering, in proofreading, publishing, and the Christian Workers' Course, 2006–2011.[143]

When Deane Meatheringham left the team in 1992, Geoffrey, now seventy-three, again took over the role of Executive Director. Two years later: 'In January 1994 Laurel and I thought it best for our health's sake to go to the milder climate of the plains and so we moved to Kingswood ... Colin and Robyn Jones with their six children moved into our house at the Centre'.[144] Colin gives this account:

My contact with Geoff began in 1976 when hearing him speak on 'Liberating Love' at the Churches of Christ Pastors' Camp in NSW, during my final year at Bible College. What I sensed from that time was the absolute authority and liberating power of the word of God—and the grace it declares ... Then, some time later, I arranged for a group of Churches of Christ pastors to spend a morning with Geoff at his home, to hear him speak on the principles of biblical counselling. He outlined the 'operational grid' of proclaiming God, Man created, Man fallen, Man redeemed etc, with a view to seeing people brought into the freedom of grace. Driving down Ackland Hill Road that day, I knew that the rest of my life must be given to the proclamation of these very things![145]

From this grew what became 'The Way to Human Freedom', 'a doctrinally and vocationally comprehensive, integrated, clear and pass-on-able body of teaching—to be used in local churches and mission situations, for the establishment of Christian workers . . . a framework for proclamation that was to be increasingly used by others':[146]

My joy at seeing it all there before me was enormous—and from that day I've not been able to resist the proclamation of it at every opportunity! The more I have declared these things the more wonderful, liberating and transforming they have become for me personally—and the more I've seen them powerfully impact the lives of others.[147]

Colin's thirteen years on the team (1994–2007), which included four and a half years of suffering Chronic Fatigue Syndrome, saw him proclaiming in diverse cultural situations within Australia and in India, Zimbabwe, Ghana, South Africa, Mozambique and Papua New Guinea, often among those who had limited education and English:

. . . I cherish memories of hearing Geoff powerfully and prophetically preach the word—with wisdom, immediacy, authority and fire—and knowing that nothing less must represent the ministry of every servant of God! I hold dear the experience of community we have enjoyed as a Team, which has itself been an explication of the Gospel we proclaim. I am also, so grateful to the Lord for the deep yearning that has grown within me—through this ministry—that the whole of the *apostolic witness* become the personal, joy-filled testimony of every believer, and that—in this—Christ's people be liberated into full human life, community and vocation! It is my conviction that such a yearning is at the heart of the New Creation movement.[148]

By 1997 Geoffrey had noticed 'a shrinkage in numbers of attendances in the Classes':

I am not in a position to say why a shrinkage in numbers began, and I am not saying it was necessarily a bad thing . . . I have always thought that with the input into many churches from our ministry, that pastors and people would be affected, and that a groundswell of grace would grow and a consensus of grace and love would move the churches out of mediocrity, deficient teaching and current entertainment and marketing techniques to promote the congregation. I still believe that but I face, realistically, the fact that we have, in the eyes of some, become as those rejected.

It was true that, among the churches, 'the majority scarcely know we exist and others just couldn't care'. At the same time, Geoffrey said, 'We should not be down-hearted':

I believe a very real factor which shows that the Lord persists with us, and would have us persist with the vision He has given us, is the coming of Martin to the Ministry . . . If God had wanted us to tail off the NCTM ministry He would have shown us that our witness was to be ended, and this for His own reasons. Instead He has sent us Martin, who, with his family, powerfully feels the call and command.[149]

Martin Bleby with his wife Vivien came from twenty-seven years of Anglican parish ministry in country, outback and suburban settings. He came with a teaching gift that was already being exercised in New Creation Schools and Classes: 'I love nothing more than to be with a group of people with an open Bible, teaching them from the Scriptures'. He saw his joining of the New Creation team as coming more deeply to the heart of 'prayer and the ministry of the word'[150] for which he had been ordained, to be able to serve the church and its ministers more widely. Geoffrey had played a key role in Martin coming to a deeper understanding of what happened on the cross,[151] and an important element in Martin's call to New Creation was 'to honour Geoffrey in that ministry God has given him, and to be with Geoff in whatever God is doing among us in our day'.[152] After Geoffrey resigned as Executive Director in 2001, Martin was given the leadership as Director of

Ministry, jointly with John Skewes as General Manager, for the next ten years, over 'a significant time of transition and of conserving and passing on' all that had been given in this ministry.[153] Andrew Klynsmith, who with his wife Elizabeth had joined the team in 2009, took up this position of Director of Ministry at the beginning of 2011, while Martin continued on the team to help groups of people in local churches to develop their evangelistic and teaching ministries, using resources he had developed over those years.[154]

The growth and ministry of the New Creation team is a key to understanding and appreciating Geoffrey in this final and culminating stage of his life and ministry. While exercising a unique and outstanding ministry of his own, he never sought to be a loner. He was never happier than when surrounded in ministry by those whom God had raised up with him.

The team is also a thirty-year or more miracle:

> From the beginning none of us on the Team has received any stipend or monetary help from NCTM funds. We have trusted our heavenly Father for our needs and he has supplied us faithfully as he has moved his people to minister in this way. Most members of the team have worked only at the Centre but some have done 'tent-making', that is, have worked to earn money in order to minister on the Team.[155]

A number of wives have also worked in paid employment as part of their participation in the ministry.

'No staff-worker asks for help either directly or by hints.'[156] While this has been called a 'Mueller type faith ministry',[157] in Geoffrey's mind it probably had more to do with the writings of Roland Allen (1868–1947),[158] who advocated the appointment of ministers 'who will live on their own resources and do the work of ministry without pay',[159] while not excluding 'dependence for livelihood upon the offerings of the faithful',[160] especially in expanding rather than settled church situations.[161] Geoffrey had made a study of Allen's 'voluntary principle' of ministry,[162] and no doubt it was this that inspired him to structure the finances of the New Creation Teaching Ministry in this way. As a practical testimony to the faithfulness of God, it may serve as an example as to how ministry could operate adequately in the wider church.

Beyond the 'team' was a great company of 'helpers':

> None of this would have been possible without the back-up of folk who helped us do the physical building of our facilities, who have typed, corrected, proof-read, and collated the materials.[163] We have needed those who have come one or two (and even more) days a week. Some have laboured on the property, others have helped with production, mail orders, library cataloguing, covering of books, recording in the studio and at missions, the selling of study and reading materials, and a host of other things ... Most of all, of course, are those who have prayed for the work, believing it was not the *dream* of a person or persons, but the *vision* given to a company of people.[164]

Geoffrey gives one example: 'hundreds of thousands of books have been sent out, demanding millions of sheets printed and collated. One man, Les Smith, has stood for years and years, just collating books, booklets and notes.' He also mentions 'those quiet givers who help us to work as Team members, and enable us to buy needed equipment, finance the producing of books and cassettes, and meet expenses entailed in running classes'.[165]

NEW CREATION AND THE CHURCHES

'NCTM ... is not a church, not an institution and not a kingdom':

> Since it has no Elders and does not celebrate the Sacraments it guarantees that it will never be a church, but rather an aide to the churches who care to use its resources of persons and biblical materials.[166]

To underscore that New Creation is not a church, Geoffrey makes the point:

All team members are also members of their own churches, and these are of different denominations. Some team members are elders and leaders in their parishes, and as such are wholly loyal.[167]

This was true also of those who came to New Creation events— the aim was to make them better members of their own churches, and this is generally what happened.

If New Creation is not a church, then what is it? Geoffrey does not accept the tag of 'para-church':

> We need to recognise that the early church had special ministries for teaching. They were (a) apostles, (b) prophets, (c) evangelists, (d) pastors and teachers.[168] Whilst we cannot here say what each taught we must see that *all* taught. The first three were almost certainly itinerant, visiting the churches but not ministering in one church continually. The first apostles cannot be replaced but there is a secondary ministry of apostles—'the sent ones'. We need prophetic ministry today as much as ever, i.e. persons being the immediate mouthpiece of God. This is the word which is not second-hand. It also corrects as well as encourages churches. Evangelists taught in early days; they did not manipulate the will of their hearers. They based their proclamation in the truth. Pastor-teachers are indeed teachers in the local church, and that is their continuing place. There may, however, have been itinerant teachers. Certainly the church elders are to be 'apt to teach'.[169]

Thus 'New Creation Teaching Ministry is a movement of such people in ministry amongst the churches. As such, it is . . . part of the ministry supplied by Christ to his church':[170]

> Today we miss the itinerant teaching gifts for the most part . . . We have to come to terms with the fact that the local church is not the beginning, the middle and the end of all teaching. *The local pastor cannot compass everything*, even though basically he is *the primary teacher* where the church is.[171]

'My own travels through many parts of the world and our own land have convinced me (rightly or wrongly) that our levels of teaching and understanding often leave much to be desired':

We also have to recognise that critical theology of the past two centuries has all but undone some who have been trained under it. Whilst we must all exercise our critical gifts we must not sieve the truth ... many churches need supplementary teaching. By this I do not mean only in doctrine and theology, but in truth and its practice, which in fact is true teaching ... we believe the New Creation ministry has a prophetic teaching role which can be supplementary to the churches.[172]

Geoffrey was puzzled, then, to find that 'churches feel themselves threatened by what we teach and do'. His perceptive explanation was, 'I think one strong objection is that we are not a church, and a second we have an ecclesiology that is an affront to them':

I doubt whether many pastors—let alone the people—have an ecclesiology. All of us have a rough one, but it may be better called 'a denominationology' ... I think every church has its own culture which is often a sub-culture of its denomination ... People feel secure in their local pattern of church culture, and resent changes ... The local church is often the first-post as well as the last-post of member loyalty.[173]

In contrast to this:

I think I have broader views of the church, the people of God and eschatology pertaining to the same than have most pastors and theologians—grateful as I am to them all ... I think many are frustrated because they cannot pin us down.[174]

Even so:

I believe the churches—whatever their shortcomings and even practices may be—are still under the Lord of the churches who walks among the golden candlesticks.[175]

'For this reason we live in our local churches, love folk there, relate to them and with love bear any reproach that may come to us.'[176] And in the end:

After all NCTM is a 'something–nothing', and all true Christian belief and work meets the general 'scandal of the Cross' for its 'foolishness' . . . If there is any 'scandal' or 'foolishness' attached to NCTM, then it should only be that of the Cross. We should recognise the folly of many of our own acts from time to time but deny that the Cross is essentially a scandal or folly.[177]

Geoffrey was in no doubt as to 'the primary purpose of the church' and its 'primary resource':

. . . the life and health of our churches depends not primarily upon the brilliance of theologians, the social action which shows our concern for disadvantaged people, the organising of church growth, and the use of other techniques and marketing strategies. Whatever value these things may or may not have, the primary purpose of the church is to preach the gospel throughout the world and to bring its saving power to persons outside the message of salvation and the community of Christ. The primary resource is the Word of redemption, the Word of God's love, and his grace which brings guilty human beings into the peace of forgiveness and justification. This Word makes them to be part of Christ's community—the church. This is the community of love and care, but its first care is that men and women and young people should come into the peace of forgiveness. The rest will follow.[178]

Where churches and pastors did become involved in this wider ministry, they were greatly enriched:

My conviction is that all the human resources we need are already within the churches. Many a good evangelist is left to convert his own congregation and none other! Many a teacher teaches only his own congregation, whereas both evangelist and teacher would be greatly freshened by having wider opportunities than their respective congregations, and the gospel would be going out into new places. Churches which go beyond their own local bounds become enlarged in spirit and heart: they become vitalised.[179]

FULL-ORBED THEOLOGY

Is there, then, what some have called a 'New Creation teaching'?

> No, we desire to so teach that biblical truth will come through, and that a warm, loving, strong people of God will further proclaim that gospel—*the* gospel—which will draw others to Christ and His people, so that the gospel will be extended to yet more others.[180]

The New Creation 'Doctrinal Stance' is remarkably formal and orthodox, but with a certain freedom and fullness:

> The 'objects' outlined in the Inaugural Meeting Minutes and the Constitution make it clear that NCPI–NCTM believe in the authority of Scripture for faith and practice. They therefore hold to the historic Creeds of the Church known as Apostles', Nicene and Athanasian. Their doctrine is biblical and Reformed, without prejudice to the movements of God's Spirit which come at times of revival and renewal of the Church. Whilst recognising these and wishing to share in them as they follow the truth, they do not feel bound to accept theological rationalisations of any movement or group. They believe that a full-orbed theology must be Trinitarian, and that while theology is not the truth itself, it can deeply affect—for good or not—the approach of Man to truth, that is, to God Himself.[181]

The expression of this 'full-orbed theology' in teaching is wide-ranging and inexhaustible:

> It is at once the setting forth of the Three Persons of the Trinity as stated in the Creeds and shown in the Scriptures as co-working in Creation, Covenant, Israel, Redemption, the People of God, the justification, sanctification, glorification and perfection of the elect and of all the creation, so that all creation is renewed to be 'the new heaven and the new earth'. This may be described as 'from the action of creation to the climax of it in the new creation'.[182]

'Within this general theological structure are particular treatments of subjects and themes':

... there are NCTM books and written or recorded Studies on the Trinity, on the Person and Work of each Person of the Trinity, on the *ad intra* and *ad extra* works of the Triune Godhead, and this thrust flows into numerous thematic studies on such topics as Creation, Covenant, Law, Salvation History, the Story of History, the Kingdom of God, Prophecy, the Order of Salvation (*ordo salutis*) and so Christ's Atonement, Resurrection, Ascension and Heavenly Session. In regard to Salvation there are the themes of the Fall, Sin, Death, Conscience, Grace, Repentance, Faith, Baptism, Forgiveness, Reconciliation, Justification, Sanctification, Adoption, and the Gift of the Spirit.

'Leading on from this Salvation treatment is the nature of the Church':

... that is, the Community of Christ which is in the Father and the Holy Spirit and which is always on Mission. This 'Mission' is the plan of God to bring reconciliation of the nations under the Lordship of the Son. Linked with this is the matter of the Kingdom and the defeat of Satan's kingdom. The Social Nature of the Church, its Practical Christian Living—which is especially active in the triad of Faith, Hope and Love—are studied. At this point the theme of the Holiness of God and Man is covered, personal holiness of the Church and its Members also being treated, linked of course with the formerly mentioned Sanctification of all Creation. The theme of Relationships Human and Divine arises from the Doctrine of the Trinity, and so Human Marriage, Family and Society are examined. All of these are under the covering principle of Covenant and the Kingdom of God.[183]

'In all these theological Studies the "NCTM ethos" seeks to be biblical':

At the same time it seeks to take into consideration historical, textual and literary criticism, yet it must be stated that the Studies on the whole are not in the critical metier found in academia. For this reason they might erroneously be thought to be simplistic. They work on the principle that the Scriptures are a remarkable unity and however the text may have been formed it is now the sacred text which demands humility from those who study it; not the humility of a bibliolater, nor the presuming arrogance of the intellectual, but the humility of a sinner under grace who desires to know God and His mind for the world He has created and loves, and which He redeems, sanctifies, glorifies and perfects.[184]

Teaching requires a teacher, in person: 'A general observation is that when it comes to the teaching of Scripture *a teacher* is better than *a course*'.[185] Those who proclaim and teach 'must live in constant union and communion with God':

> ... those who teach in and of the 'NCTM ethos' are those who were first affected by it, and then those who could not proclaim apart from God, that is, in union and communion with Him. Whilst the 'form' of the biblical truth can always be taught apart from union with God, the 'substance' or reality of it cannot be communicated by such teaching. A teacher must know God existentially in order to impart living truth. He—she—is a witness to God and the truth by living in God and His truth.[186]

This is not to say that God cannot use any person who is not in this mode: 'Of course, the *authenticity* of the truth is not dependent upon it being proclaimed by a certain kind of person, and it may please God to use any medium He chooses'.

How is the teaching expected to come through?

> We believe that in the Apostolic age the gospel was proclaimed through the ministry of apostle, prophet, evangelist, pastor and teacher in such a way that willing listeners grasped 'the whole counsel of God' and responded. Intellectual brilliance is not required to know the truth of God and live in it. The Three Persons of the Godhead lead us into all the truth. We seek in our teaching and learning to follow this 'prophetic principle' as teachers and listeners come under the Word of God. We believe that what we learn springs directly from the Scriptures as our way and rule of life, and that the living truth of Scripture helps us in approaching the contemporary scene. We see our teaching as bringing us into interpersonal relationships with the Triune God, with the community of Christ—the Church—and with the general community.[187]

EAGER TO PREACH[188]

When it comes to primary evangelism, Geoffrey has little regard for methodologies:

> I have watched the ecclesiastical parade of the years with the vast variety of methodologies and theologies (generally imported from North America) that gleam, glitter, attract, and are employed but only to fail, become effete and outdated. All of them—without exception—fail to produce lasting and dynamic effects, even though they give great promise at the start. Let it be understood that where the Cross is not central nothing of power ever eventuates. Plenty happens apart from it, but it eventually runs out of 'puff'.[189]

What, then, should take the place of such methodologies?

> I personally believe that teaching is the best form of evangelism. I am not convinced that extremely simple presentations of a few points with strong pressure to 'make decisions' is the best way [to] bring life to the churches and the churches to life. [190]

This is not to say that God does not work in other ways: 'Even so, I believe God uses all kinds of human endeavours, often in spite of ourselves, our ideas and our methods'.

Geoffrey gives this advice to budding evangelists, from his own experience and practice:

> ... what we want is a short, lively, interesting, simple and humanly warm gospel message ... The kind of meeting—the music, the singing, the friendly warmth, and the sincerity of the preacher and helpers—should make folk feel at home, and yet impress them with the serious nature of the gospel, which is a command, a warning and an invitation all at once.[191]

A gospel presentation will be different from a sermon or a study:

> Each gospel message will refresh believers, and will be doing its work in the unconverted. There are so many subjects, aspects and the like which we can proclaim, such as knowing God, His love, His grace, His judgement, His salvation, Man's sin, his lostness, the

danger of death and hell, the Prodigal and the Father, the joy of the forgiveness of sins, of being justified, of the cleansing, the sonship, the warmth of the Shepherd, Christ the life, the truth, the way, the bread, the door; the Cross, the resurrection, the heavenly home, safety, certainty, the hope of glory—and so on. As we proclaim these themes they must be simple and clear, no apologetics, no complicated reasoning, but a loving sincere message from a heart which has gospel fire burning in it.[192]

None of this can be done apart from love:

There could be many motives for proclamation, such as proselytising, adding to our numbers, seeking to strengthen our groups or gain support for our ministry. There could be self-proving (self-justifying) ministries, and many more such motives. Paul said, 'Let all that you do be done in love'. Outside of that love there is no point to any action.[193]

Absent from the New Testament is 'the idea of being converted through evangelism and becoming a member of a local church group, which itself was a socio-religious group intended to foster itself as a self-contained spiritual unit':

The church was the dynamic witnessing unit of the Spirit who, through them, confronted the world with Christ, that is, his past victory of the atonement, and his present action in defeating evil in history and bringing in the Kingdom of God fully and for ever . . . none of this will make much sense to us unless we have received the powerful 'washing of regeneration and renewal in the Holy Spirit' and the power for witness which comes with the gift of the same Spirit, for it is he alone who can 'convict the world of sin and of righteousness and of judgment', and by so doing bring them to the obedience of Christ.[194]

In summary:

. . . true evangelism is the overspill of a heart too full to contain what is good. This can be said of God as well as of man. The Father is the Great Evangelist, and the Son and the Spirit no less than He . . . The true evangelist is a person who knows the great thrusts and themes of God's Word, and who holds evangelism in that perspective . . . All must be recruited in the interests of proclaiming the love of God, but then that love must not be limited to a restricted line of proclamation, and then held within those confines. The true *kerugma* as a teaching embraces 'from eternity to eternity' . . . God is Sovereign, and His Kingdom without end. In the ultimate He will unite all things. In the meantime we must proclaim His love, and share it with needy, beaten and defeated humanity until its sins are forgiven, and its defilement cleansed. Our task is to set men and women free in the name of the Father, of the Son, and of the Holy Spirit.[195]

THE GREAT RIOT OF BULLABAKANKA

Geoffrey Bingham left the Adelaide Bible Institute because he and his ministry could not be contained within it. This is because the gospel he proclaimed, and the God whose gospel it is, cannot be contained within a Bible College. Nor can it be contained within any local church. Nor, for that matter, could it be contained within the New Creation Teaching Ministry. Even within the Ministry that had been purpose-built around him, Geoffrey was still always straining at the leash. Much as he 'burned in the work',[196] NCTM was still for Geoffrey a 'something-nothing'.[197] From time to time he would remind people of the windup provisions in the NCPI Constitution, by which 'The group may be wound up by resolution of a majority of members present at a meeting called for that purpose' and the assets 'given or transferred to some other institution or society with similar objects'.[198] The gospel of the resurrected Jesus Christ, and those who proclaim it, cannot be content with anything less than the complete 'new heavens and a new earth in which righteousness dwells'.[199]

Geoffrey tells a short story, in which a man's love for his ordered vegetable garden is outshone by his wife's apparently 'higgledy-piggledy' riot of flowers and shrubs:

I like my orderly garden. Look at the plants, row upon row, generally standing to attention. Only the potatoes are slouches, but if you keep hilling them they seem to stand upright enough. Strawberries will get out of hand if you don't keep them in rows, thick pea straw holding them in line. Of course, there is nothing to compare with sweet corn. They are soldiers at any estimate. Firm, upstanding, tassels rigidly aloft, cobs at the ready. They almost salute you. They almost present arms.[200]

It is only after his wife has died that the man comes to appreciate her work:

I walked across the vast lawn and looked up towards the house. I wondered whether a miracle had taken place. There was her garden, all higgledy-piggledy but something about it mystified me. It was not higgledy-piggledy. It was a mass of colours and supporting green background. The garden was lovely, beauty itself. I started and stared again. Nothing had changed. It was still entrancing. I kept looking at it, unable to believe my eyes. I held my breath for fear it was a momentary illusion.

It was none of that. It was a glory of loveliness . . .

There are allusions to the 'Last Post' and 'Reveille', signifying life on the other side of death. 'I suddenly, though quietly, understood the freedom of which she had spoken':

'A great riot of beauty at old Bullabakanka,' I said, thinking how gentle a riot it all was, but then a riot for all that.[201]

[1] Leaflet, 'New Creation Teaching Ministry: A brief history and explanation of the work', February 1994.

[2] *The Ministry of New Creation*, vii.

[3] Photocopied page from *Vision and Duty* 1970 [?]: 'In the course of a strategic two months visit to South-East Asia Mr. Bingham visited seven countries, took part in two consultative conferences in Singapore and a convention at Malang, Java, spoke to many missionary groups and contacted at least 17 A.B.I. graduates, including four Asian students'.

[4] *The Ministry of New Creation*, vii.

[5] 'An Account of the New Creation Teaching Ministry and New Creation Publications Incorporated, from 1973 to 1996', paper by Geoffrey Bingham, April 1996.

[6] 'Confidential Observations on A.B.I. by Principal G. C. Bingham' 25/1/73, p. 2.

[7] 'Observations on A.B.I.', p. 1.

[8] 'Observations on A.B.I.', pp. 3, 4.

[9] 'Observations on A.B.I.', p. 4.

[10] 'Observations on A.B.I.', p. 3.

[11] 'Observations on A.B.I.', p. 1.

[12] 'Observations on A.B.I.', p. 2.

[13] 'Observations on A.B.I.', p. 4.

[14] 'Account of the New Creation Teaching Ministry', 1996, p. 1.

[15] 'Observations on A.B.I.', pp. 1, 3.

[16] 'Observations on A.B.I.', p. 3.

[17] Bible College of South Australia, which the Adelaide Bible Institute later became. Geoffrey Bingham, Letter to Former Students of ABI, April 1990.

[18] *The Ministry of New Creation*, vii.

[19] 'Account of the New Creation Teaching Ministry', 1996, p. 1.

[20] *The Ministry of New Creation*, 2.

[21] Letter from Rev. Andrew Wilson [Methodist Church, Kapunda, South Australia], February 1973.

[22] Andrew Wilson Letter, 1973, p. 1.

[23] 'Account of the New Creation Teaching Ministry', 1996, p. 1.

[24] Andrew Wilson Letter, 1973, pp. 1, 2.

[25] Andrew Wilson Letter, 1973, p. 2.

[26] Andrew Wilson Letter, 1973, pp. 1, 2.

[27] Andrew Wilson Letter, 1973, p. 2.

[28] 'Account of the New Creation Teaching Ministry', 1996, p. 1.

[29] *The Ministry of New Creation*, 2.

[30] 'Account of the New Creation Teaching Ministry', 1996, p. 1.

[31] *The Ministry of New Creation*, 2.

[32] *The Ministry of New Creation*, 2.

[33] Conversation of Martin Bleby with John and Beryl Skewes, 16th February 2012.

[34] *The Ministry of New Creation*, 1.

[35] *Laurel's Story*, 111.

[36] *The Ministry of New Creation*, 2.

[37] Conversations with Geoffrey Bingham and John Skewes recalled by Martin Bleby.

[38] Later published as Christian Teaching Series 1–7: *The Weakness of Man and the Power of God; Can a Man Know God?, The Meaning and Significance of the Trinity; Commanded Repentance and Full Forgiveness; Faith, Justification, Conversion and the New Birth; The Christian and the Holy Spirit; The Christian Doctrine of Holiness*. These, with a full range of Biblical references, give a solid and comprehensive grounding in each of these vast and significant topics.

[39] *The Ministry of New Creation*, 3. *I Love the Father* was first printed by the Lutheran Publishing House.

[40] *The Ministry of New Creation*, 3.

[41] 'Extracts from the Inaugural Meeting, January 19th, 1974', in *The Ministry of New Creation*, v.

[42] 'History: The New Creation Story', New Creation Teaching Ministry Program 2000.

[43] *The Ministry of New Creation*, 3.

[44] *The Ministry of New Creation*, 4.

[45] *The Ministry of New Creation*, 4.

[46] *The Ministry of New Creation*, 3–4.

[47] *The Ministry of New Creation*, 5.

[48] Elizabeth married Geoff Diment, and Carol married David Leeder. Anne had married Eric Rasmussen while the Binghams were still at ABI; Geoff and Laurel later travelled to Nimbin in Queensland to marry Richard and Susan; *Laurel's Story*, 108–109, 117.

[49] *The Ministry of New Creation*, 4.

[50] *The Ministry of New Creation*, 5.

[51] 'Account of the New Creation Teaching Ministry', 1996, p. 2.

[52] *Laurel's Story*, 116.

[53] 'Account of the New Creation Teaching Ministry', 1996, p. 2.

[54] 'Account of the New Creation Teaching Ministry', 1996, p. 2.

[55] 'Account of the New Creation Teaching Ministry', 1996, p. 3.

[56] Letter to Former Students of ABI, April 1990, pp. 1-2.

[57] 'Account of the New Creation Teaching Ministry', 1996, p. 1.

[58] Geoffrey Bingham, 'Personal Message for Team Consideration 28/10/97', p. 1.

[59] *The Ministry of New Creation*, 4-5.

[60] 'Personal Message for Team Consideration 28/10/97', p. 1.

[61] 'Personal Message for Team Consideration 28/10/97', p. 1.

[62] 'Foreword to the Living Faith Series', *Living Faith Studies*, 1981.

[63] *The Ministry of New Creation*, 7-8.

[64] Acts 20:27.

[65] Martin Bleby, personal recollection.

[66] Information in this and the preceding paragraph is from personal recollection and records of these Schools, held by Martin Bleby; also *The Ministry of New Creation*, 9; 'Account of the New Creation Teaching Ministry', 1996, p. 5.

[67] Brian Arthur, email to Martin Bleby, 22 February 2012.

[68] Martin Bleby, NCTM Commissioning, 13th December 1997.

[69] 'Teaching Missions' 1972-2004, list compiled by Peter Farmer, 25/5/2007.

[70] See *Eager to Preach*, 7-10; 'Parish Missions' and 'Home Meetings', in 'The Principles and Practice of Evangelism', *Living Faith Studies*, vol. 5, 261-265.

[71] Year date: email from Ian Pennicook to Martin Bleby, 7 April 2012.

[72] 'Revival in the Human Spirit', unpublished manuscript, n.d., p. 1.

[73] 'Revival in the Human Spirit', p. 2.

[74] 'Revival in the Human Spirit', p. 3.

[75] 'Revival in the Human Spirit', p. 4.

[76] Redeemer Baptist Community; see below.

[77] 'Revival in the Human Spirit', p. 4.

[78] 'Revival in the Human Spirit', p. 4.

[79] 'Revival in the Human Spirit', p. 5.

[80] 'Revival in the Human Spirit', p. 7.

[81] 'The First Meeting' (a continuation of 'Revival in the Human Spirit'), p. 1.

[82] 'The First Meeting', p. 2.

[83] 'The First Meeting', pp. 2, 3.

[84] 'The First Meeting', pp. 3–6.

[85] 'The First Meeting', p. 7.

[86] Mr Noel Cannon, Principal of Redeemer Baptist School, North Paramatta, in Nomination for Order of Australia Award, Reverend Doctor Geoffrey Cyril Bingham, submitted by Beverley Priest, Martin Bleby and Rob Linn, October 2003, 'Geoffrey Bingham—Roles and Activities', p. 25.

[87] 'The First Meeting', p. 1.

[88] Impact Statements: What has been the impact of Geoffrey Bingham's ministry on my life? Redeemer Baptist Church, n.d.

[89] Deane Meatheringham in conversation with Martin Bleby, 2011.

[90] See for example New Creation Teaching Ministry 2001 Program.

[91] *The Ministry of New Creation*, 9; Letter to Former Students of ABI, April 1990, p. 2.

[92] Greg John, 'Publishing and Recording New Creation Music: The Story in Brief', prepared for NCTM End-of-Year Gathering, November 5th 2006. Twenty-nine of Kay's songs are published in the *New Creation Hymn Book*, with twenty-three of these recorded on the CD *Songs of Worship 4*.

[93] Don Priest, Convenor, 'Introduction to the 2001 Edition' of the *New Creation Hymn Book*.

[94] *New Creation Hymn Book*, 2nd edition, 2010; see: <www.newcreation library.net/music/index.html>.

[95] See Chapter Two.

[96] Max Hart, *A Story of Fire Continued: Aboriginal Christianity*, NCPI, 1997, 3.

[97] John Harris, *One Blood: 200 Years of Aboriginal Encounter with Christianity: A Story of Hope*, Albatross Books, Sutherland NSW, 1990, 669–670.

[98] Nomination for Order of Australia Award, p. 10.

[99] Personal recollection, John Skewes, 2012.

[100] Conversation of Siew Kiong Tham with Martin Bleby, 18 July 2012.

[101] Personal recollection, Martin Bleby.

[102] *Living Faith Studies*, vol. 5, 269.

[103] Personal recollection, Martin Bleby.

[104] 'I Am Not Proof Against Your love', *New Creation Hymn Book*, 166.

[105] Lol Bettany, Testimony, c. 2006.

[106] Letter to the New Creation Team, 16/8/99, name withheld.

[107] See *Program 2009 New Creation Teaching Ministry*, p. 14.

[108] *The Ministry of New Creation*, 14.

[109] *The Ministry of New Creation*, 14–15.

[110] Marcus L. Loane, *These Happy Warriors*, 93.

[111] Geoffrey Bingham, 'A Salute to Readers of *The Artist in the Garden*', brochure prepared for the launch of that book, 9th April 2005.

[112] 'A Salute to Readers of *The Artist in the Garden*' (published 2005).

[113] Letter to Former Students of ABI, April 1990, p. 5.

[114] <www.newcreationlibrary.net>.

[115] <www.sermonaudio.com/newcreation>.

[116] Look for 'New Creation Teaching Ministry'.

[117] Andrew Klynsmith, email to Martin Bleby, 25th February 2012.

[118] *The Ministry of New Creation*, 6.

[119] Kay Carney (nee Robinson), Testimony, 2007.

[120] Kay Carney (nee Robinson), Testimony, 2007.

[121] 'Account of the New Creation Teaching Ministry', 1996, p. 2.

[122] 'Account of the New Creation Teaching Ministry', 1996, p. 2.

[123] John and Beryl Skewes, Testimony, 2007.

[124] 'Revival in the Human Spirit', p. 7.

[125] John and Beryl Skewes, Testimony, 2007.

[126] John and Beryl Skewes, Testimony, 2007.

[127] 'Account of the New Creation Teaching Ministry', 1996, p. 2.

[128] *The Ministry of New Creation*, 6.

[129] Deane Meatheringham, Testimony, 2007.

[130] *The Ministry of New Creation*, 6.

[131] Deane Meatheringham, Testimony, 2007.

[132] *I Saw, in the Night, Visions*, 43.

[133] 'Account of the New Creation Teaching Ministry', 1996, p. 2.

[134] 'Account of the New Creation Teaching Ministry', 1996, p. 3.

[135] Deane Meatheringham, Testimony, 2007.

[136] Peter and Helen Farmer, Testimony, 2007.

[137] Peter and Helen Farmer, Testimony, 2007.

[138] Ian and Zara Pennicook, Testimony, 2007.

[139] Ian and Zara Pennicook, Testimony, 2007.

[140] Ian and Zara Pennicook, Testimony, 2007.

[141] 'Revival in the Human Spirit', p. 7.

[142] 'Account of the New Creation Teaching Ministry', 1996, pp. 2–3.

[143] 'New Creation Team Members', list prepared by John and Beryl Skewes, 2011.

[144] 'Account of the New Creation Teaching Ministry', 1996, pp. 3, 4.

[145] Colin Jones, 'Account of Involvement in the Ministry of New Creation', 2007.

[146] See: <www.humanfreedom.org.au>.

[147] Colin Jones, 'Account of Involvement in the Ministry of New Creation', 2007.

[148] Colin Jones, 'Account of Involvement in the Ministry of New Creation', 2007.

[149] 'Personal Message for Team Consideration 28/10/97', pp. 2, 4, 5.

[150] Acts 6:4.

[151] See Martin Bleby, *The Vinedresser: An Anglican Meets Wrath and Grace*, NCPI, 1985.

[152] Martin Bleby, 'NCTM Commissioning' 13th December 1997.

[153] NCTM General Mailing, 6th July 2010.

[154] *New Creation Teaching Ministry 2012*, p. 6.

[155] 'Account of the New Creation Teaching Ministry', 1996, p. 2.

[156] *The Ministry of New Creation*, 13.

[157] Email from Pastor Tom Kartzmark, Senior Chaplain, Ottawa International Airport, Ontario, Canada, 17 January 2006. George Mueller (1805–1898), philanthropist and preacher, of Bristol UK, supported himself and over 2,000 orphans on the basis of faith and prayer, relying on voluntary contributions from his followers.

[158] Conversation of Geoffrey Bingham with Martin Bleby, 2009.

[159] 'The Voluntary Clergy: i Letters to and from Roland Allen', in David M. Paton, ed., *Reform of the Ministry: A Study in the Work of Roland Allen* (Lutterworth Press, London, 1968), 88.

[160] 'The Case for Voluntary Clergy', in David M. Paton, ed., *The Ministry of the Spirit: Selected Writings of Roland Allen* (World Dominion Press, London, 1960), 147.

[161] Paton, ed., *Ministry of the Spirit*, p. 137.

[162] Files seen by Martin Bleby in Geoffrey's archives, no longer extant.

[163] 'Account of the New Creation Teaching Ministry', 1996, p. 4.

[164] *The Ministry of New Creation*, 7.

[165] 'Account of the New Creation Teaching Ministry', 1996, p. 4.

166 *Principles of New Creation Teaching Ministry: Some Thoughts from the Discussion of Geoffrey Bingham and Ian Pennicook*, January 1998, p. 1.

167 *The Ministry of New Creation*, 8.

168 See Ephesians 4:11–16.

169 *The Ministry of New Creation*, 9–10. Quote from 1 Timothy 3:2.

170 *New Creation Teaching Ministry 2011*, p. 1.

171 *The Ministry of New Creation*, 10.

172 *The Ministry of New Creation*, 10.

173 'Personal Message for Team Consideration 28/10/97', pp. 2, 3, 4.

174 'Personal Message for Team Consideration 28/10/97', pp. 3, 4.

175 'Personal Message for Team Consideration 28/10/97', p. 5. Reference to Revelation 1:12–20.

176 'Personal Message for Team Consideration 28/10/97', p. 5.

177 'Personal Message for Team Consideration 28/10/97', p. 5.

178 *Eager to Preach*, 12.

179 *Eager to Preach*, 7.

180 'Personal Message for Team Consideration 28/10/97', p. 4.

181 *Principles of New Creation Teaching Ministry*, p. 16.

182 *Principles of New Creation Teaching Ministry*, pp. 13–14.

183 *Principles of New Creation Teaching Ministry*, pp. 14–15.

184 *Principles of New Creation Teaching Ministry*, pp. 15–16. See further: *How to Study the Bible*, 1980. This is followed up by Martin Bleby, *God Speaking: Authority and Interpretation in the Scriptures*, NCPI, 2006.

185 *How to Study the Bible*, 26.

186 *Principles of New Creation Teaching Ministry*, p. 9.

187 New Creation Teaching Ministry Christian Workers' Course leaflet, 2004.

188 Title of a booklet written by Geoffrey 25 November 1996, taken from Romans 1:15.

189 Letter to Former Students of ABI, April 1990, pp. 2–3.

190 *Eager to Preach*, 13.

191 Letter from Geoffrey Bingham, 'NCTM Gospel Nights 1999'.

192 Letter from Geoffrey Bingham, 'NCTM Gospel Nights 1999'.

193 *Proclaiming Christ's Gospel in Today's World*, 75.

194 *Proclaiming Christ's Gospel in Today's World*, 29.

195 'The Principles and Practice of Evangelism', *Living Faith Studies*, vol. 5, 275.

[196] Geoffrey Bingham, conversation with Martin Bleby, 2009.

[197] 'Personal Message for Team Consideration 28/10/97', p. 5.

[198] 'New Creation' Publications Incorporated, *Constitution and Rules*, Adopted 7th April, 1989, Amended 16th February, 2001. At a meeting of the NCPI Council on 15th July 2012, the Council voted to implement these windup provisions of the NCPI Constitution, as from early in 2013, 'taking care that the resources be made available for future generations' (NCPI Letter, 20th July 2012).

[199] 2 Peter 3:13.

[200] 'The Great Riot of Bullabakanka', *The Lion on the Road*, 79.

[201] *The Lion on the Road*, 82–83.

CHAPTER 13

THE *Person* OF ROMANS SEVEN

> I do not do the good I want, but the evil I do not want is what I do
>
> Romans 7:19

WRETCHED MAN THAT I AM!

'SO, IS ROMANS 6 in conflict with Romans 7? No!'

Geoffrey had just turned eighty-eight. He was giving what was to be his last public address: a study at the 2007 New Creation Teaching Ministry Summer School on 'The Law of the Spirit of Life in Christ Jesus'.[1] This is a phrase found in Romans 8 (verse 2). Nevertheless, Geoffrey on this occasion spent quite some time expounding Romans 7, particularly verses 13–25, as something not to be glossed over:

> I find it to be a law that when I want to do right, evil lies close at hand. For I delight in the law of God in my inmost self, but I see in my members another law at war with the law of my mind and making me captive to the law of sin which dwells in my members. Wretched man that I am![2]

Geoffrey was well aware of the different accounts given of this chapter:

> Some see the passage as Paul prior to conversion, still struggling with law. Some see it as representative of all men in their struggle with law. A few see it as Paul having some 'desert experience,' i.e. he has been trying to work things through. Some see it even as Paul in a defeated and possibly backslidden state. So far as I understand it, Paul is describing what happens to him whenever *in the face of law* he seeks to be obedient.[3]

Geoffrey clearly understood it as Paul after conversion as a believer, and as the condition of every believer, himself included:

I have discovered that I want to do good. I find I don't do good. I don't want to do evil but I find I do it. Now, all of those who have passed that point in their lives—they've gone through that; that's all over—raise your hand! But beware! Because I will be seen to be your enemy . . . if you've never come to the place where you despair of yourself and you see that you sin, you do really need somebody to tell you the truth . . . have you come to the place where you cry out: 'Oh, wretched man that I am! Sin is always at me. The Law is always my enemy. Am I never going to get out of that?'[4]

Geoffrey asks, 'Now, as a Christian, could you say that was your situation?'

Maybe you've not been keeping a record. But if you are keeping a record you would find that every time that you want to do good, it is a law that sin will attack you. Every time you want to do good, you will never be let free to do it. The powers of darkness, the use of the Law, the twists that there are in life—all of those things—it's a law that you cannot do good and you cannot desist from evil.

Geoffrey was not speaking academically here. He was speaking from his own experience.

CAPTIVE TO THE LAW OF SIN

Geoffrey was always quite open about his weaknesses and failings—sometimes embarrassingly so. They were evident from an early age. One who knew him in those early days writes, 'I only met him, as a child, in the guise of a turbulent school boy, as many of us were':

Geoff and I were at different schools and as we wandered home in the afternoons sometimes some of us met and behaved badly towards one another.

On one occasion in the early 1930s a well-aimed stone thrown by dear Geoffrey struck me on the forehead and I ran home with blood running down my face to report to my shocked mother on Geoffrey's prowess in battle.

He adds, 'In later life I heard nothing but good of him. He now rests in God's arms where I hope to join him shortly.'[5]

Geoffrey writes, 'as a child I must have been a pest in many ways':

> I judged my father according to my ideas of what he should have been. I can now see that I was an individualist, a person determined to do what he would do, and I would let nothing stand in my way . . . I was fashioning situations and things my way, as far as I could. I can now see what a problem I must have been to my father, when all the time I thought he was the problem.[6]

King David prayed, 'Remember not the sins of my youth'.[7] The sins of our older age can be more subtle and insidious. Geoffrey recalls:

> One of my most devastating experiences was in Kranji POW camp. A fine physiotherapist by the name of Ken Topliss once said to me quietly, as he was massaging my partly paralysed right leg, 'You must be about the most egotistical man I have ever met!'
>
> I restrained myself from sitting bolt upright, but inwardly I was shocked. My mind said, 'Me? Egotistical? Of course not!' I was numbed by Ken's words. I did not dare ask him in what ways he thought I was egotistical. I knew that what he said was true enough to him. He was a man of fine character and no carping critic.[8]

Geoffrey took some time to work this through:

> For weeks I wandered around quite lacerated by his critique. Slowly I began to see something of what he meant. Of course I was egotistical: I was essentially self-centred. In one sense I was self-centred in not being self-centred. I went out to others, tried to help folk who were mentally and physically suffering, and I think my actions were sincere and genuine, but behind those actions I was living up to my self-devised eikon of myself. That eikon was pretty close to being self-righteous.[9]

Elsewhere he explains:

> I must have been congratulating myself that I was not as other men were . . . *I* thought that *I* kept myself in good order. That was not

the case. I was in the midst of self-righteousness, virtually a Pharisee ... Self-righteousness is a most deadly sin and it mocks grace ... Over the nearly sixty years that have followed I have discovered that the proud human heart wants nothing to do with grace. It is the ego that is kept alive by religious pride.[10]

Some things did not change much over the years:

... I rang a surgeon who had been in our Kranji prison camp. He was in his nineties and physically and mentally quite active. I had not seen him since 1945 and he was surprised, and delighted, that I had rung him.

'I remember you well', he said. 'You were a person who, when you got an idea in your head, could not be talked out of it. You would press it, never letting it up. You would carry everything before you.'

I was momentarily stunned. Recovering quickly, I chuckled a little and said, 'Well, I guess I have mellowed a bit since then. I suppose I have matured somewhat.'

When I told my wife she was the one to chuckle. 'I wouldn't think you have changed much.'[11]

Geoffrey was wary of ambition, for he found it strong in himself. 'At a pastor's school I recall him shocking everyone when he said that if we have one ounce of ambition then our ministry has had it.'[12] Strong-mindedness ran in the family:

All members of our family have been strong-minded, each in his or her own way. I doubt whether any was less strong-minded than I was, and am. We might all be called 'ambitious' in some measure. I think that to some degree we have matured and mellowed as the years have passed, but the drive is still there.[13]

Such strength of drive, while making things happen, could also be a weakness and a failing. Geoffrey was quite capable of putting people in their place, even of making them feel put down:

I certainly do not think my life has been wholly egocentric, or that everything I have thought and done has sprung only from me. I am sure I have always known love for people, however awkwardly or badly I may have expressed it. Of course I have driven roughshod over some, without even being conscious of doing so. I have been

critical and even censorious where I ought to have been understanding and—without any desire to excuse myself—I think that
that has been the case with most of us.[14]

It is not only the individual who is involved. Unwittingly
or not, a whole organisation or ministry can participate in the
insensitivity that leaves people hurt. One willing helper of the
New Creation Teaching Ministry wrote of 'a number of sad,
unexplainable outcomes that I really don't know how to
describe', and went on to speak of some who were exhausted,
burnt-out or otherwise harmed by demands placed upon them
by the Ministry, and who subsequently 'don't want anything to
do with NCTM'.[15] Whether 'such a sad occurrence' is part of the
polarisation that comes with declaring the gospel,[16] or is a clash
of people's 'interpersonal mannerisms',[17] or is ultimately inexpli-
cable, no doubt Geoffrey and those with him in the Ministry bear
part of the responsibility.

Sometimes the lapses can be very close to home. Geoffrey was
most disturbed when he read what Laurel had to say about his
'moods' in the account of their life that she wrote in 2000. Laurel
had summed up:

> I think the big thing is that after fifty-three years of marriage I now
> understand his moods, as I guess he does mine.[18]

After reading what Laurel had written in the account, Geoffrey
resigned as Executive Director of the New Creation Teaching
Ministry at the beginning of 2001, at the age of eighty-two, so
they could spend more time together.[19]

Geoffrey makes reference to the Scottish preacher Alexander
Whyte (1836–1921), who told his congregation more than once:
'You'll never get out of the seventh of Romans while I'm your
minister!'[20] This is because Geoffrey realised that, in all his
eighty-eight years, Romans 7 had remained as true of him as it
ever was.

But Geoffrey also knew that this was not the whole story.
'These things matter', he says, and goes on, 'but they should not
crush us':

The fact that we can see our failures, sins and shortcomings must mean much. The fact that we can laugh at our foolish egotisms is surely a hopeful sign.[21]

There is a story told of a team member who arrived one morning for a prayer meeting, threw himself down in a chair and said, 'I feel so un-holy!' Geoffrey replied perceptively: 'You must be a very holy person to be able to say that'.[22]

There were times when Geoffrey found the nights particularly difficult, when his sins would come and visit him. He would need to remind himself again: 'Therefore, since we are justified by faith, we have peace with God through our Lord Jesus Christ ... There is therefore now no condemnation for those who are in Christ Jesus' (Romans 5:1; 8:1):[23]

> Sometimes when all the world's asleep,
> Sometimes when terror's passions deep
> Come stealing to us from their grave—
> Those sins from which He came to save
> Our race of doom and dreadful death—
> We cry as though our latest breath
> Had come at last, and we are lost,
> Upon guilt's storm forever tossed.
>
> But grace comes throbbing through that night,
> And sin's forgiven, and holy light
> Breaks to us from Your Cross and Tomb
> As You come to our upper room.
> O Christ now risen from the grave,
> You gave Yourself ourselves to save,
> And all the pains of memory
> Are banished in that holy Tree.
>
> The shame of guilt cannot return,
> Nor fire of curse within us burn.
> You sin and guilt and curse became
> To save us from eternal shame.
> Our spirits in Your Cross rejoice,
> And with us all creation's voice
> Is lifted in the highest praise
> For love and grace and all Your ways.[24]

Because Geoffrey knew the forgiveness of his sins, he was willing to acknowledge and admit them. Within a day or so of a falling-out he would generally ring up or write and say 'Sorry', and seek to continue in the relationship. One such instance:

> For myself, I am so often aware of my sins, shortcomings and idiosyncrasies and trust that [you] will see it all as the battle with the old Adam. Forgive them all, and where they offend culturally put them down to crass action on my part.[25]

I, OF MYSELF

At the 2007 Summer School, Geoffrey was warming to his theme:

> Paul . . . called himself the chief of sinners—'I am'! Not, 'I was'—and there's a mystery there.[26]

'Who is this man who said he is sold unto sin?' asks Geoffrey. 'Can that be our great St Paul?'

> Then he says: 'I know that in me nothing good dwells. That is in my flesh.' In myself as a *sarkinos* creature, I know that nothing good dwells within me. That is to say, of me there is nothing good.[27]

Geoffrey notes Paul's use of the Greek word *sarkinos* in Romans 7:14, meaning 'made of flesh'. He takes it here to be a neutral word, as in 1 Corinthians 3:1 where it refers to infants: 'you're like a little baby . . . you are born into the world and you are helpless and you can do nothing of yourself'. He contrasts it with 'the hard word *sarkikos*, meaning 'fleshly', which is 'deliberately evil, deliberately disobeying God', used in 1 Corinthians 3:3 to relate to jealousy and strife.[28]

This distinction is a key to Geoffrey's understanding of Romans 7. If, as Jesus said, 'No one is good but God alone'[29]—all goodness is derived only from God—then we are faced with the reality of our 'moral helplessness' of ourselves:

We must never assume that *of ourselves* we can accomplish anything of goodness, righteousness, holiness, love and truth . . . We will have good intentions, but not the power, *of ourselves*, to accomplish the good or desist from the evil. Evil, *of itself*, is stronger than we are, of ourselves.[30]

Elsewhere he explains that *sarkinos* in Romans 7:14 'does not have evil connotation so much as connotation of *moral inability*':

I of myself am human and weak. I delight in the law of God and seek to desist from sin and do good, but when I try *of myself* then I find sin is always with me, is stronger than me, and forces my hand . . . I wish to be out of a body where such is the case, and I will be rescued from this body, but meanwhile I recognise the facts, and live with them.[31]

THE LAW OF THE SPIRIT OF LIFE IN CHRIST JESUS

Geoffrey recognises that by now some in his audience at the 2007 Summer School 'might be feeling quite uneasy':

. . . yes, because what does it say in Romans 6? 'Sin shall not have dominion over you—for you're not under law, but under grace.'[32]

Geoffrey reassures those who have this concern. He says, 'Well, stick to Romans 6!'

Paul says, 'But by the grace of God I am what I am, and his grace toward me was not in vain . . . ' (I Cor. 15:10) . . . We accomplish nothing of a moral nature without the grace of God.[33]

For Paul, as for us, 'a brilliant miracle has taken place' on the cross:[34]

Wretched man that I am—here am I! . . . 'I want to do good.' Hey! That is something! *I want to do good!* . . . that's the biggest miracle that happens to a man, that he who sins so easily would now want to do good—delight in the law after the inward man . . . Your thrust is to do good—if it wasn't to do good you wouldn't be a believer. Is that clear? I hope it may be liberating.[35]

Even so, the goodness must still come from God:

> ... believing man with his new life does not *innately* possess goodness, as such. Hence he cannot *of himself* overcome evil and do good.[36]

By the same token, neither is sin innate in the person with a purified heart:

> It appears that Paul sees it as *an inmate* but not as *innate*. He says, 'It is no longer I that do it, but sin which dwells in me' (Rom. 7:17). He thus divorces sin as being foreign to him, and not intrinsically part of him ... he knows that his heart rests on the justificatory grace of God. It does not cease to be a pure heart because it is subject to sin's pressures.[37]

Not only that, but true life and action can now flow:

> The thought he pursues in Romans 8 is that through the Spirit, in fact and in deed, he can 'put to death the deeds of the body'.[38]

'But if by the Spirit you put to death the deeds of the body', Geoffrey says, 'well, there's your sanctification, practical holiness and righteousness'.[39] So he comes into Romans 8:

> 'There is therefore now no condemnation' ... The Holy Spirit has come to that man and he has set him free from the law of sin and death. I can acknowledge the fact that I delight in the law of God after the inward man, and I would do good and I wouldn't do evil. If that's not a miracle for Geoff Bingham, then there are no miracles.[40]

We now know that we are 'wholly dependent upon God to live as His image and likeness', and we see that 'God always works in the believer' and that 'power for the believer is never lacking'.[41] Referring to Romans 8:4 Geoffrey writes:

Believers are to 'fulfil the just requirements of the law'—believers 'who walk not according to the flesh but after the Spirit'... It is precisely because they are justified that they can and they must fulfil 'the just requirements of the law'. The one who pleases God, then, is the one who walks according to the Spirit and fulfils the just requirements of the law.[42]

But this is never in a legalistic way: 'There's not one command in Romans 8—Paul is just glorying in what is the reality':[43]

His innate problem of accomplishing the defeat of sin, and the triumph of effective obedience, is *through the Holy Spirit*.[44]

Being through the Holy Spirit, who blows where he wills, we can expect it to be anything but hidebound and predictable:

And so, life is vibrant! 'You never know what the Spirit will do', is one of things one could say. I've been thinking a lot about my past life and I realise that the thing that has always been on my heart is the word of life—the gospel. Because the Spirit of truth, when it comes, it comes to bring the gospel to us ... the Spirit of God has come into us and we speak the truth of God, we speak the word of God, we show the holiness of God and the righteousness of God, but—in all of that—the love of God, that He won't leave us to say what a 'wretched man that I am'.[45]

This is not just in word, but in action:

... when the Spirit of God, comes to us, we are not just talking anymore. *We know God!* His love has been poured into our hearts— we can *live* in this world—we can minister in this world.[46]

ALL OF THE SPIRIT

'So, is Romans 6 in conflict with Romans 7?' Or is Romans 8 in conflict with Romans 7?:

Romans 6 and 8 speak of a triumph over sin, but in both cases the 'I, of myself' is not present. In the first case it is the defeat of sin by

Christ and his Cross, in the second it is the empowering of the Spirit so that one can desist from evil, and can do good. Yet to know that in no case can one do good *of oneself* is a salutary and valuable lesson![47]

Elsewhere Geoffrey summarises Romans 6, 7 and 8:

What we must keep constantly in mind is that in Romans 6, Paul is speaking of the clearance of guilt, and the loss of sin's power through that event. In Romans 7, he is analysing the man who seeks to obey the law, but is unsuccessful, i.e. he obeys it in *intention*, but cannot obey it in *action*. In Romans 8, he is speaking of man living in, and depending upon, the Spirit, in which case man can now 'put to death the deeds of the body,' i.e. he can live in a state in which sin and flesh are defeated when obedience through the Spirit is effected. We must see these three situations as different, yet, when all together, just the one. Hence if we look at the believer as in only Romans 6, or only Romans 7, or only Romans 8, then we will get the whole matter quite out of focus.[48]

In winding up his Summer School 2007 address, Geoffrey was keen that none present should miss out on the blessing:

So, if you look a bit tense—as some of you do when I'm saying some of these things—is it because your situation doesn't add up to Romans 8? You can't even overcome the sorrow that you have that you don't do good and you do evil from time to time? No, he has condemned sin in the flesh—that is finished ... if you don't have the Spirit of Christ, you still haven't come to the point of that infilling, that flooding of love and holiness and righteousness actuated and made to be operative and real, by the Spirit. 'If the Spirit of Him who raised Jesus from the dead dwells in you, he who raised Christ Jesus from the dead will give life to your mortal bodies also through his Spirit which dwells in you.'[49]

And he harked back to his experience of the Spirit in the days at Miller's Point:[50]

All of that is of the Spirit.

I can remember years ago when I was a minister in a church, and I knew there was something wrong and I didn't know what it was, and I just got on my knees one day and I said, 'Well Lord, I should be a man filled with the Spirit and full in the knowledge of you and of your love and in action. But Lord, that's not so with me.' And I said, 'But you said in your Word, "If any man believe on me, out of his belly shall come rivers of living water"'—that's what I'm talking about.

I'm not talking about paddling Christians—you know, little bits of this and little bits of that, and being boosted up by different schools and other things like that. I'm talking about the Spirit of God coming into us in all fullness so we understand the mysteries of God, and we are men and women and children and old people who walk in the fullness of the Spirit. That's what I'm talking about.

And I said, 'Well Lord, I believe in you. I believe all of that—I really do. But You will have to make rivers of living water flow out of me.'

Geoffrey concludes: 'And he did. And he does. And it's real!'[51]

[1] *For Freedom Christ Has Set Us Free*, New Creation Teaching Ministry Summer School 2007, MP3 disc 957, Study 12. Transcribed by Lol Bettany.

[2] Romans 7:21–24.

[3] *The Splendour of Holiness*, 127.

[4] Summer School 2007.

[5] Marsden Hordern, of Warrawee, NSW, Letter to Martin Bleby, 26 October 2011.

[6] *My Beloved Family*, 166.

[7] Psalm 25:7, KJV.

[8] *My Beloved Family*, 164.

[9] *My Beloved Family*, 164.

[10] *Love Is the Spur*, 72.

[11] *My Beloved Family*, 165.

[12] John Dunn, email to Martin Bleby, 25 May 2012.

[13] *My Beloved Family*, 167.

[14] *My Beloved Family*, 169.

[15] Testimony, 2007, name withheld.

[16] As in Matthew 10:34–36; John 9:13–41.

[17] Testimony, 2007, name withheld.

[18] *Laurel's Story*, 131.

[19] Martin Bleby, personal recollection.

[20] Summer School 2007; see G. F. Barbour, *The Life of Alexander Whyte D.D.*, p. 305, quoted: <www.geocities.com/athens/olympus/4199/sothen.htm>, accessed 27 February 2007.

[21] *My Beloved Family*, 169.

[22] Martin Bleby, personal recollection.

[23] Conversations and teaching recalled by Martin Bleby.

[24] 'O Cross of Christ, O Place of Bliss', *New Creation Hymn Book*, 327.

[25] Personal recollection, and Letter from Geoffrey Bingham to Martin Bleby, 31 January 2000.

[26] Summer School 2007; referring to 1 Timothy 1:15.

[27] Summer School 2007.

[28] Summer School 2007.

[29] Mark 10:18.

[30] *The Splendour of Holiness*, 83.

[31] 'The True Nature of Law', *Living Faith Studies* 28, vol. 3, 176.

[32] Summer School 2007; referring to Romans 6:14.

[33] *The Splendour of Holiness*, 83.

[34] *Living Faith Studies* 28, vol. 3, 176.

[35] Summer School 2007.

[36] *The Splendour of Holiness*, 128.

[37] *The Splendour of Holiness*, 220.

[38] *The Splendour of Holiness*, 220.

[39] Summer School 2007.

[40] Summer School 2007.

[41] *The Splendour of Holiness*, 84, 83.

[42] *An Introduction to the Epistle to the Romans* (unpublished manuscript), Chapter 8, 2, 3.

[43] Summer School 2007.

[44] *Introduction to the Epistle to the Romans*, Chapter 8, 3.

[45] Summer School 2007.

[46] Summer School 2007.

[47] *Living Faith Studies* 28, vol. 3, 176.

[48] *The Splendour of Holiness*, 128–129.

[49] Summer School 2007.

[50] See Chapter 8, 'The Day of the Spirit'.

[51] Summer School 2007.

CHAPTER 14

All
THINGS ARE
Yours

Looking into the distance

TOTTERING OVER A HILL

'As you go up the hill, you see the blue sky arching away from you. As you advance, it recedes, but it doesn't really. It comes to you also. You get closer to it, and yet you never arrive.'[1]

Geoffrey had written a number of short stories about the approach of death. This is one of them. He was picturing an old man climbing to the top of a hill, as he had often done before:

Once you had raced up a hill. Sometimes on foot, sometimes on a cycle. Even on a horse, a high gelding or a smooth mare. Then betimes in a vehicle. First a shaky, noisy car, then a solid, steady car, and then finally a long, sleek, smooth car which thrust itself upwards effortlessly. But today you walked, on your own. There was no one to come with you. Tottering over a hill.[2]

This time it is more difficult:

The crest of the hill looks down at you, as you look up at it. Then, with an effort of breathing and pushing your old legs forward, you make it to the top of the hill. Then there is a bit of a gasp as you regain your breath.[3]

He sits on a rock, and surveys 'the sweeping flats beneath':

Before the flats there are low hills, undulating, making curved lines across the landscape. Clusters of green trees pattern the whole world of grass-green. A river lies in it all, like a flat silver tract of water. This is what you hadn't seen, pressing up the hill.[4]

'Glow of the sun, warmth of the rock, ease of the body' eases him down into 'comfortable memory'[5] from the years of his life. Throwing a young bull to the ground for branding, 'feeling

325

strong'; milking a cow in the early morning, 'steam rising from the hot dung as the first sun rayed up through the mist'; the country church on a Sunday with its 'religious colour', seemingly removed from the daily 'mysteries about life and death'. Then the city, with its 'clustered small houses'. Early attempts to communicate with people in writing and preaching. 'The mystery of the Cross suddenly breaking open to you, and sunlight streaming down into your soul' in a little mission hall where a man 'told powerfully the love of the eternal God'. Later, in the army, 'the process of being brutalised for the killing to come', then 'the sudden action . . . Smashed steel, spiked trees with fractured limbs'. 'Then the prison . . . barbed wire . . . miracles of love, and the dreadful acts of hate . . . deterioration of spirit . . . searching for an answer':[6]

> Here, in the sun, with your tired body relaxing, it all seemed so far away. The despair, the bitterness, and then the sudden, full discovery of God as He is . . . you knew the inflow into your spirit, power to know, to feel, to tell.[7]

'Here, lying on the hills, it came flowing back, sweetly':

> Message after message flashed through. Themes vibrating sweetly in his mind. The hills of the Scripture were as real—if not more—as these which stretched before him to his own naked eyes. The King and His Kingdom. The Father and His Family. The Lover and His beloved. The Lord and His liberated. The Spirit and His renewed men of flesh. Stripped of guilt, purged of their past, shining and new as true men and women . . . 'These trust their souls to a faithful Creator,' he felt like crying to the blue arch of the sky.[8]

There were days he called 'Spirit-days':

> God was amongst them, touching men in the depths, pressing away fear from eyes, bringing healing to bodies and minds, brushing off worry and timidity. He had seen men and women grow strong, ready for action, ready to repeat God's victories. Christ was vibrantly present. The Father was watching and caring. The Spirit was unveiling the mysteries so that they came through, sparkling and clear.[9]

Then, closer to home:

> The eyes he had loved beyond all other eyes. They were quiet, strong and grey. They had followed him gently wherever he went. Something behind the eyes had followed him. With her had come their children, growing up, growing past him, going out with what he had tried to give. Sometimes he had been too busy and they had sought to find without him. This was the bitter-sweet pang. But she had not failed. She had given, for it flowed from her without words; soundless ideas, you might say, that they had caught.[10]

In this manner the whole of his life, for better or worse, passes before him, as he sits on that warm rock, at the summit of the hill. To which we shall return.

DEATH COMES SO GENTLY

Geoffrey was no stranger to near-death experiences. Not only in the war, but also with health issues and other events subsequently. 'I—for one—have been close to death, and am still often this way.'[11] 'My being wounded on the 11th February 1942 put me to bed for months and made me to be a person with a decided limp and a steady history of pain for some 66 years.'[12] One of 'a series of close shaves with death'[13] occurred when Geoff and Laurel were on a return visit to Pakistan for ministry among missionaries for three months in 1983:

> It came to an abrupt end with a near-fatal accident in a head-on collision. Geoff sustained a fractured skull, and Laurel severe lacerations: they were flown home as soon as they were fit to travel, and slowly made good their recovery with proper care and treatment.[14]

Geoffrey wrote in 2006:

> The last three years at least have been difficult ones for Laurel and me (Geoff) so far as health is concerned. Laurel is now 84 and has battled hard with her health, whilst coping with my operations and illness. In July 2005, I had surgery of the cervical spine

327

(cervical laminectomy) and in October 2005 I had surgery of the lumbar spine (lumbar laminectomy). Indications were that these operations were essential. The surgery to the upper spine relieved a problem of numbness in arms. The second operation was not as successful. These happenings at my age of 87 meant that I was deeply affected by anaesthetics and drug treatments. In late 2006 I had to undergo investigation of the prostate area because of deep pain and it was discovered that I had cancer of the prostate and bone. I have since undergone hormone therapy and radiotherapy.[15]

At the beginning of 2008, he suffered a severe fall, from which it was thought he might not recover:

It was a fall in the night and affected my head deeply . . . I entered into a bad state of mind and body.
I was so nursed and cared for that I recovered.[16]

After this he was admitted to higher care in the Burnleigh Nursing Home, Parkside, just up the road from his eldest daughter's home, where Laurel and family could visit him daily. Laurel continued to live in their home at Kingswood.

Geoffrey accepted all this in the light of God's known goodness and faithfulness:

One battles with God and with pain—no small matter! . . . I have engaged with God and myself as to the matter of God's faithfulness. I have never thought of taking God to task and so have worked from the premise that God has something enriching to teach me. This, in fact, has been the case . . . We know 'All will be well!' He doeth all things well! So says the trusting patient of his surgeon! So there is a beautiful outcome to a demanding stress of many ages of sorrowful strain, and holy sorrow, and training.[17]

Not that he underestimated the fear of death:

The Hebrew was frank. He said, 'My heart is at anguish within me, the terrors of death have fallen upon me. Fear and trembling come upon me, and horror overwhelms me'. David talked about the sorrows, the cords, and the snares of death, as though he were being trapped into death.[18]

This is because 'Death is linked with the sin of man'.[19] Geoffrey quoted Paul Tillich:

> Man lives in fear of death, not simply because he has to die, but because he deserves to die.[20]

What is fearful is not so much the process of dying as the judgement of death itself:

> ... man is in fear of death because he is in fear of what lies beyond it, that is the logical conclusion of judgement. His conscience tells him he is a creature not only of time but beyond-time, and the issues of his conscience matter much. Somehow beyond time is the situation where there will be a reckoning. As Hebrews 9:27 has it, 'It is appointed unto man once to die, and after that comes judgement ...'[21]

'This fear of death is highly exacerbated by Satan, who thus keeps humanity in bondage (Heb. 2:14-15, cf. Jude 9)':

> We refer to the guilt of man as giving Satan power to accuse and so to alarm man up to judgement. Such negative use of fear increases man's terror and loathing of God, distorting the glory of God into petty cruelty, vengeful intents, and tyrannical judgement. Thus evil distorts in order to increase fear, add to man's existential anguish, and to increase his terror of life. Hence Satan, his accusing principalities and powers, conscience, law, the curse and God's wrath are all wrought into one strong force to keep man in misery, fear and rage. These manipulate him within the fear of death.[22]

What Christ has done in his death on the cross makes it 'so that sin is no longer effective in its depredations of the human spirit':

> ... every death was taken up into and encompassed by the death of Christ. The death of sin was experienced by him, and indeed was played out to the end, so that death as such was obliterated ... He destroyed death in his death. Thus the New Testament speaks of all believers having been taken up into that death (of the Cross) and so dying with him, their sins having been neutralised and destroyed so

that death's sting has been borne and thus withdrawn...The penalty of sin has been borne, the evil of sin has been expended, the power of sin has been broken, and the pollution of sin has been expunged. All the elements of death, then, have been banished...death's fear is removed, its indignity destroyed...life is known, and views of immortality are breaking upon the eyes of the redeemed.[23]

The outcome of this is as Jesus said: 'if any one keeps my word, he will never see death':[24]

'He who believes in me shall never die',[25] brings us to the true triumph of the gift of life. Whilst man experiences the death of the body as a fact seen by others, he does not personally experience it as a felt fact himself. We mean that others see his (physical) death, *but he does not! He goes on in the life he has known (as eternal) and goes into the life that is eternal.* There is transition as he crosses some unseen line, but no bump (so to speak) as he does this. No wonder he needs not to fear death.[26]

Thus Geoffrey writes: 'I can say of the times I thought death was almost a breath away that I felt wonderfully calm. There was no terror, and only serenity':[27]

Death comes so gently.
I hear the quiet footfalls,
Not light pattering—as though inconsequential,
Nor heavy padding as foreboding,
But gracious unintruding suggestion
Of one coming purposefully.

Often when long shades have fallen
Over the obsessive busyness
And the compulsive accomplishing
I have paused in the sudden quietness
Wondering why I am visited
By this soft stranger.

Never in these visitations
Has there been fear.
Nor has the bland confronted me
As though of no point (blank guilelessness),

330

But a clement spirit has met me
And grown into me as a dear friend
Accepts the welcome but does not invade . . .

Death is not death, but God
Coming for His own, His Father's arms
Reaching to His beloved. His quietude
Surrounds where fear might invade
And Love gently claims
That which was always His.[28]

THE GLORY THAT IS TO BE REVEALED[29]

Eschatology—the doctrine of the last things—held a key place in Geoffrey's theology and teaching, and in his understanding of all history. In describing what he hesitated to call 'the NCTM *schema*' of teaching, Geoffrey writes:

> Eschatology really covers, 'The Beginning of the End and the End of the Beginning'. That is, Eschatology is dependent upon Protology; it begins with it and is fulfilled in the end. The so-called 'last things' are there, in essence, at the beginning of history in 'the first things'. This is the key to understanding history—all things are to be seen in eschatological perspective, and these, in turn, in the light of the plan and intention of the Triune God, in the works of the Persons in unity. The Reconciliation of all Creation—its being summed up, filled up and harmonised in Christ—is treated in the overall ethos of God . . . The works of God come to their completion in the *telos*, in the new heavens and the new earth, in the marriage of the Bride and the Lamb, the Holy City, the Temple—which is God and the Lamb—and the eternal Paradise of God.[30]

Geoffrey sees the end of things being already present, in an anticipatory way, at the beginning. For example, the union of the man and the woman in Genesis 2:23–24 'was to be the type of the one who was to come, whose marriage as Bridegroom to the purified Bride would be the goal and meaning of history'.[31] The first person created is thus described as 'this visionary man . . . at once the man-that-is-now, the man-that-will-not-be, and yet the man-that-is-yet-to-be ... the noble and regal figure that emerged',[32] in God's image, from God's creative and purposeful action. On this is based Geoffrey's whole appreciation of human dignity, nobility and destiny—sin and degradation notwithstanding. Geoffrey characterises his teaching as being 'from the action of creation to the climax of it in the new creation', or 'from Eden to the new Eden'.[33]

And what is the goal and purpose of God's action in the whole of history? It is God's people, whom He treasures above all as His 'beloved possession':

> God planned all history from the creation of the first couple to the climax and completion of all things at the *telos*, and He has now created a people who are so partakers of His divine nature that they can be—and are—partners in His purposes for both time and Eternity.[34]

One way Geoffrey pictures humanity in its pristine glory, sorrowful degradation, and culminating elevation, is as a great castle:

> Through these swirling mists of darkness came a terrible sight. It was that of a castle which had been beleaguered ... Huge dark apertures gaped like the wounds of a ravaged citadel. Mists wreathed and wound about its broken towers, and the glory that had been a fine edifice was now only darkly silent, and its silence was tired and futile.[35]

After 'the deep sorrow, and the great suffering'[36] of the cross, comes a different vision, of 'the restoration of the great castle':

> I came upon it suddenly, and when I saw it everything was bathed in a great light. At the very first sight of it I became breathless, and very much it was as when a man beholds for the first time the beauty of a woman, and in particular the woman he has come at that point to love ... The castle stood, whole and complete. It stood firm and calm and serene. It flowed out a rich new tranquillity such as one might take an eternity to acquire ...
>
> It was the impression of full might, and strong impregnability which flowed out to me. As I looked I knew it was as though that

castle had never been violated. No one peering closely would see the tiniest touch of restoration . . . I do not say it was new, nor was fresh, but I do say it was whole, as though it had never been ravaged . . . My gaze roved hungrily over every beloved part of the great structure—its masonry, its windows, its towering peaks, its rugged battlements. Without doubt you must call it noble, and you could not but feel its gentle but strong reality, and you knew that the man was again the man as it had always been intended he should be, and as had been planned in the quietness of the no-time (or, the before-time).[37]

He has a momentary glimpse of the castle's former state:

For a fraction only of time . . . I saw the castle as it had been in its derelict state . . . The cold dank mists came swirling about again, and the dreadful sunken eyes of the gaping apertures looked out hollowly as do the vacant eyes of a rotted skull. The wretched, ragged battlement, chipped, smashed and exploited, all filled me with a sickening sorrow . . . when suddenly the eyes cleared of their mist, and the blur washed away, and there, unchanged, was the castle and its native splendour.[38]

This is God's vindicating defeat of evil and death:

The great castle before me—that mighty rearing edifice, that noble gathering of inviolability—gave the lie to the serpent's fang, and to the horror of its coils.[39]

None of this is mere idealistic wish-fulfilment. It is grounded securely in the historical reality of the resurrection of Jesus Christ from death:

It is clear that without the Resurrection of Christ the matter of hope has no basis at all . . . We have been raised with Christ in regard to our former moral–spiritual death. This is the proof to us that we shall be raised from bodily death and be equipped with a body of glory. The first Resurrection which was Christ's includes all the elect in that Resurrection. It has been well said, that what Christ began in that Resurrection he will complete in the ultimate resurrection. It is in this assurance, by faith, that we now live, and for us also, 'faith is the assurance of things hoped for'.[40]

It is perhaps in his songs that Geoffrey's hope comes through most vividly. He used to tell the story of a pastor who had the heart of an evangelist, and used to evangelise his congregation every Sunday as if they had never heard the gospel before. Eventually they got sick of it, and told him so. He went to a trusted colleague and asked what he could do. The wise old counsellor responded: 'Tell them about the banquet!' From this came a new song:

> Tell them about the banquet,
> Tell them the feast that will be,
> The rejoicing and tasting and feasting
> As the wine of the Kingdom flows free.
> With the endless rejoicing of meeting,
> The communion so sweet at the core,
> Of talking and laughing and wonder
> And the songs of the evermore.

Here will be the summation of all that is in the Scriptures:

> Tell them about the Speakers:
> The Patriarchs rising will give
> Of the visions of Yahweh's great splendour
> And communion that caused them to live
> Where the idols were gaudy and shabby,
> Or fierce in their ruling of men,
> For the Patriarchs knew of the glory
> The Spirit imprinted on them.
>
> The Kings will be there with their speeches
> Who know of the Kingdom of God,
> And the Priests will laud in their wonder
> The law and its power of blood;
> The Prophets will dance for the sorrows
> Messiah would share in His flesh
> To give garments of joy to the mourners
> And bring primeval beauty afresh.

At the heart of it all will be Christ himself, with his people:

Messiah will rise in the Spirit,
His tender hand soft on His Bride,
He will bow to acknowledge the Father
Who gave her to be at His side.
He will hand all the glories of Kingdom
To His Father, ineffable King,
And millions of sons and of angels
Will join as the galaxies sing

In the songs that are ever and endless
Of the banquet of worship and praise,
Of the union of God with His image—
The Bride and her people—always.
'Ah tell them about the banquet!'
The Seer cried in weeping delight,
'Tell them the banquet is coming,
Yet the banquet is here day and night.'

The reality of the coming age is what keeps us going in the present:

The songs of the banquet we're singing,
In faith with love's full hope in sight,
The foretaste keeps life in the suff'ring
And Heaven makes darkness all light.
The thousands and myriads are singing
As angels and creatures adore,
And wisdom and honour and glory
Flood heaven and earth evermore.

The Three rise as One in the banquet
In union the One are the Three,
The love and the power of communion
Encompass the Love-Family.
All creatures are one in the Father,
All things unified in the Son.
One fellowship are in the Spirit
And the banquet has only begun.[41]

Another very personal expression of this 'sure and certain hope'[42] comes in a song Geoffrey wrote after the funeral of a friend:

335

One day we'll see Him face to face,
And then our hearts will beat as one,
That day we'll know the glory of His grace,
As we on earth have never known . . .

The years of sorrow and of strife,
The sin that brought a holy shame,
The guilt our hearts could never wholly hide
Will never visit us again.

Dear Lover, Saviour, Jesus Christ,
Our present life is hid in Thee,
But oh! the wonder when we are unveiled
In glory of our liberty.

Till then we live in present hope,
In patience of the coming sight,
And those who share with You Your glory now,
We then will meet with great delight.

Delight and bliss and joy and love,
As now our hearts cannot contain,
Will flood us as we see Him face to face
And we are wholly one again.[43]

Geoffrey hungers to be able to express what it is to 'set your hope fully upon the grace that is coming to you at the revelation of Jesus Christ' (1 Peter 1:13):

It is literally 'the grace that is being brought', meaning that it is coming to us now, and is being revealed to us, as Christ himself is being revealed to us. It is not, then, all in the future. At the same time, so much is to be revealed which as yet we do not know, and which we have not yet experienced.[44]

One of the most appealing features of the 'new heavens and a new earth in which righteousness dwells'[45] will be the utter purity and total absence of any uncleanness:[46]

What the sheer joy and relief of a believer will be at coming to ultimate and irreversible holiness we cannot say, but we can imagine it. Jesus said the pure in heart will see God, and John says, of the saints, 'They shall see his face, and his name shall be on their foreheads' (Rev. 22:4). To be in the intimate presence of God, to know nothing of impurity is present, and to be finished with the old struggle with it, will be a glorious state in which to live. The rare times of feeling utterly utterly pure, and being shed of old impurity, are enough foretaste of the coming reality to make us rejoice in the grace that is coming to us at the revelation of Jesus Christ, for he is the complete revelation of utter holiness.[47]

This has powerful implications for living now:

> In the ultimate, Man will be perfect. He will function correctly. Even so this does not mean that Man cannot discover what he really is, and seek to live out now—in the age in which we live—the very best of relationships with God and his fellow creatures. No one is primarily and only interested in what Man will ultimately be. We would all like to know how best to live now, to seek out the ways in which we can have the best relationships whether they be personal, marital, familial, communal, national and even international. The Christian knows he has to seek these relationships under grace. He who is not a Christian must seek to live the best relationships within the limited capacity which is his.
>
> Even so the goal is an incentive and an impetus for present living. If we know what we are going to be, we can set about being that now. This calls for 'great grace' because the handicaps of our past as a race are with us now.[48]

One practical outcome of this for Geoffrey was his resistance to sectional party-mindedness, his drawing on a wide range of teachers and writers, and his insistence that 'all things are yours' (1 Corinthians 3:21–23):

> When Paul chided the Corinthians for being party-minded, it was because they were clutching after the riches of one teacher. That teacher did not see those riches the way his listeners did. He saw Christ as his riches, salvation as his fullness, and life in the Spirit as pouring out to others the fullness they needed ... That is why he told the immature and spiritually stunted believers at Corinth, 'All things are yours, whether Paul or Apollos or Cephas or the world or

life or death or the present or the future, all are yours; and you are Christ's; and Christ is God's'.[49]

'If all of this sounds high-flown and impractical', he says, 'then let a believer try to live without God's fullness':

> Let him treat his union with the eternal God with indifference, and let him seek to draw for his needs upon his own reservoir! Then he will know his own innate poverty. Then he will know his meanness of spirit. His life will be occupied with trivia, his mind will dwell on things mediocre, and he will seek to draw some sort of fullness from objects and persons.[50]

There is a better way:

> If, however, he luxuriate in the grace of God, if he receive from the fullness of love, and if he be given over to 'the fullness of the blessing of the Gospel of Christ', then rivers will first flow into him, and then out through him. The measure of such a man will be the measure of the gifts God has poured out upon him. His vision of God will be of His length, breadth, depth and height, so that together—with all saints—he will come to know the love of Christ which surpasses knowledge, the outcome of which is that he will be filled unto all the fullness of God, and his glory will be in the endless variety, diversity and unity of the fullness.[51]

LIVING IN THE *TELOS*[52]

Geoffrey's approach to death was attended by the usual frailties, uncertainties and indignities that accompany dying in old age. Earlier on, as his eyes, ears, teeth and feet increasingly needed artificial help, Geoffrey had often referred to 2 Corinthians 4:16— 'Though our outer nature is wasting away, our inner nature is being renewed every day'—and on that basis he claimed that he was 'newer' than many who were younger than he was! No less than in earlier days, he needed to hear the reassurance of the gospel from his friends, and he welcomed it. At the same time, his mind remained keen, and his astute pastoral sensitivity enabled him still to speak into their lives with prophetic edge where needed. He continued to read, and found a kindred spirit particularly in the American puritan theologian Jonathan Edwards (1703–1758), whose biography and writings he kept close to his bedside.[53]

Geoffrey's health issues left him somewhat incapacitated: 'One problem has been that the result of accidents and surgery to heal the injuries has completely destroyed my computer skill'. Recovering from the damaging fall that landed him in Burnleigh Nursing Home, 'I woke one morning with a new surge of power ... I began to write by hand'.[54] His right arm was in pain, but when asked if it affected his writing, he replied, 'Strangely, no'.[55] Another book was in the making:

> I knew what I wanted to do. It was to write a book on the depths of God's true Fatherhood. It was not that I believed I now knew all the depths of God as Father of His children, but that God, in His mercy, would teach me more and more, if I were permitted to live in spite of my cancer and my present near death.[56]

He titles it, *Finding the Father: Living in the Telos.*[57] Gillian Borgas, whose own father had recently died, encouraged Geoffrey in his writing, with weekly visits, and was in turn pastored by him. As he wrote each part she had it typed out and brought it back to him for checking.

It is a discursive work, ranging over incidents of his life, from his relationship with his own father through to his present situation, interspersed with theological insights and biblical exposition, along with observations on life and relationships. It reads at times almost like a 'stream of consciousness' novel. It will suddenly switch from one theme to another. All of it with a certain lightness of touch, matched by a purposeful earnestness. It could come across to some as disconnected fragments from a faltering spirit. Geoffrey denies this:

> ... the placement is deliberately mixed. This is the plan of the writer who lives in a mixed world as it would seem ... Tidiness is an attempt to persuade readers our world is led by a 'collected' and 'tidy' deity ... I hope that bits and pieces of this book may give us a

new and powerful outlook on the amazing mysteries which will appear to our yet-to-be-opened-eyes.[58]

He writes as one standing on the edge of eternity and straining to communicate what he can just begin to see. 'It is untellable', he says, 'but we must tell'.[59]

What is this '*telos*' in which we live? It is:

> ... the Divine climax for all people for all time ... a loving unity of all folk that on earth do dwell ... where glorious beauty is the way of life for all, and holiness is the order for all creatures, and all things are eternal and no creature ever perishes. Moreover love is the one and only way for all.[60]

While this is of the end-time—'the fascinating *telos* promising a great future to the whole human race'[61]—nevertheless it is very much of the here and now:

> The *telos* is that which has always been and always will be. There is no *finale* which does not come from the original ... there is not such a thing as a *beginning* to the *telos*, nor an *ending* to the same. It is all eternal![62]

This is because the *telos*, as Geoffrey has come to appreciate, is the very being and action of God operative towards us now:

> It is never apart from us, nor are we apart from Them, i.e. the Godhead and the members of the Kingdom.[63]

In some of his final Monthly Ministry Studies in 2005, Geoffrey had sought to set forth the reality of 'The Living God and His Living Powers' present to us in the church and through all history, as 'the true River', 'the Bread of Life', 'the Word of Life', 'the Breath of God', 'the Tree of Life', 'the Blessing of God', and 'the Blessings of Light'.[64] Now he says:

> ... the 'tree of life', 'river of life', 'the word of life', indicate that humanity—as a member of the eternal (living) Kingdom—will never be short of ... the substance required for Kingdom vocation.[65]

This *telos*, then, is essential for present living, 'our own on-way of going':[66]

> ... *that which is to be, is to be!* Eternal life when seen here is what forms the pattern now, that it may issue now what we will be there, *then* ... I am glad, even if it is late in life, that I have come to know the principle of *telos*—the continual work of God from the beginning of time to the so-called 'end', 'fulfilment', 'closure', 'climax'. The time from 'the start' to 'the finish'. One, as a creature of God, needs to know where he or she is in God's plan. Then each of us ... will know the present will of God.[67]

The *telos* is nothing other than 'Father and Family for ever',[68] shown by 'the sealed and sanctified action of the Cross of love, of perfected love, perfected by the shedding of Jesus' blood'.[69] So 'the true kingdom of God is a place of true relationships. This is the true life of the *telos*':[70]

> My conclusion is that all human beings are interdependent one upon the other ... God's law is essentially love and so we can—*and must*—live in love together ... Every man is of love and, in union with God, he can love ... One may spend all one's life probing the hiddenness of personal relationships and the power of love that suffers.[71]

Geoffrey is keenly aware that this is contested:

> ... the *telos* is 'the heavenlies' which is the place of conflict, also, between God and evil powers who are in conflict.[72]

But he is confident of the outcome:

> God so works that all evil—we repeat, ALL EVIL!—is destroyed and defeated FOREVER.[73]

> All that is evil will be rendered helpless. Only love will be effective and affective. The triune way of unity and love is the goal of God and His thrilling *telos*. As the *telos* draws itself to its own close we will be tasting the vast gifts of the Godhead in ways unbelievable.[74]

Geoffrey himself is impacted: 'I feel the first of the tremors of the ultimate creation as the event draws nearer'.[75]

This, for all its grandeur, is set in the homely context of life in the nursing home, reminiscences of his past life, and the comings and goings of Laurel and the family. All of this he sees woven into and contributing towards life in God's great *telos* day by day:

> We are sure that movement into eternal life does not obliterate family love but only enhances it.[76]

The imminence and reality of the *telos* of God leaves him dissatisfied with aspects of his earlier theology and writing:

> ...theology is a small skill...I must admit that as I have been writing this book...I have had a certain unease with my biblical interpretation, my choice of vocabulary and my theology.

But he adds: 'I have had no misgivings over the final outcome, i.e. the biblical conclusion which is the action and shape of the *telotic* Kingdom'.[77] His pain and limitations drive him and those who visit him 'back to the washing board of the Bible to learn afresh the lessons of that incredible book, the lessons of the Kingdom which is true *telos*'.[78] He is not afraid to spell out what is still needed in our day:

> I believe it is time we began building back into our society the basic elements of our Christian Gospel. At the end of a long life I am convinced its tenets are sound and functional and the best to follow. I also believe they are adaptable from generation to generation.[79]

And he urges his readers, whoever they may be, to respond appropriately:

> Be born again, here, now. What is to be is prepared for us here, now, although it is here that it might be there, fully, then...Be born again! Having been born again, hasten out into all the world and partake here, in this world, of heaven in all things. Drink deeply of all life. Watch the Kingdom of all life and join in all its eternal life.

Become a child of God and of the family of life. This is fantasy for sinners, but the Cross is given for sinners—the place of transformation and eternal life! Here is the Father—your Father and our Father—the Head of the Eternal Family, for ever![80]

For, 'Once in the *telos*, we are in it forever'.[81]

DOWN THE HILL

We return to the man who has made it to the top of the hill:

The warm sun quivered the air, and the day grew unnaturally bright. He had a sensation that death was coming to him as life. The hills flashed beyond themselves into something they were always destined to be. Their bondage snapped and they began an ecstatic paean to the faithful Creator. The skies arched away and slipped together again, in new meaning. The little river broadened and rushed and rolled and floated. The trees bent crazily together, drew back, and literally laughed.[82]

He finds himself caught up into this largeness of life:

It all bore in on him. His limbs suddenly flowed with new power, enriched vibrancy. A heady sweetness rushed through his body, and his heart grew and grew, until he was standing up, his arms to the sky. His understanding flourished beyond his former greatest moments, and full comprehension poured into him.

'I know you!' he cried, as the creation about declared the glory of God. Voice called unto voice with the mighty revelations he had always sensed. Every blade of grass had meaning, every rock a message, and every breath of air was the wine of understanding.

Geoffrey's physical health was failing by the 3rd June 2009. Laurel and members of his family were there. 'How fitting', they wrote, 'that some of his last words were, "Ruthie" and "Abba! Father!"':[83]

Then came all the voices—human, yet humanity flushed to its full being. Incredibly sweet their praise that poured over the undulating hills with its own powerful curving. Around him it flowed, and he shared in it with his own released utterance.[84]

'We believe he saw heaven and, as he would say, never felt the bump as he moved from this life to the next':[85]

Down the hill he plunged, his arms in joyous waving. Long green grass of a texture he had never known, and a colour he had never felt, was like a gentle waving sea about him. Into it he plunged with joy, falling, and rising and falling again, and rising . . . [86]

[1] 'Tottering Over a Hill', *I Saw, in the Night, Visions*, 31.

[2] *I Saw, in the Night, Visions*, 32.

[3] *I Saw, in the Night, Visions*, 31.

[4] *I Saw, in the Night, Visions*, 31.

[5] *I Saw, in the Night, Visions*, 32.

[6] *I Saw, in the Night, Visions*, 32–37.

[7] *I Saw, in the Night, Visions*, 37–38.

[8] *I Saw, in the Night, Visions*, 38.

[9] *I Saw, in the Night, Visions*, 38.

[10] *I Saw, in the Night, Visions*, 38–39.

[11] *Finding the Father: Living in the Telos*, unpublished manuscript, 2009, p. 43.

[12] *Finding the Father*, 193.

[13] *Finding the Father*, 270.

[14] Marcus Loane, *These Happy Warriors*, 94.

[15] Geoff and Laurel Bingham, Christmas Letter 2006.

[16] *Finding the Father*, 146.

[17] *Finding the Father*, 47, 103.

[18] *Dear Death or Dark Devourer?*, 21.

[19] *Dear Death or Dark Devourer?*, 21.

[20] *Dear Death or Dark Devourer?*, 24.

[21] *Dear Death or Dark Devourer?*, 21.

[22] *Dear Death or Dark Devourer?*, 21–22.

[23] *Dear Death or Dark Devourer?*, 22, 23.

[24] John 8:51.

[25] See John 11:26.

[26] *Dear Death or Dark Devourer?*, 27.

[27] *Dear Death or Dark Devourer?*, xiv.

[28] *Dear Death or Dark Devourer?*, 50, 51.

[29] Romans 8:18.

[30] *Principles of New Creation Teaching Ministry*, 15.

[31] *The Profound Mystery: Marriage Love, Divine and Human*, 24.

[32] *Bright Bird and Shining Sails*, 10.

[33] *Principles of New Creation Teaching Ministry*, 14.

[34] *The Beautiful City of God*, 133.

[35] *Bright Bird and Shining Sails,* 14.

[36] *Bright Bird and Shining Sails,* 48.

[37] *Bright Bird and Shining Sails,* 49–50.

[38] *Bright Bird and Shining Sails,* 50.

[39] *Bright Bird and Shining Sails,* 51.

[40] *Comprehending the Resurrection,* 33, 35.

[41] *New Creation Hymn Book,* 286.

[42] The Order for the Burial of the Dead, *Book of Common Prayer,* 1662.

[43] *New Creation Hymn Book,* 183. Written in 1986, after the funeral of Bill Andrews, for his widow Grace.

[44] *Great and Glorious Grace,* 297.

[45] 2 Peter 3:13.

[46] See Revelation 21:27.

[47] *Great and Glorious Grace,* 302.

[48] *God's Glory, Man's Sexuality,* 23–24.

[49] 'All Things Are Ours', *This Building Fair,* 165.

[50] *This Building Fair,* 165–166.

[51] *This Building Fair,* 166.

[52] A Greek word meaning 'end', 'goal', 'fulfilment', as in 1 Corinthians 15:24; 1 Peter 1:9; Romans 10:4.

[53] Martin Bleby, personal recollection.

[54] *Finding the Father,* 108.

[55] Gillian Borgas, in email to Martin Bleby, 1 August 2012.

[56] *Finding the Father,* 166.

[57] Unpublished manuscript 2008–2009.

[58] *Finding the Father,* 101–102, 103.

[59] *Finding the Father,* 91.

[60] *Finding the Father,* 149.

[61] *Finding the Father,* 124.

[62] *Finding the Father,* 120, 128.

[63] *Finding the Father,* 128.

[64] NCTM Monthly Ministry Studies, July, August, September 2005.

[65] *Finding the Father,* 89.

[66] *Finding the Father,* 64.

[67] *Finding the Father,* 64, 135–136.

68 *Finding the Father*, 152.

69 *Finding the Father*, 37–38.

70 *Finding the Father*, 206.

71 *Finding the Father*, 120.

72 *Finding the Father*, 110.

73 *Finding the Father*, 100.

74 *Finding the Father*, 86.

75 *Finding the Father*, 264.

76 *Finding the Father*, 222.

77 *Finding the Father*, 104.

78 *Finding the Father*, 91.

79 *Finding the Father*, 89.

80 *Finding the Father*, 150.

81 *Finding the Father*, 108.

82 *I Saw, in the Night, Visions*, 39.

83 'Geoffrey Bingham: A Family Eulogy', 10th June 2009.

84 *I Saw, in the Night, Visions*, 39.

85 'Geoffrey Bingham: A Family Eulogy'.

86 *I Saw, in the Night, Visions*, 39–40.

BIBLIOGRAPHY

PUBLISHED WRITINGS BY GEOFFREY BINGHAM CITED OR REFERRED TO IN THIS BOOK:

For a more complete listing, and to download titles, go to
www.newcreationlibrary.net

Unless otherwise stated, all books are published by
New Creation Publications Inc., Blackwood, South Australia

Troubadour Press Inc. later became an imprint of
New Creation Publications Inc.

Ah, Strong, Strong Love!, 1993.

All Things of the Spirit, 1997.

Angel Wings, 1992.

The Artist in the Garden, 2005.

The Authority and Submission of Love, 1982.

The Baptism in the Holy Spirit: Christ Pouring out His Spirit in the Last Days, 2003.

The Beautiful City of God, Redeemer Baptist Press, Castle Hill, 2001.

The Beloved Community of God: Yesterday, Today and Forever, Redeemer Baptist Press, Castle Hill, 2002.

Beyond Mortal Love, Troubadour Press, Blackwood, 1996.

Beyond the Cross, 1988.

A Biblical Way of Counselling, 1985.

The Boy in the Valley and Selected Short Stories, Troubadour Press, Blackwood, 1992.

The Boy, the Girl, and the Man, 1988.

Bright Bird and Shining Sails, 2007.

Christian Teaching Series:

    1. *The Weakness of Man and the Power of God,* n.d.

    2. *Can a Man Know God?,* n.d.

    3. *The Meaning and Significance of the Trinity,* n.d.

    4. *Commanded Repentance and Full Forgiveness,* 1986.

    5. *Faith Justification Conversion and the New Birth,* n.d.

    6. *The Christian and the Holy Spirit,* n.d.

    7. *The Christian Doctrine of Holiness,* 1985.

Christ's Cross over Man's Abyss, 2003.

Christ's People in Today's World, 1985.

The Clash of the Kingdoms, 1989.

Comprehending Justification, 2002.

The Concentration Camp and Other Stories, 1993.

Constraining Love, 1985.

Creation and the Liberating Glory, 2004.

Creation and Reconciliation, 1987.

The Day of the Spirit, 1985.

The Days and Dreams of Arcady, 1985.

Dear Darling Idols: lords and gods piffling and appalling, 1981.

Dear Death or Dark Devourer?, 1989.

Direct Biblical Counselling, 1986.

The Dominion of Darkness and the Victory of God, 1977.

Dry Bones Dancing!, 2003.

Eager to Preach, 1996.

The Everlasting Presence, 1989.

Father! My Father!, 2006.

For Pastors and the People, 1989.

Freely Flows Forgiveness, 1981.

The Glory on the Inside, 2012.

The God and Father of Us All, 1982.

God and Man in Signs and Wonders, 1988.

God and Man in the Mission of the Kingdom, Redeemer Baptist Press, North Parramatta, 2003.

God and the Ghostown, 1984.

God Sends Revival, 1984.

God's Glory, Man's Sexuality, 1988.

Great and Glorious Grace, 1988.

The Heavenly Vision, 1987.

The Holy Spirit, Creation and Glory, Redeemer Baptist Press, Castle Hill, 1999.

How to Study the Bible, 2007.

I Love the Father, 2008.

I Saw, in the Night, Visions, 1986.

I, The Man! 1996.

Laughing Gunner and Selected War Stories, Troubadour Press, Blackwood, 1992.

The Law of Eternal Delight, 2001.

Liberating Love, 1988.

The Lion on the Road, Troubadour Press, Blackwood, 1994.

Living Faith Studies, vols 1 to 5 (10 studies in each volume), 1981.

Love Is the Spur, Eyrie Books, North Parramatta, 2004.

Love unto Glory, 2003.

Man of Dust! Man of Glory!, 2006.

Man, Woman and Sexuality, 1986.

The Meaning and Making of Man: A Series of Seven Studies on Christian Counselling, 1996.

Mr. Hicken's Pears, Troubadour Press, Blackwood, 1995.

Mr Piffy Comes Home, Troubadour Press, Blackwood, 1993.

My Beloved Family, 1999.

New Creation Hymn Book, 2010.

Oh, Father! Our Father!, 1983.

Oh, No, Lord! Not Law, Lord?!!, 1979.

The Person and Work of the Holy Spirit, 2009.

Practical Christian Counselling, 1981.

Primarily for Parsons, 1987.

Proclaiming Christ's Gospel in Today's World, 2005.

The Profound Mystery: Marriage Love, Divine and Human, 1995.

The Return of the Lorikeets, 1995.

Revelation: A Commentary (undated).

The Revelation of St John the Divine: Commentary and Essays on the Book of the Revelation, 1993.

The Revival God Gives, 2003.

Reviving the Humble, 1991.

Spirit Baptism: Spirit-Living, 1989.

The Splendour of Holiness, 1985.

The Story of the Rice Cakes: The Search for Moral Sanity in a Prisoner of War Camp, 2006.

The Stranger in the Cemetery, 1991.

Strong As the Sun, Troubadour Press, Blackwood, 1994.

Sweeter than Honey, More Precious than Gold: The Law of Love and the Love of Law, 1995.

Tall Grow the Tallow-woods, Troubadour Press, Blackwood, 2000.

The Things We Firmly Believe, 1992.

This Building Fair, 1988.

3 Special Stories, 1990, republished 2012 as *The Glory on the Inside*.

Trinitarian Theology: Human Unity and Relationships (NCTM Pastors' School), 1991.

True Preaching: The Agony and the Ecstasy, 1988.

Truth—the Golden Girdle, 1983.

Twice-Conquering Love, 1993 (all quotations taken from the hard cover edition; page numbering in the 1992 paperback edition may be different).

The Vandal, 1990.

Where I Love I Live, 1986.

The Wisdom of God and the Healing of Man, 1990.

Wonderful Counsellor: Studies in Effective Biblical Counselling,
2004.

The WORD and the Words of the Cross, 1995.

The Wrath of His Love: Studies in the Wrath of God and of Man,
2003.

BOOKS BY OTHER AUTHORS

Babbage, Stuart Barton. *Memoirs of a Loose Canon,* Acorn Press,
Brunswick East, 2004.

Bingham, L. E. C. *Laurel's Story,* private publication, 2000 (used
by permission).

Bleby, Martin. *Marriage and the Good News of God,* NCPI,
Blackwood, 2010.

——. *The Vinedresser: An Anglican Meets Wrath and Grace,*
NCPI, Blackwood, 2003.

Bromiley, Geoffrey. *God and Marriage,* T. & T. Clark, Edinburgh,
1981.

Cameron, Marcia. *An Enigmatic Life: David Broughton Knox
Father of Contemporary Sydney Anglicanism,* Acorn Press,
Brunswick East, 2006.

Edwards, Brian H. *Can We Pray for Revival?—Towards a
Theology of Revivial,* Evangelical Press, Darlington, 2001.

Farley, Edward. *Ecclesial Man: A Social Phenomenology of Faith
and Reality,* Fortress Press, Philadelphia, 1975.

Forsyth, P. T. *Positive Preaching and the Modern Mind,* NCPI,
[1907], 1993.

Hart, Max. *A Story of Fire Continued: Aboriginal Christianity,*
NCPI, Blackwood, 1997.

Harris, John. *One Blood: 200 Years of Aboriginal Encounter with
Christianity: A Story of Hope,* Albatross Books, Sutherland,
1990.

Jenson, Robert W. *America's Theologian: A Recommendation of
Jonathan Edwards,* Oxford University Press, New York, 1992.

Judd, Stephen and Cable, Kenneth. *Sydney Anglicans: A History of the Diocese*, Anglican Information Office, Sydney, 2000.

Kevan, Ernest F. *The Grace of Law: A Study in Puritan Theology*, Carey Kingsgate Press, London, 1964.

Loane, Marcus L. *These Happy Warriors: Friends and Contemporaries*, NCPI, Blackwood, 1988.

Maxwell, L. E. *Born Crucified: The Cross in the Life of the Believer* [first published 1945], First British Edition, Oliphants Ltd., London, 1958.

Motyer, J. A. 'The Biblical Concept of Law', in *Evangelical Dictionary of Theology*, ed. W. E. Elwell, Baker Book House, Grand Rapids, 1990.

Packer, J. I. *Knowing God*, Hodder and Stoughton, London, 1973.

Paton, David M. (ed), *Reform of the Ministry: A Study in the Work of Roland Allen*, Lutterworth Press, London, 1968.

——. *The Ministry of the Spirit: Selected Writings of Roland Allen*, World Dominion Press, London, 1960.

Piggin, Stuart. *Spirit of a Nation: The Story of Australia's Christian Heritage*, Strand Publishing, Sydney, 2004.

——. *Firestorm of the Lord: The History of and Prospects for Revival in the Church and the World*, Paternoster Press, Carlisle, 2000.

Raiter, Michael. *Stirrings of the Soul: Evangelicals and the New Spirituality*, Matthias Media, Kingsford, 2003.

Reid, John R. *Marcus L. Loane: A Biography*, Acorn Press, Brunswick East, 2005.

Shedd, Russell Philip. *Man in Community*, Epworth Press, London, 1958.